Henry James Coleridge

The Public Life of our Lord Jesus Christ

Vol. 5

Henry James Coleridge

The Public Life of our Lord Jesus Christ
Vol. 5

ISBN/EAN: 9783337771133

Printed in Europe, USA, Canada, Australia, Japan

Cover: Foto ©Lupo / pixelio.de

More available books at **www.hansebooks.com**

THE TRAINING OF THE APOSTLES.

(PART I.)

BY

HENRY JAMES COLERIDGE,

OF THE SOCIETY OF JESUS.

LONDON
BURNS AND OATES,
PORTMAN STREET AND PATERNOSTER ROW.
1879.

✠

NULLUM PUTO, FRATRES CARISSIMI, AB ALIIS MAJUS PRÆJUDICIUM, QUAM A SACERDOTIBUS, TOLERAT DEUS : QUANDO EOS QUOS AD ALIORUM CORRECTIONEM POSUIT, DARE DE SE EXEMPLA PRAVITATIS CERNIT : QUANDO IPSI PECCAMUS, QUI COMPESCERE PECCATA DEBUIMUS, NULLA ANIMARUM LUCRA QUÆRIMUS, AD NOSTRA QUOTIDIE STUDIA VACAMUS, TERRENA CONCUPISCIMUS, HUMANAM GLORIAM INTENTA MENTE CAPTAMUS. ET, QUIA EO IPSO QUO CETERIS PRÆLATI SUMUS, AD AGENDA QUÆLIBET MAJOREM LICENTIAM HABEMUS, SUSCEPTÆ BENEDICTIONIS MINISTERIUM VERTIMUS AD AMBITIONIS ARGUMENTUM, DEI CAUSAM RELINQUIMUS, AD TERRENA NEGOTIA VACAMUS, LOCUM SANCTITATIS ACCIPIMUS, ET TERRENIS ACTIBUS IMPLICAMUR.

(S. Greg. Magnus *in Homilia in Lucam* xxvii.)

PREFACE.

THE space of time in the Public Life of our Blessed Lord which is considered in the present volume, was probably not very long in its actual duration, though we cannot fix its beginning or ending with perfect certainty. But it was a period which was hardly surpassed by any other in the importance of the issues which were decided in its course, though its prominent incidents were few, and though it is possible to pass it over without much remark in framing a general narrative of our Lord's life. It extends from the delivery of the Sermon on the Mount to the point of time at which, after the first conspiracy against His life made by the Pharisees and Herodians, our Lord began to retire before the opposition which His teaching as to the Sabbath, and the miracles which He had wrought on that day, evoked in those who were ever after to be His bitter enemies and persecutors, the Chief Priests and ecclesiastical authorities of the holy nation.

The first part of this period of a few weeks or months, as the case may have been, was employed by our Lord in His usual course of missionary preaching in Galilee, and we have therefore but few records of distinct incidents. But it was also remarkable for some very striking and significant miracles, which stand out from the general history with a prominence of their own, on account of the Divine truths which our Lord seems to have wished to connect with them. These are the miracles of the first marvellous fishing in the Lake of Galilee, of the healing of the leper, and of the healing of the paralytic who was let down in his bed through the tiles of the house where our Lord was preaching, in the presence of a large assembly of scribes and Pharisees gathered from different parts of the Holy Land as well as from the towns of Galilee. The second part of the time of which we are speaking, embraces our Lord's visit to Jerusalem for the feast of the Pasch, the second in the three years of His preaching—a visit which was signalized by the first open breach between Him and the authorities of the Synagogue. It was at this time that our Lord healed the man at the Pool of Bethsaida on the Sabbath Day— perhaps the Sabbath of the feast itself—and further, ordered the man whom He had healed to take up his bed and walk before all, as if with the express design of arousing public attention, and bringing on the disputation which followed. This occasion first brought our Lord into direct collision with the Chief Priests, and it is from this that we must date the long difference which ensued, and which was terminated only by His Death. It seems to have been soon after this that the incidents occurred of the disciples plucking the ears of corn in the fields, and the second public miracle on the Sabbath Day, when our Lord, after the question had been formally raised by His adversaries, healed the man who had a withered hand. After this we find Him retiring from the more public and open manner of preaching which He had hitherto followed in Galilee, and doing this in so remarkable a way as to draw to it the attention of His disciples, who saw in it, as we may judge from the words of St. Matthew, a special fulfilment of the prophecies concerning the Messias.

Even if it could ever have been otherwise, the treatment which He experienced on the part of the Chief Priests and rulers at Jerusalem must have concentrated our Lord's hopes and cares very mainly on the small body of disciples whom He had gathered around Him. They were not yet formed into the band of Apostles, distinctively so called, but most of them were already, perhaps, His inseparable companions. It is natural to consider the incidents and the teaching of this time as having been specially addressed to them in our Lord's intention, and to look upon their special training for their lofty office as having been already begun. It was mainly for them that the first great miracle of this period, the miracle of the fishing, was worked. They were more likely than any others to profit fully by the teaching implied or directly conveyed in the other miracles and actions of this time, such as the healing of the leper and of the paralytic. It was in reference to them that much of the incidental teaching of the same period was delivered, such as the doctrine conveyed in our Lord's defence of His indulgence to them in the matter of public fasts and penances, and in the eating the ears of corn in the fields on the Sabbath Day. To them, more than to any others, did He look for the fruitful intelligence of the great dogmatic truths which He also set forth at this time. Hence this volume has been called by a name in reference to this view of the subject-matter of which it treats, and the name will apply to those which succeed it, until the narrative reaches the point of the great confession of St. Peter.

The great doctrinal document of this period of the Gospel narrative is the long discourse which is contained in the fifth chapter of St. John's Gospel. Apart from the treasures of dogmatic teaching which are to be found, as theologians know, in that famous discourse, it seems to have an historical importance which has not always been duly recognized by the Christian historians of our Lord's life. It seems to put on record, briefly but completely, the principal features of the position in which the Jewish rulers were placed by the Providential action of God, in setting before them the various kinds of testimony to our Lord's Divine mission to which He there appeals, as well as the effect upon His own counsels and movements of the attitude of defiant resistance assumed by those rulers. In a certain sense the whole of the Gospel history, as far as it took the tone and line which it did actually take in consequence of the action of the priests at Jerusalem towards our Lord, is summed up in this single chapter, the whole of the preceding events leading up to it, and the whole of those that follow taking their colour from it. It has been natural and even necessary, in a work like the present, to dwell on this chapter at considerable length. It has all the characteristic difficulties which belong to the discourses of our Lord as reported by St. John, and in no part of his work will a writer who undertakes the task before me feel less satisfied with his own performance. But it would be a sign of certain failure if such a writer thought he had succeeded in fathoming all the depths of these Divine words. I shall be content if the labour which I have bestowed upon them should induce other commentators to work in the same direction, and I am confident that there will be found few passages in the Gospels which throw more light upon the history, which point more clearly to the elements of a full comprehension of the dealings of the Jewish authorities with our Lord, and of His dealings with them.

It is indeed sad to have so vividly brought before us the truth that, in this respect also, our Lord fulfilled beforehand the prophecy which He made as to what should befal His disciples, that 'a man's foes should be those of his own household,'—to see so plainly how the rulers of the holy nation were the main instruments, first in the apparent defeat of our Lord's attempts for its salvation, and then in His murder and in the final reprobation and repudiation of that nation for its guilt in its treatment of Him. It is clear that the people were ready enough to receive our Lord. They had flocked to the Baptism of St. John, and that had prepared them for Him Who was to come after St. John. They understood the Divine meaning of the miracles as evidences, and the character and personal demeanour of our Lord won their hearts, as they could hardly fail to win them. But their natural leaders, the members of the Mosaic hierarchy, set themselves against Him, and used the whole power of their position most unscrupulously, first to discredit Him, and ultimately to take away His life. Nowhere in all history is there a more signal instance of the influence of a dominant class in determining the action and the fate of a nation. But in this instance it was the priesthood which God had established, which was responsible for a national sin no less heinous than the judicial murder, by the forms and powers which He had Himself set up, of the Redeemer of mankind, the Incarnate Son of God. This issue is as yet in the future in the narrative of this volume, but it is already determined upon, and our Lord, in the discourse of which mention has been made, has pointed out the evil principles from which it was to proceed.

Such is the certain truth of the history, and it is far better to examine carefully the spiritual and moral evils, on which our Lord sets His mark in this discourse, in their working out the issue, than to shrink from the full lesson which such truths bring home to ourselves. The history of the treatment of our Lord by these men is the history, in principle, not only of the evil effects of ambition, self-seeking, and the other vices by which they were infected, as repeated over and over again in the annals of the Church, but it also furnishes us, when considered in the light of His own comments on their conduct, with the key to the resistance to the Christian and Catholic evidences, in all times and by all sorts of men. In a very few words, fewer, perhaps, even than those in which our Lord Himself set forth these truths, St. John has recorded for us this most important revelation of the human heart made by Him Who knew what was in man.

The essay on *The Sequence of the Miracles*, which will be found at the close of the present volume, would perhaps more naturally find a place in a new edition of the two introductory volumes called the *Life of our Life*. It is placed here for the convenience of the reader, as some little time may elapse before a new issue of those volumes.

H. J. C.

London, Feast of the Immaculate Conception of our Blessed Lady, 1879.

CONTENTS.

CHAPTER I.

Characteristics of our Lord's teaching after the delivery of the Sermon on the Mount.

St. Matt. viii. 2—4, ix. 1—13, xii. 1—21; St. Mark i. 40, iii. 12; St. Luke v. 1, vi. 11; St. John v.; *Vita Vitæ Nostræ*, §§ 37—45.

	PAGE
Occupation of our Lord after the Sermon on the Mount	1
A period of ordinary preaching	2
Particular character of His teaching of this period	3
Manifestation of His own prerogatives	4
Intention of the miracles of this time	6
The miraculous fishing, the leper, the paralytic	6
Miracles on the Sabbath Day	8
Conspiracy of our Lord's enemies and His retirement before it	8
Teaching as to the Church implicitly begun	10
Separation of enemies and friends	11

CHAPTER II.

The miraculous draught of fishes.

St. Luke v. 1—11; *Vita Vitæ Nostræ*, § 37.

	PAGE
Significant actions of this time	12
Narrative of the miracle	13
The Apostles' experience of our Lord's preaching	15
Their joy at hearing Him	17
The command to launch out	17
Human labour unable to command success	20
Obedience of St. Peter	21
The net almost broken	22
Effect of the miracle on St. Peter	23
Our Lord's promise to him	25
Details of the scene in Christian contemplation	26
The position of St. Peter in the Church	27
Series of the lake miracles	29

CHAPTER III.

The healing of the leper.

St. Matt. viii. 2—4; St. Mark i. 40—45; St. Luke v. 12—16; *Vita Vitæ Nostræ*, § 38.

	PAGE
Importance of this miracle	31
Its place and circumstances	32
Our Lord's injunctions	34
Not all obeyed	34
His retirement	35
The Israelites and leprosy	35
Sanitary reasons of the Mosaic legislation	36
Other reasons	36
Compassionate character of the law	37
St. Basil and his hospital	38

	PAGE
Sermon of St. Gregory of Nazianzus	38
Mercifulness of separating the lepers	40
Leprosy considered as a type of sin	42
Our Lord as Physician	43
Effect of the miracle	44
Virtues of this leper	44
Our Lord's answer to him	45
The miracles as signs	46
Our Lord's touch	47
Signification of this	47
Also, a lesson of charity	49
Christian charity and the lepers	50

CHAPTER IV.

The healing of the paralytic.

St. Matt. ix. 1—9; St. Mark ii. 1—14; St. Luke v. 17—28; *Vita Vitæ Nostræ*, § 39.

Interval after the healing of the leper	52
Careful order of our Lord's actions	53
Our Lord's prayer at this time	54
His return to Capharnaum	55
Great assembly of ecclesiastics	56
Variety of character	57
Subject of our Lord's discourse	58
The paralytic brought in	59
Faith of the hearers	60
Dispositions of the paralytic	61
The forgiveness of sins	62
Connection between physical and moral evils	63
Thoughts of the scribes	64
Power to forgive sins unprecedented	65
Not impossible	65
Our Lord reading their hearts	66
His remonstrance to them	67
The meaning of the question	67
Force of the argument	68
The miracle proving the doctrine	69

	PAGE
Connection of the miracles	70
Effect on the multitude	71
Appreciation of the doctrine	72
The miracle sacramental	73
Hostility to the doctrine of forgiveness	74
Passage from Cardinal Newman	76
Men made judges	77

CHAPTER V.

The call of St. Matthew.

St. Matt. ix. 9; St. Mark ii. 14; St. Luke v. 27, 28; *Vita Vitæ Nostræ*, § 39.

Call of St. Matthew following on the miracle on the paralytic	78
Circumstances of the call	79
St. Jerome on St. Matthew	80
Opportunities of knowledge of our Lord	82
Effect of the Sermon on the Mount	83
Interior struggle	85
The call of our Lord	86
Typical character of St. Matthew's call	86
Vocation a personal command	87
Foundation of the doctrine of vocation	88
St. Paul's question	89
The answer to it	89
Importance of the moment of vocation	90
Personal following of our Lord	91
Motives of loyalty	92

CHAPTER VI.

The Feast at St. Matthew's house.

St. Matt. ix. 10—13; St. Mark ii. 15—22; St. Luke v. 29—39; *Vita Vitæ Nostræ*, § 40.

The publicans and our Lord	93
St. Matthew's banquet	94

	PAGE		PAGE
Invitation to his friends	95	The principle requires meditation	122
Our Lord at the feast	96	The last part of the answer—	
Hypocrisy a dominant vice	97	'Not the just, but sinners'	124
Our Lord contradicting the fashion	98		
Actions of His saints grounded on this	99		

CHAPTER VIII.

The Children of the Marriage.

St. Mark ii. 18—21; St. Luke v. 33—35; *Vita Vitæ Nostræ*, § 40.

	PAGE		PAGE
Importance of Apostolical conversation	100	Occasions of the Jewish fasts	127
Its dangers	101	The question put to our Lord	129
Rules for it—to act under obedience	102	Contrast between our Lord and St. John	129
Care not to lose fervour	103	Our Lord's answer	130
Gentleness of manner	104	He does not deny the advantages of fasting	130
Need of familiarity with God	106	Nor the fact as to the disciples	131
And prudence	106	His manner of referring to His own separation from them	132
Letter of St. Francis Xavier	106	Image of the Bridegroom	132
Preparation for this conversation	107	Reference to St. John's words	133
Different characters to be approached	108	Other images here used	134
Letter of Blessed Peter Favre	109	Three heads of our Lord's answer	136

CHAPTER VII.

'Mercy, and not sacrifice.'

St. Matt. ix. 11—13; St. Mark ii. 16, 17; St. Luke v. 30—32; *Vita Vitæ Nostræ*, § 40.

	PAGE
Present condition of the disciples	136
Joyousness their characteristic	137
Difference between our Lord and the Scribes	110
Occasions of joy in Christian life	138
Who are meant by 'sinners'	111
Gentiles, or worldly persons	112
Time of our Lord's public teaching	139
Criticism of the Scribes and Pharisees	114
His own great affability	140
Our Lord's answer threefold	114

CHAPTER IX.

New wine and new bottles.

St. Mark ii. 21, 22; St. Luke v. 36—39; *Vita Vitæ Nostræ*, § 40.

	PAGE
The first part, as to the need of a physician	115
The conditions of the office of physician	116
Various maladies of the soul	117
First part of our Lord's answer	142
Courtesy of our Lord to His critics	118
Characteristics of His future system	143
Second part of the reply— 'Mercy, and not sacrifice'	119
Second part of His answer, twofold	145
Passages in the prophets	120
Their meaning	121
The cloth and the garment	145

	PAGE
The wine and the bottles	145
Introduction of a new system	146
First principle, no patchwork	147
Necessity of freedom from old traditions	149
And from all particularism	150
Second principle, 'the wine to fit the bottles'	150
The Judaizers	150
Whatever has life, has a spirit of its own	151
The third principle, as to the 'old wine'	153
Great tolerance of the Church	154

CHAPTER X.

The miracle at the Probatic Pool.

St. John v. 1—15; *Vita Vitæ Nostræ*, § 41.

Our Lord looking forward to the Church in His miracles	156
Regard for the Sabbath	157
The Probatic Pool at Jerusalem	158
Characteristics of the miracle	159
Its chief incidents	161
The man who had been healed	162
Position of the Jewish authorities	163
Our Lord meeting the man in the Temple	165
Information to the authorities	166
Their attention again challenged	167
Note I.—*On the Feast mentioned in St. John v.*	168
Note II.—*On the genuineness of the fourth verse of St. John v.*	173

CHAPTER XI.

Our Lord and the Chief Priests.

St. John v. 16—30; *Vita Vitæ Nostræ*, § 42.

Discourses of our Lord in the Gospel of St. John	176
Discourse after this miracle	177
Spirit and character of the Jewish hierarchy	178
The Synagogue was to them an end, not a means	179
The priestly failing, jealousy	180
Moral difficulties to them	181
The same motives always operative	182
Our Lord's presence a trial to them	184
His language lofty and Divine	185

CHAPTER XII.

The work of the Father and of the Son.

St. John v. 16—18; *Vita Vitæ Nostræ*, § 42.

Our Lord must have chosen the special point at issue	186
Institution of the Sabbath	187
Its witness to important truths	188
The Sabbath of the new creation	189
Our Lord's answer concerning the work of His Father	190
Twofold resemblance to His Father	192
Our Lord understood by the Jews to claim a natural filiation to the Father	193
Contrast to His answers at other times	193
Cogency of the proof of His assertion	194
Activity of God in His Kingdom	195
And of our Lord in the new Kingdom	196
A twofold picture	197

	PAGE
CHAPTER XIII.	
Unity of the Divine operation.	
St. John v. 18—30; *Vita Vitæ Nostræ*, § 42.	
Great depth of our Lord's words	200
Doctrine disclosed in answer to His enemies	201
Divisions of the discourse which follows	201
Truths of two kinds	203
Great condescension of our Lord in His explanations	204
Light thrown on this passage by Christian theology	205
What is generation?	206
The idea of the Word of God aiding the explanation	207
Three elements in generation	208
Perfection of the Divine generation	209
The communication of the Divine essence	210
Our Lord here states this doctrine both affirmatively and negatively	211
Assertion of the unity of operation	213
Love of the Father for the Son	214
Our Lord explaining the Incarnation	215
Different classes of souls among His audience	217

CHAPTER XIV.	
Resurrection and Judgment.	
St. John v. 29—31; *Vita Vitæ Nostræ*, § 42.	
Further communications of our Lord on this occasion	218
Comparison with the discourse to Nicodemus	219
The greater things still to be manifested	221

	PAGE
The raising of the dead	223
The exercise of the power of judgment	225
The General Resurrection	226
Our Lord's frequent mention of the judgment	227
Equity of His judgment	227
Danger of forgetting intellectual responsibilities	229
The trial of the Chief Priests	230

CHAPTER XV.	
Witnesses to our Lord's Mission.	
St. John v. 31—39; *Vita Vitæ Nostræ*, § 42.	
Recapitulation of the evidences of our Lord's mission	232
His own witness to Himself	233
Five heads of testimony here adduced	235
The witness of St. John	236
How treated by the Jewish authorities	238
The witness of the miracles	240
Our Lord's Divinity implied in His miracles	241
The witness of the Eternal Father	243
Reference to the promise of Moses	243
The Father drawing men to our Lord	246
The witness of the Scriptures and of Moses	248

CHAPTER XVI.	
Causes of our Lord's rejection.	
St. John v. 39—47; *Vita Vitæ Nostræ*, § 42.	
Our Lord as the wise Physician	251
Disease of the will in the Jews	252
Slavery to human respect	253

	PAGE		PAGE
The Jews and heretical teachers	255	Its meaning here	288
Action of the will in faith	256	The Sabbath made for man	289
Action of Divine grace	258	Application of this principle	291
The love of God	259	The Son of Man Lord of the Sabbath	293
Proof of its absence, the rejection of a messenger in the name of God	260	Importance of this principle	294
Our Lord coming in the name of His Father	261	Benefit to the Church	295

CHAPTER XVIII.

The man with the withered hand.

St. Matt. xii. 9—14; St. Mark iii. 1—6; St. Luke vi. 6—11; *Vita Vitæ Nostræ*, § 44.

Those who come in their own name	261
Arrogance of false teachers	263
Dominant fault of the Jewish rulers	265
The applause of men	266
Miserable power of human respect	267
The glory which is from God alone	269
Our Lord will not be their accuser	270
The accusation of Moses	273
Principle on which to reject our Lord was to reject Moses	274

Importance of this miracle	297
The question of the Pharisees	298
Our Lord's challenge to them	299
The miracle worked	299
Discomfiture of the enemies of our Lord	300
Impossible to question the miracle	301
Their league with the Herodians	302
Their example constantly followed in history	304

CHAPTER XVII.

The Disciples in the Cornfields.

St. Matt. xii. 1—8; St. Mark ii. 23—28; St. Luke vi. 1—5; *Vita Vitæ Nostræ*, § 43.

CHAPTER XIX.

The Servant of God.

St. Matt. xii. 15—21; St. Mark iii. 7—12; *Vita Vitæ Nostræ*, § 45.

Position now taken up by the Jewish rulers	277
The disciples at this visit to Jerusalem	278
Our Lord's departure	280
Passage through the cornfields	281
The Pharisees	282
Our Lord's answer	283
Five heads of doctrine adduced	285
The example of David	286
The priests in the Temple	287
'Mercy, and not sacrifice'	288

Our Lord's conduct under opposition	305
Descriptions of St. Mark and St. Matthew	306
Prophecy of Isaias applied by St. Matthew	309
The servant of God	310
The bruised reed	310
Teaching for the Apostles	311
The patience of God in the Book of Wisdom	312
The character of our Lord	314
The character of the Church and of the Saints	315

Contents.

APPENDIX I.

Sequence of the Miracles.

	PAGE
Multitude and diversity of the miracles	317
Their order not accidental	318
The first and the last	318
Miracles described in detail—their number	320
Those which are not so described	320
At the first Pasch	320
At the beginning of the Galilæan preaching	321
On other occasions	322
Mention of large numbers often introduced casually	324
Or when we happen to have the events of a day related	325
Effect of these multitudes of miracles on contemporaries	327
Special purpose in the more singular manifestations of this kind	328
The miracle at Cana	329
The cleansing of the Temple	330
The ruler's son	330
The Mount of Precipitation	331
The opening miracles at Capharnaum	332
The miraculous fishing	332
The healing of the leper	333
The healing of the paralytic	334
The Pool of Bethsaida	335
The withered hand	335
The centurion's servant	336
The widow's son	336
The embassy from St. John Baptist	337
The blind and dumb demoniac	338
The tempest stilled	339
The legion of devils	339
Last miracles at Capharnaum	339
And at Nazareth	339
Feeding of the five thousand and of the four thousand	340
The miracles wrought with difficulty	341
Splendour of the unsolicited miracles	342
Importance in the history of the Sabbatical miracles	343
Our Lord leaving Galilee	344
Narratives of St. Luke and St. John	344
The miracles related by St. John in this period	345
Those related by St. Luke	347
Parallel to others in St. Matthew	348
Reason for this	348
The last miracles of our Lord	350
Important features in the history connected with the miracles	351
The Sabbatical miracles	352
Other miracles connected incidentally with important events	353
Sacramental miracles	354
Prophetical miracles	354
A great number of these unsolicited	355
These miracles mentioned by all the historical evangelists	358
Witness of St. John's Gospel	359
Evidential value of the miracles—St. Matthew's use of them	361
Instance of the Gospel of St. Mark	363

APPENDIX II.

Harmony of the Gospels.

From *Vita Vitæ Nostræ*, §§ 37—45.

	PAGE
Sect. 37.—The miraculous draught of fishes	365
Sect. 38.—The healing of the leper	366
Sect. 39.—The healing of the paralytic and the calling of St. Matthew	367

Sect. 40.—The feast at St. Matthew's house . . 369	Sect. 43.—The disciples plucking corn on the Sabbath . 374
Sect. 41.—The miracle at the Probatic Pool . . . 371	Sect. 44.—Another miracle on the Sabbath . . . 375
Sect. 42.—Our Lord's dispute with the Jews . . . 372	Sect. 45.—Our Lord retiring before His enemies . . 376

CHAPTER I.

Characteristics of our Lord's Teaching after the delivery of the Sermon on the Mount.

St. Matt. viii. 2—4, ix. 1—13, xii. 1—21; St. Mark i. 40, iii. 12; St. Luke v. 1, vi. 11; St. John v.; *Vita Vitæ Nostræ*, §§ 37—45.

THE time of the delivery of the Sermon on the Mount has been conjecturally fixed as in the month of October of the year, in the early summer of which our Lord began His Public Ministry in Galilee. This date may not be at all certain, but there is sufficient probability about it to make us hesitate as to rejecting it altogether. If it be assumed as probable, and if the other conjecture be admitted, for which there is a greater amount of direct evidence, that the feast of which St. John speaks in his fifth chapter, at which the miracle on the man who had lain so long at the Pool of Bethsaida was wrought, was the second Pasch which occurred after the Baptism of our Lord, we have a considerable space of time to account for in His preaching as the interval between the Sermon on the Mount and that miracle. This period of time would be about half a year, and it may seem at first sight as if the events which can be assigned to this interval are comparatively few. But it has already been said more than once that we cannot expect to have in the Gospels a full chronicle of the events of those periods of our Lord's teaching which were most uniform in the character of their incidents and occupations.

We have a very full account, for instance, of the week of the last preaching and Passion of our Lord. Almost every day in that week had its peculiar and most important incidents, and the history of one day is by no means the history of the rest. The story of a week of our Lord's ordinary missionary preaching in Galilee would, however, be very much the story of another week, at least as to its chief features. Day would follow day with more or less of uniformity of hard and continuous work for the conversion of sinners, the instruction of those already converted, the care and healing of the sick, the relief of the poor, and the like. Each town or village might have its own tale of graces received, of miraculous cures, and of authoritative teaching, but there would not be any great variety in the principal elements of the story of one, as compared with that of another of the same kind. Nor have we anywhere in the Gospels a description of even one day of our Lord's ordinary missionary teaching, as distinguished from such teaching as that which is contained in the Sermon on the Mount or, again, in the Parables. There is every reason for supposing that, if the remainder of the time which intervened in the first year of our Lord's teaching after the Sermon on the Mount, and before the second Pasch, was as long as the conjecture which has just been mentioned would make it, very great portions of it were spent in much the same way as the interval which had preceded the Sermon and followed the beginning of the Public Ministry. There were, no doubt, breaks in the continuity of our Lord's missionary exertions at this time, and this, indeed, is noted by the Evangelists; but there would be very much in the occupations of these months which would be uniform, whether the number of months was great or small. When we consider what has come down to us as historically true concerning the populousness of the tract of country in which our Lord was now working, and the very strong words in which the Evangelists express the universality of His teaching over the whole of that tract, it will seem rather a matter of astonishment that He should have been able to make His personal presence felt everywhere in that country, even in the longest space of time that can be allotted to His ministry there, than that there should seem to be so few special details concerning the miracles and the doctrine of such a period.

It will be a further help to the explanation of the apparent difficulty of which we are speaking, if we can find that there is any one predominant characteristic about the miracles and other actions of our Lord at this time, which may serve to furnish a special reason for the mention of them by the Evangelists, while others, in themselves perhaps equally wonderful, may have been passed over by those historians. Now it is undoubtedly the case, that there is a particular character about what is recorded as to the teaching and bearing of our Lord in the period of which we are to begin to speak in the present volume. The period immediately following the delivery of the Sermon on the Mount is, as we may say, the closing period of the time when, if ever, our Lord could teach and work His miracles with comparative immunity from opposition and persecution. In the early months of His Public Ministry all had seemed to hail Him with ecstatic delight, and His progress from town to town and city to city was like that of some triumphant sovereign returning, the idol of His people, after a long absence, to His own dominions. We have noted the marks which are discernible in the Sermon on the Mount of our Lord's own full prevision of the storms which were so soon to arise and overcloud the fair prospect. But as yet all this was future. It was not till His next appearance at Jerusalem that any open break was to take place between Himself and those who were ever afterwards to be His bitter enemies—the priests and ecclesiastical authorities at Jerusalem, the very persons to whom He might have looked with the greatest confidence for support and adhesion. He had, as has been seen, provoked their jealousy from the very first, and the first manifestation of that feeling had come in the shape of a question as to the authority which His actions evidently claimed. This took place on the cleansing of the Temple at the first Pasch after His Baptism. On that occasion, our Lord by no means disavowed the claim which was imputed to Him, though He answered His questioners enigmatically, and speedily retired from the neighbourhood of the capital city. He could withdraw, but He could not anywhere or at any time teach and act as if He were less than He was. In the same way, as has been seen, His teaching in Galilee had the same characteristic which had struck the jealous priests in His actions at Jerusalem. The people were astonished at His way of teaching, for He taught as One Who had authority and power of His own. The record of this wonder on the part of the multitudes cannot have been made for us by the Evangelists without a special purpose, and it cannot surprise us if we find that they at once go on to record acts and sayings of our Lord at this time which also implied claims to this or that special exercise of that Divine prerogative, to His possession of which the whole of His teaching witnessed. No time could be more opportune for the manifestation of His prerogatives, if we are so to speak, than the period on which we are now to enter. As yet there was no formal opposition to His teaching, no attempt to draw the people away from Him by calumnious charges. He was to a certain extent left to choose His own opportunities for unfolding, as occasion allowed Him, one after another of the manifold and most momentous truths which He was charged to deliver, whether to the people at large or to those who were to take His place as their teachers after Him. Most difficult indeed it was to force all the particulars of the Divine message on the dull hearts and heavy intelligences of the people—difficult to find, even in the Apostles themselves, the qualities of mind and heart which were requisite for the reception of truths which might have seemed most elementary as to His Person and authority. But the claims which were essential for the completion of the work which He was to leave behind Him, were in many respects new and unexampled, and the whole welfare of the Church and of society, as she was to form it, depended on their recognition. It would seem as if the period of time on which we are now entering was very mainly chosen by our Lord for the promulgation of the truths on which these claims rested. It was His manner, as it always is the manner of God, to declare Who He was, and what were His rights, rather by actions than by words. His arguments with the Jews, of which we have a perfect specimen in the discourse which St. John has preserved to us in his fifth chapter, turned rather upon the evidence which His Father had furnished to them as to His authority, than on the details of the points on which that authority was to be exercised. The miracles which stand out in the history of these months or weeks seem to have been directed by a Divine purpose to the enlightenment of the minds of those who were capable of understanding them, as to some at least of these details. If this was the case, if it was really our Lord's purpose during this interval to assert in various ways His supreme authority, as the Son of Man, on many points as to which that authority transcended the power of any teacher who had gone before Him, then we have a clue which connects these miracles by one uniform intention, and also an explanation of the fact that these and not others have been recorded, as having made an impression on the minds of the Apostles, and as having had a special bearing and influence on the course of the Evangelical history.

It will not be difficult to trace this apparent purpose in the series of miracles and teaching on which our attention will be occupied. It may be supposed that the ordinary teaching of our Lord was going on as usual during these months, except those parts of it as to which it is especially noted by the Evangelists that He spent them in retirement or prayer. But the more salient features of this time are to be found in the circumstances as to which the narrative is more full. The chain of miracles of the entire part of this period is not a long one. The narrative begins with the miracle of the miraculous fishing in the Lake of Galilee, a miracle altogether unsolicited, and which, if for that circumstance alone, would naturally be considered as symbolical and pregnant with a deeper teaching, in connection with the work of the Apostolate, than that of a simple evidence of preternatural power. The next miracle is the healing of the leper, itself full of symbolism on account of the disease which was cured, and this is followed by the significant command of our Lord to the person for whose benefit it was wrought to go to the High Priest himself and inform him of the cure. The next in order is the healing of the paralytic, a miracle clearly wrought with a view to the teaching engrafted upon it, as to the power of the Son of Man on earth to forgive sins. Here we have a most distinct assertion of a power which was altogether new to the Jews, a power the possession of which was to be one of the chief glories of the Church, one of her chief claims on the allegiance and homage of mankind, and, consequently, one of the chief points on which the enmity of the world and of Hell has fastened. For the doctrine which is connected with this great power shows us that the Son of Man has indeed left behind Him on earth, in the sacrament in which the exercise of this prerogative is contained, a remedy which had no parallel at all in the Old Law for the worst of all human miseries. The miracle of the cure of the paralytic may have been very closely connected with the call of St. Matthew. It is at all events natural to suppose that the joy and wonder of the people who witnessed the miracle may have lasted on for some little time, and have been an element in the enthusiasm which prevailed at the time of the banquet which the new disciple gave in honour of our Lord. It appears to have been at this time, also, that the first question was put to our Lord as to His indulgence, in not making His disciples fast, like those of the Pharisees and of St. John Baptist. In the answer with which our Lord met this criticism, as well as in the words which follow, in which He uses the image of the new wine and the old bottles, it is easy to see a tone of entire independence of precedent, the assertion of the power of the legislator of a new system, the whole character of which was to be fresh and original. For the power of an authoritative teacher and lawgiver is not less shown by the dispensations and indulgences which he grants from previous rules, and his independence of traditional customs, than by any new laws of greater strictness which he may enforce for the first time. And the language in which our Lord takes up the beautiful title which St. John Baptist had been the first to confer upon Him, of the Bridegroom, bringing in thereby and applying to Himself a very large number of references which were scattered over the Prophetical books of the Old Testament, has the same character of independence and high authority.

But the most striking of the features in our Lord's conduct at this time, in reference to the claim of authority of which we are speaking, is undoubtedly to be found in the series of miracles which He now began to work on the Sabbath Day. These miracles, like that of the fishing on the lake, were altogether unsolicited, and our Lord took the initiative in exercising His powers in these acts of mercy, evidently with the direct purpose of attracting the attention of others, besides those on whom they were wrought, to His power as the Son of Man over the Sabbath Day. We shall have to speak in detail on this claim, as well as of the miracles by which it was supported and enforced, and it is mentioned here only as throwing light on the general subject of the main features of this period. It is also significant that St. John should have mentioned what was apparently the first instance of a miracle of this class, and should have done so, as it seems, for the purpose of subjoining to it the dispute which afterwards ensued between our Lord and the Jewish authorities. The Evangelist here sums up for us the arguments to which our Lord appealed as furnishing evidence to Him, and as rendering it obligatory on all, who did not wish to set themselves against the counsels of God, to acknowledge His authority.

One stage of the period of which we are speaking is concluded by the conspiracy of his enemies, the Pharisees sent down from Jerusalem into Galilee to watch and thwart Him, with the courtiers and officials of the Herod who ruled over this part of the country, to bring about His death, and our Lord's retirement from the more public spheres of action in which He had hitherto been moving, in consequence of this conspiracy. We are thus brought to a very important point in the Gospel history, and the period which immediately succeeds to this, though it is a space of time illustrated by some of the most splendid of the miracles and other actions of our Lord, has all through a new character which is given to it by the malice of His persecutors, the as yet not quite perfect faith of the disciples, and the gradual falling away of the people from His teaching. It appears that as this period drew on, our Lord retired more and more from the places in which He had during the previous year been most frequently seen. It appears also that everywhere He was persistently haunted and pursued by watchful and captious enemies. But all this time another process was going on, on which, as it seems, the thoughts and prayers of our Lord were centred in a singular manner. During all this time He was forming, more and more completely, the band of Apostles, who were first formally called to be His immediate and inseparable companions soon after that conspiracy of His enemies against His life which was just now mentioned. For some time after the formation of this select band they continued with Him in another of the missionary circuits in which so much of His time was spent. Later on, he called them together and gave them the powers which were befitting for the exercise of their Apostolic ministry in the more restricted sense of the terms, during a short period, when they were sent out, as if for the express purpose of trying them, two and two, to preach and labour after the example of their Master. It was to the Apostles that our Lord explained the meaning of the parabolic teaching which He now adopted in His instruction of the people, and the whole history of this time may be considered most usefully as being that of their gradual but silent advance up to that perfection of faith in His Divinity which was at length expressed, in the name of all, by St. Peter on the memorable occasion when our Lord asked them who they thought Him to be.

One further remark with regard to the characteristic features of this period of our Lord's preaching will be enough by way of preparation for the closer study of those words and actions of His on which we are about to be engaged. It is well known that it was not until the full profession of faith in His Divinity on the part of St. Peter, of which mention has just been made, that our Lord is recorded to have spoken in public, at least, of His Church. But it will not be difficult to trace in the incidents of this time a constant tacit forethought on the part of our Lord as to her characteristic powers, her mission, and the principles of her constitution and action. It seems indeed, sometimes, as if He was preparing the way for what was afterwards to be conspicuous in her, and especially for much that was to be new and contrary to the expectations of the Jews and the traditions of the Synagogue. Her fecundity is foreshadowed in the miraculous fishing, her use of natural elements in the healing of the leper. The miracle on the paralytic directly prepared the minds of men for her new claim to have power on earth to forgive sins. The entire novelty, as well as the great gentleness of her disciplinary system, is contained by anticipation in the doctrine concerning the children of the bride-chamber and the new wine and new bottles. Her power as to the right observance of the Sabbath and other such positive institutions seems to have been purposely asserted by the conduct of our Lord in working miracles on that day, despite the prejudices of the Jews which He went out of His way to brave. This part of the Gospel history reads as if it had been put together with the direct purpose of vindicating the liberty of the Church, and of asserting our Lord's own example and teaching as to the gradual removal of the obligations of the Old Law. These things ran counter, as has been said, to the darling prejudices of the Jews, and yet our Lord deliberately did and said so much in this direction, at the very time that He was preparing to retire before His enemies, and showing the greatest possible tenderness not to offend the persons who were most hostile to Him. Such a line of conduct can hardly have been adopted, except with a direct reference to the policy which the Church was to be guided to pursue after the Holy Ghost came to dwell in her on the Day of Pentecost.

Thus it was that, as our Lord went on teaching and working out the great object of His mission by the Father, the people with whom He had to do gradually separated themselves more and more into distinct camps, so to speak—those who became more and more hostile, and those who became more and more closely and singly devoted to His service. His enemies became more embittered, His followers grew into disciples and then into Apostles. The Synagogue, by its rulers, became committed more and more to a line of conduct which ended at last in His murder and in its own reprobation, while out of the little band of the fishermen of Galilee, and of others who clung to our Lord in ever more perfect faith, was formed the nucleus of what afterwards became the Holy Catholic Church. We are now to trace the history of this gradual sifting of the true and simple hearts from those in which self-love and human respect made faith impossible, and of the ineffable love, wisdom, mercy, and condescension which marked the conduct of our Blessed Lord in this part of His earthly course.

CHAPTER II.

The Miraculous Draught of Fishes.

St. Luke v. 1—11; *Vita Vitæ Nostræ*, § 37.

AT the close of his account of the Sermon on the Mount, St. Matthew tells us that great multitudes followed our Lord when He came down from the mountain on which that Sermon had been delivered. This is probably meant to show us that He continued His course of preaching throughout the country for some space of time after the Sermon, and that during that course He was followed from place to place by large crowds, forming a body of continual listeners to His teaching, in distinction from those which were gathered together in each place through which He passed by the fame of His arrival. We have already pointed out how the main features of the history would in such a case be the same day after day, and that thus there would be no special reason for recording the details of the teaching. Laborious as such seasons of continued preaching must have been, it is only natural, therefore, that what is preserved to us concerning the incidents of this period should relate to actions of our Lord which must have stood out as singular and remarkable at the time, and which had a significance of their own, in the unfolding of the mysteries by which He manifested the powers and prerogatives of His Sacred Humanity—powers and prerogatives which He was to hand on to His Church after Him. We have now to speak of one of these significant actions, the great importance of which lies in itself rather than in the particular moment at which it occurred, though it has a very remarkable bearing on the preparation of the Apostles for the great work to which they were being gradually drawn.

It may perhaps have been in some short pause in the course of active preaching of which we have spoken, that our Lord was for the moment at Capharnaum. The disciples who had accompanied and assisted Him in the circuit from which He had returned had not as yet been called by Him to abandon their homes and ordinary occupations at such times. The two pairs of brothers, Peter and Andrew, James and John, had returned for the few days of this stay at Capharnaum to their boats and nets. It was the practice to begin the fishing at night, and they had spent the night before the morning of which we are now to speak on the lake, but without any success. It had been a night of toil and watching, and all in vain. When the morning came, they put back to the shore, and washed and folded their nets. There they found our Lord, and, as He was about to teach, the crowds, as usual, gathered round Him, eager to hear, till the pressure became great, and He stept up into the boat of Simon Peter, asking him to push off a few yards from the shore, that He might address the people with greater ease. He went on with His instruction to the end—probably for a long time, as was His wont. When it was time to dismiss the crowd for their mid-day meal, our Lord turned to Simon Peter, and bade him put out towards the middle of the lake and let down his nets. Peter at once obeyed with joy. He told our Lord that they had toiled all night and had caught nothing, but he would gladly cast his nets again at a word from Him. 'We have laboured all night and caught nothing, but at Thy word I will let down the net.' The words are full of plaintive simplicity and enthusiastic faith, the natural fruit of that attentive listening to our Lord which had made him forget all his trouble and filled him with devotion. The nets were let down, and when the fishermen began to draw them in, they found that they contained an immense number of fishes. The net was in danger of breaking. Indeed, it seems to have been already broken. Peter and Andrew signalled to their partners, who were still in the other boat, close to the land, to come to them. Both boats were soon filled with the fishes, and were in danger of sinking before they could reach the shore. The evident miracle struck the humble Apostle with fear and reverence at the close presence of Him Whom he had been gradually led by the teaching of the Eternal Father to recognize as more than man. He threw himself at our Lord's feet, saying, 'Depart from me, for I am a sinful man, O Lord.' His astonishment was shared by his partners, his brother, and the small crew of the boat. Our Lord bade him fear nothing: 'From henceforth thou shalt be catching men.'

The simple narrative of the Evangelist has been pondered with loving reverence by the contemplative souls of all ages in the Church, seeking to fill in the picture where St. Luke has drawn it in outline only, to make it clear where it seems obscure, and to gather the moral lessons or the mysterious and even prophetic meaning which it may be intended to convey. The skilful fishers of the lake had sought their prey at the time and place which, according to the teaching of experience, were the most promising of success. Their failure after so many hours of weary and tedious toil may have been a serious disappointment, for their families may have been left without their aid during the weeks of their absence from home in the company of our Lord. He had already spoken to them of their future occupation in His service in language borrowed from their simple craft, for, when He had called them to follow Him at the outset of His course of preaching, He had promised to make them fishers of men. They had now for some time seen what were the conditions of that toil for souls to which He invited them. In the first place, then, it was a pursuit of immense and continuous labour; it involved bodily toil and mental fatigue—a strain on the attention, an indifference to discomfort and weariness, a sort of slavery to the calls of a multitude of persons, each too eager for his or her own needs to be at all considerate as to the trouble which it might cost to attend to them, an obligation to leave anything at any time in order to minister to sudden requirements, which involved an absolute neglect of self, even to the extent of the sacrifice of necessary rest and of the time for refreshment, of which the labours of their own hard and sometimes dangerous calling were but a very faint picture. It implied, moreover, a readiness of self-adaptation and self-sacrifice, such as that of which St. Paul afterwards spoke, when he said he had become all things to all men, for which nothing but the most consummate charity could furnish the strength, and nothing short of the most exquisite virtue could furnish the skill, the prudence, and the delicacy. Then, again, they had seen this work in the hands of our Lord marked by the most marvellous successes and the most glorious fruits. Though He spake as never man spoke before or since, still the effect of His words seemed to go beyond their intrinsic power. Movements of grace such as could ordinarily issue in nothing short of heroic acts of virtue seemed to be common on every side. The air seemed full of a new power. Nothing is so frightful in this world as the sight of an immense mass of men, swayed irresistibly by some overwhelming evil impulse. Nothing is so magnificent as a like number of men carried away by the enthusiasm of some mighty inspiration which comes from above. This is the secret of the marvellous effects which are sometimes seen when the word of God, in the mouth of a great saint, becomes for the time the master of a great audience, or when an immense multitude is collected and urged on by the attraction of some great festival or pilgrimage. In the case of the preaching of our Lord, it may be said that both these mighty influences were combined. His presence made a festival wherever He went. He was Himself the centre of the influence which draws men in all generations to great shrines which are blessed by God, and the most marvellous of His own preachers was a child by His side. And besides all this, the disciples had witnessed the wonderful prodigies of power and mercy by which His mission had been attested, the devils cowering before Him, the diseases of the body changed into health by His touch or at His word.

But at the same time, the disciples had already learnt that the evangelical calling was one which had its difficulties and even its defeats, as well as its triumphs and its incomparable glories. In this respect, it was but too like to that calling of their own to which He had compared it. It was a pursuit which, even in our Lord's hands, was not of certain or uniform success. During this first year, indeed, of His Apostolical ministry, we may fairly suppose, as has been said, that He was received with a freshness and vigour of enthusiasm which were not to last. There may have been a more even tenour of great success than was to be seen afterwards. But the issue of all such labour depends, in the first place, upon the various conditions of the souls to which it is addressed, and, in the second, on the secret counsel and choice of God, without a special drawing from Whom no one can come to our Lord. We may well feel sure that the Apostles had already witnessed much, in the reception of the teaching of our Lord by various persons and in different places, in which they might have seen a practical commentary on the picture which He afterwards drew in the Parable of the Sower. Their own fishing, during the night which they had spent on the lake, may have reminded them of occasions when even He had seemed to cast His nets with but poor success. But all this was soon forgotten, for they had joined Him as He was about to teach, with the multitudes thronging to hear Him, crowding in breathless attention to the water's edge, and forcing Him, as it were, to take refuge in the boat. Very gladly had Peter received his Master, and his disappointment sat lightly enough upon him as he listened to the words of eternal life from the lips of our Lord. The word of God, even in the mouth of a teacher of ordinary sanctity or power, often kindles a glow of enthusiasm which, while it lasts, seems to transport those whom it affects altogether out of themselves, to make them breathe the air of Heaven rather than of earth, an atmosphere in which the truths of faith shine with the brightness and the beauty in which they are seen by the angels in the presence of God. It is an atmosphere of truth and purity, of lofty conceptions and heroic resolutions, of glowing love and conscious nearness to our Lord. We soon pass out of its influence; but to have lived but a short half-hour in the light and fervour which it kindles is in itself a grace which leaves the will strengthened and the mind illuminated with the strength and light of God. If such is sometimes the fruit of the word of God, as it is spoken by His ministers in the Church, we may well imagine that a great instruction of our Lord to a large and eager crowd of simple and faithful souls must often have seemed to the Apostles to raise them to Heaven itself. We are told that, on another occasion like that of which we are speaking, when our Lord had been instructing the multitudes by the sea-shore, He was overpowered by fatigue at the close of His discourse, and we are thus able to draw a picture for ourselves of the energy, the animation, the force, and earnestness of His preaching. No preaching is ever truly efficient in which the preacher does not throw his whole heart and soul, all his powers, mental and physical, into his work; but what must it have been when the preacher was the Incarnate Son, using the whole force and power of His Sacred Humanity for the promotion of the glory of God and the salvation of souls!

In the case before us, the discourse of our Lord was to lead on to a display of marvellous power, of which, however, the Apostles, rather than the multitude, were to be the witnesses. It may even seem probable that it was partly for the purpose of retiring from the gaze of the crowd that our Lord bade St. Peter put out to sea, instead of landing from the boat and proceeding at once to the house which He made His home when in Capharnaum. Peter was now to be rewarded, with that liberal magnificence with which our Lord always repays even the slightest services which are rendered to Him, for the shelter which he had afforded to his Master when He mounted the side of his boat. The reward was to be in the same kind with his disappointment of the night, while it was also to be full of instruction as to his future ministry in the Church, and to prepare him to enter with zeal and joy on the renewal of the work with our Lord from which he had been resting for the moment. He was to learn from the issue of a fresh trial with his nets, under different conditions, what was to be the kind of toil for souls which God would bless with success. He had before laboured in vain, when all seemed to promise him success, as far as it could be secured by human skill and prudence; now he had our Lord with him, he was to launch out boldly where he had before fished in vain, and to let down his nets in the spirit of obedience and faith. Our Lord's words to His Apostle seem to speak, as it were, to a heart full of enthusiasm, hope, and faith, and to suppose in him a readiness to catch the spiritual teaching which was founded on the analogy between the material fishing which he was bidden to undertake and the labour for the salvation of souls which was figured thereby. They seem to speak the language of parable, and even of prophecy, and this character is not confined to our Lord's words, but seems to belong to the whole history of the incident. The words 'Launch out into the deep' suggest a bold confident spirit of enterprize, and remind us of the similar words addressed to the same Apostle, at the time of his vision at Joppa, before he was sent to the formal admission of the Gentiles into the Church, in the persons of Cornelius and his friends, and the voice came to him from Heaven, 'Arise, Peter, kill and eat.'[1] In each case the Apostle seems to be invited to vigorous action and venturesome enterprize, to cast aside all doubt and pusillanimity, even what might be reasonable prudence and moderation in his undertakings, if he had not a special call and encouragement and mission from on high. He is to consider the power and authority of Him Who commands, rather than his own slender

[1] Acts x. 13.

forces or the human probabilities of success. For all great works that are done for God must be done with courage and boldness, even though they are not to be undertaken without much counsel and prayer and forethought as to their method and aim, and it is almost a mark of the blessing which is to rest on them, that some human considerations and prejudices have to be set aside when they are taken in hand.

It is characteristic of all human enterprizes that their results cannot be certainly secured. They may be undertaken with the fairest prospects, the amplest means, the largest experience, the most practical skill. They may fail when all seems to promise success, or they may succeed when failure seemed their inevitable issue, but in no case can the issue be secured. If so it is with undertakings which depend upon natural causes and forces, or which at the most have only the chances and changes of the natural elements, such as the weather and the like, to oppose them, how far different must the case be in spiritual enterprizes, in the work of those who are, or who would fain make themselves, fishers of men, labourers in the vineyard of the Lord! In other cases no one can be secure that the workers may not have to confess that, at the end of a night of toil, they have caught nothing. This may be the lot of all human labour, of the toil of the brain as well as of the arm, of the man of science, or the statesman, of the searcher for truth as well as the searcher for gold. Life is a struggle and a battle for all, and its prizes are as often given capriciously as won by fair industry and intelligence. But in any undertaking which has to deal with the soul of man, and the spiritual world by which it is surrounded, human labour and industry have no promise or chance of success at all. The words of St. Peter are a motto which might be written at the head of the history of all such attempts, however honest and industrious, when the condition of the grace and blessing of Heaven has been wanting. 'We have laboured all the night and taken nothing.' The philosophers in their search for truth, the founders of sects and religions outside the Church, the missionaries who would convert the heathen, the mock hierarchies which attempt to do the work of the Church in nations already Christianized, all these, and others like them, may labour, and some, to a great extent, in good faith, and yet they will take nothing. And, as has been said, even the loyal and duly commissioned servants of the Church may often have to wait long for the reward of their labours, they may spend long nights, as it were, in toil, without success, even though there be wanting no condition on their part by which it might have been secured. For God, after all, keeps the issue in His own hands, as St. Paul says to the Corinthians, that he might plant, and Apollo might water, but God alone gave the increase.[2] We find traces of this principle of God's government even in our Lord's own life, as in His want of success at Nazareth, and in the history of the Apostles, while it is continually illustrated in the lives of the saints.

These thoughts illustrate the first part of these words of St. Peter, while the words which follow illustrate the prompt confidence and obedience which are at once inspired by a clear command from God or from one who speaks in His name. It mattered little to St. Peter that the last night had been so unfortunate, it mattered little that the best time for fishing was night, and not day, it mattered little whether the venture to which he was now invited might succeed or not. 'At Thy word, nevertheless, I will let down the net!' This was what he was told to do, without any promise that his fishing

[2] 1 Cor. iii. 6.

would be successful, but this was enough, even if the command of our Lord did not imply the promise. The faith and obedience of the fishermen were at once rewarded. But great as must have been the benefit which they thus received, and their joy at this fresh evidence of their Master's preternatural power and tender care for them, it seems hardly possible to linger long over the material boon, so full does the whole story become of evident spiritual meaning.

The details of the miracle seem as full of parabolic meaning as those of the miracle of the cursing of the barren fig-tree. The net is cast in obedience, and immediately it incloses a prodigious multitude; it is partly broken by their weight, it requires all the efforts of the fishermen under the command of Peter to receive the fishes into the boats, and these are almost submerged by the abundance of the prey. The mind at once passes on to the evangelical preaching of the Apostles and their followers in the Church, the pressure of converts of all kinds into the net, which, as our Lord describes it in one of His spoken parables, gathers in fishes of every sort, good and bad, and the consequent danger to unity and the perfect observance of the Gospel law. We seem to have a picture before us of the miscellaneous multitude of souls of which the Catholic Church is at all times made up, although the fact that so it is is more conspicuous at some periods of her history than at others. Such times are those of a large increase from without in the number of her children, or of the nations which own her sway. One epoch in her annals which was among the most dangerous in this respect was that which followed the conversion of Constantine, and the submission of the Roman Empire to the faith. Arianism immediately sprung up, and it is not too much to say that the beginning of the fatal schism of the East, which, after the rise of a swarm of other heresies, finally laid the fairest portions of the heritage of the Church at the feet of the abominable tyranny of Islam, may be dated from that time. Then indeed, if ever, the net was broken. Something of the same kind may be said of the great external magnificence of the Church in the middle ages, which led to the intrusion of ambitious, covetous, and worldly men into the high places of the sanctuary, and thus engendered that partial corruption which it required all the efforts of the Pontiffs and Saints of the Tridentine period to purge away, after many once Catholic nations had been lost to the Church. It seems as if Providence had over and over again written in letters of fire on the annals of the Church that great prosperity is injurious to her, and that very rapid progress in the conversion of large multitudes of men is not without its danger. She has a hard work to do in the continual training and care of her own children, and her advance is all the more solidly secured when it is won inch by inch against the powers which oppose her.

In the same way, the effect of the miracle on St. Peter and his companions, though natural enough in itself, is probably most easily understood in the supposition that to them, too, even at the time, the parabolical meaning of the whole scene, and its connection, in our Lord's intention, with the preaching which had immediately preceded it, and which was also so soon to follow it, were strongly and vividly present. The marvellous success of the casting of the net was in itself enough to fill them with stupor and astonishment, much more were such feelings aroused when they saw in what had happened a figure and a promise of the way in which the labours to which they were to be called for the salvation of souls were to be prospered by our Lord. This feeling probably speaks in the simple words of St. Peter, 'Depart from me, for I am a sinful man, O Lord.' Any display of supernatural or preternatural power is appalling to our weak humanity, sensible as it instinctively is of its own fallen and guilty condition. Any miracle might therefore naturally have frightened St. Peter and his companions, especially when the issue of it was a certain nearness of danger. But they had now been long in our Lord's company, and they must often have witnessed exertions of His preternatural power far more intrinsically appalling than this. The miracles, for instance, in which He put forth His authority over the powers of evil, must have been attended by circumstances of terror which are here altogether wanting. But if St. Peter's mind passed on from the fishing with his nets in the lake which he had lived on from his boyhood, to that other Divine fishing for the souls of men by means of the preaching of the word of God, which our Lord had already promised to make the vocation in the Church of himself and his friends, and if he saw, in the marvellous abundance of the prey before his eyes, a prophecy of the multitudes whom he was to be commissioned to bring into the spiritual net of the Gospel, he may well have sunk back in the sense of his own utter unfitness for the work, and of the very close nearness to the powers of the unseen world into which he was to be brought by the position for which our Lord designed him. In the same way, perhaps, it is that St. Paul, speaking of the effects of the exercise of the Apostolical ministry on various classes of hearers, cries out, 'For these things who is sufficient?'[3] But the words of St. Peter breathe the spirit of deep humility, modesty, self-accusation, and consciousness of his own weakness and unworthiness, which is characteristic of this great Apostle, and they are to be understood

[3] 2 Cor. ii. 16.

not so much as beseeching our Lord directly to grant the prayer which they seem to express, but rather as a prayer either to leave him or to make him more fit for the favours which He was lavishing on him. Thus we have instances in the lives of the servants of God in which they have shrunk back in alarm at their own success in preaching, fearing lest the work of God should suffer from the unworthiness of the hands into which it had fallen, or when they have desired that the favours bestowed on them might remain hidden, or might even be withdrawn, inasmuch as they have distrusted themselves all the more, the more highly they were raised by such gifts. That St. Peter did not wish to be separated from our Lord is clear from the history itself; for in that case he would not have drawn near to our Lord and have thrown himself at His sacred feet. And, although these words do not of necessity imply that he recognized in our Lord, as revealed in this miracle, a Divine Person, and not merely a saint endowed with preternatural powers, it still seems far safer to consider them as disclosing that penetrating faith in our Lord's Divinity which St. Peter was afterwards to confess so solemnly at Cæsarea Philippi. So to understand them makes it much easier to account for the fear with which the blessed Apostle was filled and overpowered.

The words of our Lord's reply to St. Peter seem to confirm the strong and prominent parabolical significance which we have been pointing out as belonging to the whole history before us. 'Fear not, from henceforth thou shalt be catching men.' They imply that the high vocation to which Peter was destined, was not to be withdrawn from him on account of his unworthiness; rather, his sense of his own unworthiness was to be at once the condition and the safeguard of that vocation. He had seen in parable how entirely all success in the evangelical ministry was to depend on the will and blessing of God, Whose spirit breathes where He wills, and he was not to fear, as if the work was his own, to be frustrated by his weakness or to be prospered because he was strong. He was to take courage, and gird himself up to the duties to which God called him, by a call which implied the promise of the graces necessary for the work. The marvel which he had just witnessed was to bring home to him the omnipotence of God, as well as the loving care with which it would exert itself in favour of the servants and friends of the Incarnate Son in the work of the new kingdom. We gather from the narrative of St. Luke, who says that, having brought their ships and the fish which they had caught to land, the disciples left all things and followed our Lord, that immediately after the miracle He started with them as His companions, on a fresh tour for the purpose of preaching. This confirms, again, the parabolic meaning of the miracle which had just been wrought, for it implies that they did not even linger for the purpose of making any use of the great booty which had been gained. The miracle was complete in itself, without any such use. The fish which had been caught were for the servants and the families of the Apostles, nor is there any mention in the Gospel of the presence of the multitude as witnesses of the miracle. It was for the Apostles, then, and for them alone. Before the news of the marvel could spread through Capharnaum, our Lord and His followers were already far on the road to some other city of Galilee.

Christian writers have dwelt with great minuteness on almost every detail in the scene of which we have been speaking, and they have found a significance in each. The washing of the nets, on which the disciples were engaged when our Lord began to teach, is understood of the care which preachers are to take of their own souls, while they are labouring for the good of others, especially as to the most perfect disinterestedness in the discharge of their sacred duties, or again as to the desire of praise, the temptation to vainglory, or to any sacrifice to human respect in their handling of the word of God, which are so many soils and defilements which may stain the ministry of the unwary. Again, that our Lord should have begged St. Peter to put off a little from the shore, that He might instruct the people at greater advantage, has been considered as conveying the lesson of that detachment from earthly cares and thoughts and interests which is so essential a condition of the successful preaching of the Gospel. Again, the charge to launch out into the deep has seemed to some to allude to the deep and sublime doctrine with which the evangelical preacher must not fail to feed his hearers who have received the gift of faith, in the exercise of which on the great truths of revelation a large part of the service which they are to render to God is to consist. The same meaning of the words of our Lord takes in also the teaching of the loftiest and most difficult of the precepts of the Gospel, the evangelical counsels, the doctrine of perfection, the beatitudes, and the like, from none of which is the preacher to shrink, when the occasion is before him, because he speaks in the name of Him with Whom all things are possible, and to Whom it is as easy to shed abundant streams of grace upon the souls of the hearers of the word as to fill the nets of the fishermen on the lake with thousands of fishes. These may suffice as instances of the moral and spiritual meanings which have been found in the details of this beautiful miracle.

It is also not uncommon to find the same miracle insisted on in another connection—that is, as marking a step in the implicit teaching of our Lord with regard to the position in the Church which was to be occupied by St. Peter. There are certainly some indications in the history of the pre-eminence of the Apostle over his brethren, which can hardly be considered as accidental. The boat or ship in which our Lord takes His seat for the purpose of teaching the crowds is that of St. Peter. It is to St. Peter that our Lord addresses the charge to launch out into the deep, while the injunction as to letting down the nets is addressed to the disciples in the plural number. The answer of St. Peter, who replies that he will let down the net at our Lord's word, seems to imply a sort of authority over the others. In the same way St. Peter speaks in his own name, as the master of the boat, when he implores our Lord to depart from him, as he is a sinful man; and it is to him alone that the assurance is addressed that he is not to fear, and that henceforth he is to be a catcher of men. These are the details which are recorded as to the position here given to St. Peter; and it seems natural to consider that they are not less significant than the other circumstances on which so much stress has been laid in the commentaries of the Fathers. Moreover, this miracle stands in the gospel history at a point between the first call of the disciples to the companionship of our Lord, and the formal and solemn act of election by which the four who are here named were, with eight others, to be separated from the main body of His followers and raised to the dignity of Apostles distinctively so called. It is a miracle which has a very clear reference to their future and not distant vocation, and it is full of moral and spiritual teaching with reference to its labours and duties. On this account there seems more reason for thinking that every detail has a special and designed significance with reference to the kingdom in which the

Apostles were to be the rulers, after and in dependence on our Lord, than might be the case in other events of our Lord's history which do not so directly relate to the work of that kingdom. When the four disciples were first called by our Lord to follow Him, there seems to be no distinction made between them, though even then St. Peter is one of the first pair of brothers who are invited by our Lord. When, a few weeks later than this time in the history, the twelve Apostles are promoted to their high and singular dignity, we find an unmistakeable primacy allotted to St. Peter. In the anecdote before us, it seems as if the chief of the Apostles was already, to some extent at least, distinguished as such, and we are thus prepared for the further teaching as to his primacy which is contained in the subsequent incidents of the history in which he is still more remarkably placed before the other disciples.

The miracle of which we have been speaking may also be considered as the first of the beautiful series of manifestations which took place on the lake of Galilee. The miracles on the lake are not only remarkable in themselves, but they seem to have a sort of continuity, as if they were meant to convey some special class of truths, in reference to the providence of God or the history of the Church in its struggle with the world. Such at least may seem to be the main burthen of the series which begins with this miraculous fishing of St. Peter, which goes on to the incident of the storm during which our Lord was asleep in the boat and which was at once stilled by His word, which includes that other most wonderful voyage across the lake when the Apostles toiled all the night against winds and waves, and were at last relieved by the presence of our Lord, Who came to them walking on the waters, and which ends with another miraculous fishing, after the Resurrection, which seems in so many striking ways to supplement or to contrast with the fishing of the Apostles which is related in the passage of the Gospel on which we have now been commenting. It is well to keep in mind, even in speaking of the scene before us, the relation which may be supposed as existing between the several incidents which are thus recorded in connection with the lake. The boat of St. Peter has become almost universally recognized as the figure of the Church in her toilsome and dangerous voyage over the troubled and treacherous seas of the world. In each of the scenes of which the series is made up, there is danger or anxiety or disappointment, which is allayed or turned into security and joy and triumph by the presence of our Lord. And it is certainly remarkable that, in each of these incidents, except in that of the storm, a very prominent and conspicuous part is occupied by St. Peter.

CHAPTER III.

The healing of the Leper.

St. Matt. viii. 2—4 ; St. Mark i. 40—45 ; St. Luke v. 12—16 ;
Vita Vitæ Nostræ, § 38.

It appears probable, as has been said, that the miracle of the fishing, of which we have just been speaking, was the immediate prelude to a fresh starting of our Lord with His Apostles on one of those missionary circuits throughout Galilee to which the greater portion of the first year of His Public Ministry was devoted. Out of the many incidents of these expeditions, usually, as has been said, not varied in character, the Evangelists have recorded for us some few which stand out in the history with a character and outline of their own. What their general character is, in reference to the unfolding of the counsel of God in the mission of His Son, has already been intimated. The first of these is one in itself, and in the consequences connected with it, striking and impressive, to an extent perhaps which it is not easy for us at first sight to understand. We are not familiar, either with the dreadful disease which afflicted the subject of the miracle, or with the manner in which that disease was looked on by the Jews. It was also remarkable in its circumstances, and in the sort of necessity which it seems to have entailed on our Lord of keeping for a time on the outskirts of the cities, instead of entering them, as was His wont, to teach freely in the synagogues. It was also a miracle of deep spiritual significance, and in this respect it occupies a very remarkable place in the gradually unfolding chain of the manifestations of our Lord. It follows very naturally after the miracle of the fishing, considered in its parabolic and spiritual signification, and it prepares the way for the great sacramental truth, the declaration of which seems to have been the chief object of our Lord in the miracle which follows next upon it in the historical order, the miracle on the paralytic man who was let down through the roof of the house in which our Lord was teaching. These are some of the chief heads for our consideration as to this miracle of the healing of the leper.

The place of the miracle is not named by either of the three Evangelists who relate it. It is mentioned by St. Matthew as the first of a long and very marvellously arranged chain of miracles, no two of which are exactly identical in character, which chain he subjoins immediately to his narrative of the Sermon on the Mount. It is quite certain that St. Matthew does not observe the order of time in this chain of instances of our Lord's miraculous power. Still less need it be supposed that this miracle, the first in the series, took place immediately upon the descent from the mountain of the Beatitudes. The purpose of St. Matthew in relating it made him altogether indifferent to the spot at which it occurred; and it seems possible that at the time of which we are now speaking this Evangelist had not become even an occasional follower of our Lord. St. Mark, as usual, here follows St. Matthew, filling up the story with several minute touches, in which we may certainly recognize the faithful observation and careful memory of St. Peter. But St. Luke, whose account is independent, says that the incident took place in one of the cities of Galilee, and his language seems to imply that it was a city distinct from Capharnaum. Here it was, then, that our Lord was seen as He was passing by a man whom St. Luke speaks of as 'full of leprosy;' in the most loathsome and miserable stage, therefore, of that terrible disease. For it would seem that such persons, unclean as they were considered, were not always actually banished to a distance from the habitations of men. In the case of persons of wealth and station, some private and secluded spot might easily be found near their own homes where they might nurse their misery unseen, and yet not be beyond the reach of assistance and comfort from their families. In some countries where leprosy still exists, the leper lives in some retired part of the house inhabited by the rest of his family. Thus there is no difficulty in the statement of St. Luke that this miracle took place in a city. The poor leper must have heard of our Lord, and his faith was very strong. When he saw Him he darted forth from his place of seclusion—some small building, perhaps, in a garden by the roadside—and threw himself at our Lord's feet in adoration and supplication. His prayer was short, a simple expression of faith rather than a direct petition for relief. 'Lord if Thou wilt Thou canst make me clean.' Our Lord's compassion was at once moved. He did more than He was asked, for it was His will to show in this as in some other of His miracles, the life-giving and healing power of His Sacred Humanity, by relieving the evil by actual contact rather than by a simple word or sign or precept. All the three Evangelists who relate the miracle mention this circumstance, that our Lord not only said, 'I will, be thou made clean,' but 'put forth His hand and touched him' as He spoke —an action, of course, all the more significant, because to touch a leper involved the legal defilement of the person who touched him. This legal defilement did not, of course, involve any sin; it simply implied a disqualification from taking part in public worship or from entering the tabernacle or the Temple. Still the action of our Lord in touching the leper was very remarkable in itself, as well as full of meaning in relation to the doctrine of the Incarnation.

The leprosy was immediately and perfectly cured. The whole miracle seems to have passed in a moment of time. The companions of our Lord had scarcely recovered from the shock of surprise which they must have felt at the bold action of the leper, and at our Lord's instantaneous granting of his prayer, before our Lord, in a tone of urgent authority, sent him away with the twofold injunction to say nothing to any one of his cure, and to go to the Chief Priest to show himself, —according to the provision of the law in such cases, in order that he might be declared free from his disease after the usual examination—and to make the offerings which were prescribed after the declaration had been obtained. We may suppose that the latter of the two commands was faithfully obeyed by the person who had been healed. The first, however, he was unable to observe. His wonder and joy were too great to be kept to himself, though he left our Lord's presence at once. Men who have received such benefits cannot hold their tongues, and if the leper could reason on the matter, he may have thought it his duty to make his Benefactor, the worker of so wonderful a miracle, as widely known as possible. At all events he spread the fame of what had been done far and wide. It went over the whole country that the terrible plague of leprosy had been healed at once by our Lord's touch and word. We cannot be certain whether our Lord was considered to have contracted any legal defilement. This has been supposed by some writers, as if this were the meaning of what St. Mark tells us of the consequence of the notoriety of the cure, that He was not able for a time to enter openly into the city. But the words of the Evangelist do not of necessity imply this. It is enough to suppose that the miracle attracted an unusual amount of attention, and raised the enthusiasm of the people to the highest pitch. The cure itself may have been published without any mention of the manner in which it had been wrought; and, if the manner as well as the fact had been published, the touch which could entirely cleanse the body which had been full of and covered by leprosy may have been understood, even by the Jews, to have been incapable of defiling the person of the Healer. It may have been thought that to take on Himself to heal a disease which was so especially considered as an infliction of chastisement on the part of God, the cure of which was confessedly beyond human power, a cure as to which the priests alone had authority to pronounce, was an assumption which in some respects went beyond any other which had as yet been made by our Lord. In this way there may have been a reason for His avoidance of publicity for some time after the miracle. It is certain, at all events, that He kept aloof from the towns, and remained for some time in lonely spots. He spent, as St. Luke tells us, the time which was thus gained in prayer, but the people did not leave Him to Himself. As soon as it became known where He was they crowded after Him, for the double purpose of hearing Him teach and of obtaining the cure of diseases.

It is here, then, that we meet for the first time, in the Life of our Lord, with that dreadful malady of which we have happily so little practical acquaintance, though it was well known in Europe after the Crusades, and was in many ways so tenderly and touchingly cared for by the Christian charity of the middle ages. The remarkable manner in which this disease is dealt with in the Law of Moses may be explained in two different ways. It has been thought very generally that the supposed contagiousness of leprosy was the chief reason for the elaborate provisions on the subject which are contained in the Book of Leviticus.[1] In that case the provisions in question would be political or sanitary, rather than strictly religious. It is known that the forced labours to which the Jews were obliged to devote themselves in Egypt were of a nature to occasion this particular disease, and its prevalence would not have been diminished by the hard life which they must have had to lead in their wanderings in the desert. They thus entered the Land of Promise in a condition which was very likely to make this terrible malady hereditary among them, and on this account, as is supposed, it was, that so many careful provisions were inserted in the Law, with the merciful purpose of lessening the evil by preventing its communication to persons not as yet infected by it. This is one common view of the matter, and it seems to explain sufficiently the Mosaic legislation on the subject.

On the other hand, it is now very widely and authoritatively thought that the disease in question is not contagious, and it is not difficult, on this supposition, to explain in quite a different manner the prescriptions of the law and the purpose of the lawgiver. Under no possible view of the question as to its contagiousness, can leprosy be considered as a common disease. Its extreme loathsomeness, the manner in which it makes its way from internal seeds of evil to the skin and surface of the body, until the whole man seems to be little else than a mass of festering corruption, tending to decomposition

---

[1] Lev. xiii. xiv.

by the actual falling off of one limb after another, and, beyond all, the length of time during which the sufferer might live on in this state of gradual death—often, it is said, for twenty years—while at the same time the disease was altogether incurable, these and other circumstances are enough to place it on a line of its own in the sphere of the miseries to which human nature is subject. It is clear that a malady at once so frightful in itself, so disgusting to the sight and all the senses, and so extremely slow in its course from what may most truly be called a living death to that actual separation of soul and body which, in the case of its victims, could hardly ever be anything but a most merciful release, required all the protection afforded by the special legislation which gave it a sacred character, in order to make it in any way tolerable, either to those who were afflicted by it, or to their friends, or to society at large. We might almost imagine that nothing but a true faith as to the Fatherhood and Lordship of God over all His creatures, and especially over those whom He has made in His own image, could have saved the lives of lepers, either from their own misery and despair, or from the hands of others.

What the lot of the lepers may have been in heathen countries we have little means of knowing; but it seems likely that in the East, at all events, the disease was protected, as among the Jews, by the idea that it was a special visitation of Heaven and so had a sacred character. It is easy to imagine how such diseases would be dealt with by the social economy of modern infidel philosophers, if they were ever allowed by Providence to gain the rule of the world. All this suggests the thought, that the Mosaic legislation on the subject of leprosy may have been partly grounded on those principles of mercy and compassionateness which had so much influence, in other instances, on that legislation. There are many provisions of the law which seem intended to anticipate in some measure the Christian law of charity, and it is probable that mercifulness, the care of the weak, the fatherless, the aged, the bereaved, and other such classes, were to be found in a far higher degree of development among the Jews than among any other people. But still, among the Jews, and, at a later time even among Christians, the case of the lepers must have been a very hard one. It was one of the first enterprises of the great St. Basil, after he became Archbishop of Cæsarea in Cappadocia, to build a large hospital for the reception of these sufferers at the gates of his episcopal city. He enlisted in favour of this good work the eloquence of his life-long friend, St. Gregory of Nazianzus, whose sermon on the subject is one of the noblest specimens remaining to us of the grand oratory of that generation of celebrated Christian theologians.

This sermon contains a description of the miseries of leprosy, which can hardly be read, even at this distance of time, without tears. There are degrees, the preacher tells us, of human misery, some worse and more hopeless than others. Poverty is hard to bear, but poverty is not without hope of relief. Disease is worse than poverty, for it cannot help itself. But the case is still harder when men are objects of horror, fear, and aversion to their fellows; and this is the kind of misery, in its most terrible form, which asks our compassion in the case of the lepers. 'No one who has not seen them can believe what a sight it is which they present. They are dead and living at once, mutilated of many of their limbs, so disfigured and afflicted as not to be recognized by those who were formerly their friends. They have to force themselves on our recollections by recounting the names of their parents, the places where they have lived, and the like. They have lost property, home, friends, even their own bodies; it is difficult to say whether they are more to be pitied for what they have lost of their limbs or for what remains of them. The best and most humane of men are hard and cruel to the lepers. They make us forget that we are ourselves of flesh, and clothed with vileness, and we consider that, instead of relieving them as our kindred, we owe it to our own safety to shun and flee from them. People will perhaps bear to touch a dead body, or even the bodies of wild beasts already corrupt and stinking, and yet we run from the sight and presence of the lepers and think it too much to breathe the same air with them. Their own parents lose, in their case, all their natural piety. The father drives away from him the son who has been as the apple of his eye, whom he has brought up with the tenderest care, and for whom he has poured forth prayer after prayer to God. The mother turns away in horror from the fruit of her womb, whom she has borne, not for her home, but to dwell in the deserts, on the wild mountains, and among the beasts. The people at large shout after them and revile them, not because they are wicked or criminal, but because they are afflicted and miserable. Men will admit murderers to their table, they will extend hospitality to the adulterer, but they have no mercy or kindness for these innocent victims of disease. They are driven from the cities, houses, market-places, assemblies; they are not allowed to drink of the public fountains; even the rivers are thought to be contaminated if they have tasted their water. But we treat them so cruelly, that our very cruelty brings them back upon us. We provide them with no place to live in, we give them no food, no medicines, no clothes, no coverings for their misery.

They wander about night and day, naked and homeless, showing their malady, reminding us of what they once were, calling upon the mercy of their Creator, helping one another with what remain to them of their limbs, begging, in strains which move the heart to compassion, for a morsel of bread, a little meat, or an old worn out rag to cover their shame or to shelter their sores. It is thought a great instance of mercy, I do not say to relieve them, but not to treat them with cruelty in refusing them. So, notwithstanding all their misery, and the shame which prompts them to avoid the eyes of men, they are forced by sheer need to rush importunately into the midst of our sacred assemblies on feast days, or when we are met to do honour to the Christian martyrs, reminding us well enough, if we are ready to take in the lesson, of our own frailty and of the worthlessness of all human goods, in order that they may hear the voices of men from whose society they have been banished, that they may see the faces of their fellow-creatures, may derive some consolation from the mere recital of their woes, and obtain some little help from those who are overflowing with wealth and every earthly good.'[2] These last words seem to indicate that the lepers could not be altogether excluded from the churches.

The holy Doctor goes on to remind his hearers how these miserable beings are their brethren, formed of the same clay, made like others in the image of God, and their fellow-sharers in all the blessings of the Christian mysteries. He reminds them that they are themselves the disciples of our Lord, Who has left them so many examples of mercifulness and charity. And he quotes the text of the Prophet Isaias which St. Matthew applies to Him in this very narrative, where it is said that 'He Himself bare our sorrows and took away our griefs.'[3]

[2] St. Greg. Naz. *Orat.* xiv.   [3] St. Matt. viii. 17; Isaias liii. 4.

But enough use has already been made in this place of this beautiful sermon of St. Gregory, which may certainly serve the purpose of showing how very great must have been the need of some such provisions as those which are contained in the Book of Leviticus. The lepers were taken by those regulations out of the category of ordinary sufferers. The idea which lay behind the whole of the enactments concerning their treatment, namely, that they were in a special manner stricken by God, whether for personal sin of their own or for some other cause, gave a sort of consecration to their misery, like that which in some Christian countries is commonly attached to insanity or idiocy. Their separation from their fellow-men was a severe infliction; but it was more merciful to them that it should be legalized, than that it should be left to the caprice or alarm of their families. Moreover, the legislation provided, not only for their banishment, but also for their restoration, when the time came for it, and it was a gain to them to have this solemn and authoritative process to protect them from all future question or molestation. And their very seclusion itself, which led in so many instances to their congregating together in small bands or communities, was not without its aspect of mercifulness. For it delivered them from the constant pain of the visible and sensible contrast between themselves and others, and from the suffering caused by the perception of the feeling of loathing and disgust which they inspired.

There is, however, another and still deeper aspect of the whole question, according to which leprosy was selected as being not only, in many ways, a most fearful form of disease in itself, in its effects, in its incurableness, and in the length of time during which a sufferer might remain in his misery under it, but also in particular as being one in which the malady met the eyes of men and impressed itself on the senses in a way that was altogether singular. Such a disease was on these accounts better fitted than any other to be a sort of divinely selected type of sin, which is the primary cause of all such physical evils, and, as such, to be dealt with by God in the legislation which He gave to the people which in a special manner belonged to Himself. Death itself, the worst physical consequence of sin, was treated in the Mosaic law as having a ban upon it as such, and the mourning for the dead, the touch of a corpse, or of a grave, and the like, were made occasions of ceremonial uncleanness. It has been remarked by some writers on the subject, that it would have been no more than a further step in the same direction, if all diseases, which are the forerunners of and the preparation for death, had been made, in like manner, the occasions of defilement; but that God, in His considerate mercy, took only one disease, and that the most visibly terrible of all, and, as it were, set His mark upon it, by way of protest that He was not the author of sin, and that He abominated and could not tolerate it. Thus the leper became a living and moving parable, which set forth the heinousness and mischievousness of sin, and the exclusion from the commonwealth of which God was the Lord and King, which it justly involved. He was treated as one already dead, the emblems and trappings of death were all around him; and when the time came for him to be restored, upon his cure, to the ordinary privileges of the people in communion with God, the ceremonies which were to be observed were in every respect the same as those which were enjoined in the case of persons who had been defiled by contact with a dead body. Lepers were thus among the Israelites what the Jews themselves are at present among the nations of the world—a community or class set apart by Providence, with a special brand of the Divine justice upon them, bearing witness, by their very existence, and their isolation in every land, to the truth that the Ruler of the universe can and will visit national or personal sins with conspicuous and enduring punishment. This view of the case of the lepers is not inconsistent with the truth of the other considerations on the same subject which have been spoken of above. Their treatment by the Mosaic legislation may have been regulated to some extent even by sanitary interests, and far more by motives of mercifulness to the sufferers themselves; and these again may well have been combined, in the counsels of Providence, with the still higher purpose of keeping them before the eyes and mind of the people as examples of the deadly effects of sin, its extreme banefulness, and the manner in which it is regarded by God. To a thoughtful and religious mind, this view of sin might naturally suggest itself, at the presence of any disease whatsoever. The sight of the miseries to which the body is subject leads without any forced transition to the thought of the far more serious and lasting miseries of the soul. But the lesson of this kind conveyed by the lepers, when taken in conjunction with the sort of reprobation inflicted on them by the Mosaic law, spoke much more forcibly and irresistibly even to the dullest and hardest hearts.

It was also in the designs of Providence that our Lord should reveal Himself as the physician and healer of the maladies of the soul, partly by means of His power in healing the diseases of the body. But in no instance would this teaching concerning His spiritual work, as the healer of all sins and disorders of the soul, receive more striking illustration from His mercy to the miseries of the body, than in the case of a miracle like that of which we are speaking. There is every reason for thinking that the impression made by this particular cure was far greater than that of any other of the miracles of healing which had preceded it. Our Lord may have foreseen this, and we may thus account for the great urgency of His injunction to the leper to be silent as to the mercy of which he had been the object. It seems certain that he must have been sent to Jerusalem, as that was the only place where the sacrifice enjoined by the law could be offered. And if we are to understand, as the words of St. Mark seem to imply, that our Lord sent the person whom He had healed to the Chief Priest himself, there may have been a special design in this. For the time was now approaching when He was again to visit the Holy City, and test by His presence and by fresh displays of His miraculous power the hearts of the high authorities there, on whom so much was to depend as to the reception of His teaching by the whole nation.

It is clear from the nature of the case, that the seclusion to which the lepers were condemned by their malady, and by the prescriptions of the law regarding it, together with all the suffering which it entailed, must have had very different effects in the case of different persons and characters. So it is in all afflictions, and in none more so than in the affliction of bodily disease. Such visitations are to many the school and the exercise of great virtues, of which they might not have been capable under circumstances of less external misery. The leper of whom we are speaking seems to have learnt great perfection in the trial which had befallen him. Holy writers speak of him as a bright example, not only of faith in our Lord's power, which, as far as we are told, had not before this time been exerted in the particular way of the healing of leprosy, but also of prudence, in the moment which he chose for his application, when our Lord was not engaged in teaching the crowds, who might have been scared by such an interruption, in the indirect and submissive form in which his petition was couched, in the reverent appeal which he made to our Lord's power and sovereignty, and in the simple words which he used, which stated his needs and desires without any rhetorical exaggeration. There can be little doubt that he came to our Lord with a faith which fell but very little, if at all, short of the full perception of His Divine Person; for he makes no petition for prayer, and he implies that our Lord can do as He choses in the matter of healing or not healing him. He displays great humility, reverence, devotion, confidence, and hope; and it is difficult to suppose that other virtues, which are usually found in company with those which we have named, were wanting to him. His prayer is one of those in the Gospel history which may be considered as put before us as models, to teach us the spirit and manner of the petitions which reach most easily the Heart of our Lord. Such was the prayer of our Blessed Lady at the feast at Cana, 'They have no wine;' or that of the sisters of Lazarus, when they sent to our Lord the message, 'Lord, he whom Thou lovest is sick.' He appeals to the power and loving-kindness of our Lord, and so leaves himself in His hands with entire confidence and resignation.

Our Lord's answer exactly echoes, if we may so speak, the words of the leper, for it expresses the two things of which he had spoken, the will to heal him, and the sovereign decree that he should be healed. So far, then, our Lord dealt with him according to his faith, as He was in the habit of doing with those who came to Him with such petitions. And yet He did a great deal more—though here, again, he acted as He was in some cases, though not in all, wont to act. The leper was prostrate at His feet, hiding, as some holy writers remark, his disfigured and loathsome face in the dust from the eyes of our Lord. It was as if he feared to shock Him by displaying his own misery. But our Lord leant forward, and stretched forth His hand, and touched him as he lay. It was a touch which gave health and soundness to that wretched and half-decayed body. Indeed, some holy writers have thought that the cure of the leprosy was effected by the simple word of our Lord—that the disease fled away before His touch, and that when His hand rested on the body of the leper, it found it already as clean and whole as the flesh of a newborn child. There can be no certainty as to questions of this kind, as to which the words of the Evangelists do not exclude either supposition. But, as both in this place and in so many other passages relating to our Lord's miracles, we have what appears to be the careful and express mention of actions like that of which we are speaking, it may be well to pause for a moment to consider some of the truths which are involved in His adoption of this particular method in His healing of diseases, and on other similar occasions.

We may distinguish, in the first place, those miracles of our Lord which were more simply miracles of mercy, from those which were conspicuous and intentional displays of supernatural power as well as works of compassion. Very seldom indeed did He work a miracle merely as a sign; indeed, He constantly refused to do this when it was demanded of Him by the Jews. But His miracles of healing may be distinguished from those which consisted in the deliverance of those possessed by devils, and again, from exercises of power over creatures and the elements, as when He stilled the storm on the lake, or changed the water into wine, or multiplied the loaves and fishes, or filled the nets miraculously, or withered the barren fig-tree. In these last He uses His voice only as the instrument, if we may so speak, of His inherent power; though in the miracle at Cana, and in that of the multiplication of the loaves and fishes, the miraculous effect was not directly connected even with the words which He spoke. He seems never to have touched with His sacred hands any of those out of whom He cast the devils; but when the effect which He desired to produce was the healing of disease, or the restoration of a lost sense, or even of life, we find Him ordinarily touching the person who was to be healed, laying His hands on him, and in some cases doing more, as when He put His fingers into the ears of a deaf man, or mixed some earth with spittle to anoint the eyes of one who had been born blind. The instances of cures of disease in which nothing of this kind is recorded can usually be explained in such a way as to leave it probable that, but for some particular circumstances, our Lord would have observed the rule of which we speak in these cases also, as, for instance, in the healing of the nobleman's son, or of the centurion's servant, or in the raising of Lazarus, in all of which the use of touch was either impossible or not easy.

Many reasons have been assigned by the Fathers and other Christian commentators for this practice of our Lord, some of which are general in their application, while others have reference to the circumstances of this or that particular miracle. Thus, in the instance of the leper of which we are speaking, our Lord is thought by some writers to have desired in an especial manner to insist on the truth that no legal defilement could have any place in Him. There would be the same meaning, perhaps, in His action in touching the bier on which the body of the widow's son was laid. But in other cases this interpretation would not apply. So, again, if we consider that our Lord acted in this manner out of humility and condescension, it is clear that such motives would not be enough to explain the way in which He dealt with the deaf and the blind men in the instances just now mentioned. The principle which appears to underlie all these actions of our Blessed Lord, seems to be this—that it was the law of the dispensation of the Incarnation, that His Sacred Humanity was to be the instrument and channel, as well as the meritorious cause, of all healing, of all good, of all graces and favours from God, whether spiritual or corporal. This truth it is that supports and animates the whole sacramental and quasi-sacramental system of the Church. And if it be left out of sight, men may fall back upon ideas as to our Lord and His work which are altogether un-Catholic. The religion of our Lord is, indeed, a spiritual religion, but it has a body as well as a soul, like man himself, for whose benefit it has been given, and who is bound by the law of his nature to render to his Creator the homage of both. If our Lord had not adopted the practice of which we are now speaking, the authority of His example in the acts of corporal mercy, which were the figures of the spiritual blessings with which He came to remedy the evils and miseries of the soul, might have appeared to be opposed to the invariable practice of His Church, which makes use of external signs, actions, words, and material elements, in all her ministrations for the benefit of souls—ministrations which are nothing but the application in special ways of the merits and graces of His Sacred Humanity. The diseases and evils of the soul are very far more grievous in nature than those of the body, but they are meant to be typified by the latter, and we have seen that there is reason for thinking that this particular malady of leprosy was, in a special manner, a chosen figure of sin. The manner in which our Lord healed the one set of evils was also, it would seem, meant to be a figure of the method by which, in the providence of God, the spiritual maladies of men were to be cured by Him. There was therefore a Divine reason for the rule by which our Lord acted when He so uniformly touched or laid His hands on those whom He delivered from bodily ailments.

This may be considered as the theological answer to be given to the question before us. There is also another reason assigned by some writers in this particular case, on which it may be well to add a few words. The evil under which the leper was suffering was, as has already been said, especially loathsome and revolting to the natural senses, more so probably than any other malady of the kind with which we are acquainted. To bear the sight of such a miserable object, much more to draw near to him, to breathe the same air with him, and to touch him, would be a great trial to any one who was not armed with a higher motive for such condescension than that of natural kindliness or philanthropy. Our Lord came to introduce new principles and new systems of conduct with regard to all the manifold and multitudinous phases of human affliction of every sort. He was to enforce by new motives, and by the aid of new truths and new hopes, the great practical law of Christian charity and devotion to misery of every most repulsive kind. This law can never be carried out in accordance with His intention, unless it is made almost a first principle that the most real and true exercise of mercy is that which gives, not money, or relief of any kind, so much as personal service—the service that does not shrink from the closest contact with those whom disease or decay, whether of body or of mind, or of all that makes intercourse and companionship pleasant or even tolerable, has rendered not only pitiable, but even disgusting. There are depths in the dark kingdom of misery and degradation which are hardly to be imagined by those who have not sounded them. But nothing, however loathsome to the senses, or appalling to the delicacy of the most sensitive and refined children of luxury and civilization, was to be too deep for the supernatural courage of Christian charity. But that it might be so, it was, as it were, necessary that out Lord should touch with His own sacred hands the very foulest forms of disease which came across His path, and thus at once encourage the sufferers of every extremest phase of material misery by the proof which He gave, that they also had a share in the tenderness and compassion of His Sacred Heart, and at the same time lead the way Himself in that heroic devotion to the afflicted of every sort which was to be one of the greatest glories, and one of the most incommunicable characteristics, of the kingdom of charity which He came to found.

The story of Christian charity has many beautiful pages which relate to the manner in which, when lepers came to be common in Europe, the Church and her saints provided, as far as was possible, for the relief or the alleviation of their misery. Numberless houses were built for them. St. Louis is said to have provided in his will for as many as two thousand. Confraternities were formed for the purpose of taking personal care of them in these leper-houses, and a writer of the times asserts that the pious laymen who devoted themselves to this good work endured therein, for the love of Christ, an amount of defilement, infection, and mortification, to which no penance in the world could be compared, and that this was a kind of martyrdom most precious in the eyes of God. St. Louis, already mentioned, undertook the personal charge of a leper whose disease was of a kind more especially loathsome. Sibylla, Countess of Flanders, who had accompanied her husband to the Crusades, obtained his leave to remain behind him in the

Holy Land in order to devote herself to the care of lepers. St. Francis of Assisi and St. Catharine of Siena are conspicuous among the saints who had a particular devotion to these poor sufferers, and there are here and there most beautiful anecdotes, as in the life of St. Elisabeth of Hungary, in which our Lord Himself has appeared as a leper, and been tended with exquisite care. It is not wonderful that from time to time there should have been occasions when, in seasons of plague or other terrible visitations, the superstitious prejudices of the people were aroused against these sufferers, and then severe measures were taken against them. But they had always the Church on their side, to defend their rights, and to secure them the aid of the means of grace, as well as the assistance of the charitable. Churches and cemeteries were set apart for their especial use, priests were assigned to them, and a religious order, the Order of St. Lazarus, the Grand Master of which was always one who had been a leper, was founded to serve and protect them. The actions of our Lord in His Sacred Humanity are indeed both typical and prolific; they live on throughout the Christian ages in a thousand marvellous fruits and works of piety and charity, which were present to His Heart when He went about, as St. Peter speaks, doing good and healing all that were oppressed of the devil. And we may well see the first seed of all that the charity of the saints afterwards invented for the relief of this particular form of misery, in the simple action of which the three Evangelists take special notice, when they tell us how He not only cleansed the leper by His sovereign word, when He said, 'I will, be thou made clean,' but also stretched forth His hand and touched him as He spoke.

CHAPTER IV.

The Healing of the Paralytic.

St. Matt. ix. 1—9; St. Mark ii. 1—14; St. Luke v. 17—29;
Vita Vitæ Nostræ, § 39.

IT has already been noticed that some considerable interval of time must have intervened between the miracle of the healing of the leper and the next recorded incident of the Gospel narrative. The Evangelists tell us that the public attention was so strongly drawn to our Lord by the publication of the miraculous cure of the leper that 'He could not openly go into city, but was without in desert places,' to which the people flocked to Him from all sides 'to hear and to be healed by Him of their infirmities,' and also that He spent much of His time in retirement and prayer. Many explanations may and have been given as to this effect of the publicity of so great and so startling a miracle. Our Lord may have feared to arouse the enmity of the Scribes, or the enthusiasm of the people might be feared as likely to produce some disturbance in the town of Capharnaum, of which Herod might take advantage. The crowds which flocked to Him while He kept aloof in the country parts were quite sufficient to occupy His time. Again, He may have wished to let the effect of this most symbolical miracle work on the hearts and minds of those for whom He was preparing a still more wonderful assertion of power—claiming to forgive sins, of which leprosy was but a figure. He may have wished, too, that the news of the cure might be carried to Jerusalem by the man himself who had been healed, and that there might be time for the authorities, if it so pleased them, to send delegates into Galilee for the purpose of making inquiries concerning Him on the spot where He had wrought so many wonders.

We are apt to pass from one miracle, or discourse, or parable of our Blessed Lord to another, as if there were no delicate and careful connection between the] links of the beautiful chain in which His actions were arranged by the providence of the Father andt he guidance of the Holy Ghost. But, in truth, nothing in our Lord's life was accidental or at haphazard : we may not always be able to see the connection between one part and that which follows it or has preceded it, but a connection there certainly was, worthy of the full and ecstatic contemplation and admiration of the Angels in Heaven. In the present instance, it is not difficult at all events to conjecture that, as the first of the two miracles of which we are speaking was a preparation for the other, our Lord desired that time should be given for that preparation to ripen and work itself out in the hearts of the people or their leaders. This is all the more likely, as we find that St. Luke here mentions that our Lord was at this time occupied in prayer. Prayer was, indeed, the habitual and unremitted occupation of His Sacred Heart, but it is specially mentioned that our Lord prayed on certain occasions, which were times when He had taken or was about to take some new step, the consequences of which might be important in the unfolding of the plan of His life or of His designs for His Church.

In this instance it is not forbidden us to imagine that the subject of our Lord's prayers would be connected with the miracle which He had lately wrought as to its spiritual signification. Never before had He so plainly, in a single action which lasted but for a moment, pictured the character of His mission and the manner in which its purpose was to be carried out. Later on in His course of teaching He described the fallen, helpless, bruised state in which He found the human race, in the touching parable of the man who had fallen among thieves and the Good Samaritan who relieved him. The leper prostrate at His feet, confessing his own misery and our Lord's power to heal him, and his instantaneous cure by the word of our Lord's mouth and the touch of His sacred hand, represents our condition with the same vivid completeness as the description of the wounded man in the parable just mentioned. Our Lord was not only to touch the leprosy of our nature and take it away, but He was to become as a leper for our sake, in order to remove it. The rites which were to be gone through at Jerusalem when the healed leper presented himself to the High Priest, were beautifully typical of the cleansing and absolving of the human race in virtue of our Lord's Sacrifice. Thus, this miracle, and the proof to which its effects were to be put, brought before His mind the whole scene and mystery of the Passion. Again, the man who had been healed was in a certain sense a herald to the High Priests and authorities at Jerusalem—a herald whose message might alarm and irritate them, or, on the other hand, console and prepare them for grace, according to the disposition of heart in which they might receive him. Here was another subject for special prayer. For every fresh announcement of God's marvellous mercy in the Church is in some respects a challenge to faith as well as a message of love, and the truths which were figured in the miracle on the leper involved not only the whole doctrine of the application of the graces of redemption by means of human instruments, but also the correlative duty, on the part of those whose souls were to be healed, of humble submission to the conditions on which it might please God to make the ministration of pardon depend. There are times of crisis in any spiritual or moral movement when little is said or done, but a great issue is decided in the hearts of men, and these are times when, most of all, the followers of our Lord are called upon, by His example, to give themselves to prayer.

We may suppose that our Lord did not return to Capharnaum until He had allowed ample time to elapse for the effect of this great miracle of the healing of the leper. 'Again, He entered into Capharnaum,' says St. Mark, 'after some days,' that is, after a considerable period of absence, 'and it was heard that He was in the house, and many came together, so that there was no room, no, not even at the door, and He spoke to them the word.' St. Luke's account is more precise as to the persons of whom the audience was composed. 'It came to pass on a certain day, as He sat teaching, that there were also Pharisees and doctors of the law sitting by, that were come out of every town of Galilee, and Judæa, and Jerusalem, and the power of the Lord was to heal them.' This is a very remarkable description, and it most certainly signifies that the assembly was to some extent unusual. It was not probably unusual at this period of our Lord's Public Life, for the Pharisees and teachers of the law to attend His preaching, and to do so without any evil intention or prejudice against Him. The time had not yet come for the decided break between Him and the ecclesiastical authorities. But that there should have been a gathering of such persons from all the towns of Galilee and from Judæa and Jerusalem, must have been unusual, and it may be considered as a proof of the very great extent to which public attention was now concentrated upon Him. Perhaps, also, we may see in it the effect, already spoken of, of the miracle on the leper, and it may even be thought likely that some of these Pharisees and doctors had been sent into Galilee by the authorities at Jerusalem for the express purpose of watching Him. If this be so, it gives a character of unusual solemnity to the teaching which He now addressed to an audience so important in itself and in the possible influence of its members. This may be signified in the remarkable words with which St. Luke introduces that teaching. 'He spoke unto them the word,' says St. Mark—and the third Evangelist adds, 'And the power of the Lord was to heal them'—that is, the word was directed to the healing of their souls, and it was, as it were, winged by strong influences of Divine power, which worked upon the hearts which were fit to receive it, and so prepared them to correspond to the gracious and healing doctrine which our Lord delivered.

There were there, we may suppose, as in any large audience now or at any other time, and especially any audience made up in great part of the ministers of religion, men whose souls were in the most various conditions of moral health or weakness or disease—the hardened teachers of laws which they did not themselves observe, the hypocrites whose life was so fair outside and so foul within, the ambitious or covetous or sensual ministers of the altar, the men who sought nothing so much as to rise and rule, the bouncing and swaggering prelates, whose position encouraged them never to brook contradiction or opposition, the vain, the frivolous, the worldly, the sleek silky 'devourers of widows' houses,' and those 'who made long prayers for a pretence,' who could thank God that they were not as the rest of men. But we must never judge of the mass of the Jewish ecclesiastics, —out of whom a very large number were gathered into the Christian fold by the teaching of the Apostles after the Day of Pentecost,[1]—from what is recorded for us about their rulers. Even among these there were men like Joseph of Arimathea, and it would be hard to suppose that there were not many simple souls like Barnabas among the Levites. The ministerial calling, the position of those, especially, whose lot it is to rule, has many temptations and dangers indeed; especially when the community in which they rule is prosperous as to its worldly condition or its connection with secular power. It then becomes a sphere in which ambition, avarice, jealousy of the excellence of others, a desire to monopolize opportunities of usefulness and prominence in activity, not to speak of other lower vices, are likely to find much room for exercise, and it has the peculiar danger of being ordinarily beyond the reach of admonition from others. The ranks of the ecclesiastical order are crowded with the best of men, but they do not exclude some of the worst. In the assembly of which the Evangelists are speaking there may have been some of these, but by their side there may have been found many a guileless, innocent soul, full of faith, not yet ripe for the Gospel truths, but fed upon all the rich spiritual treasures of the older dispensation. There were to be found the honest perplexed inquirers after the truth, the men struck to the heart by the purity and sublimity of our Lord's teaching, the beauty of His character, the splendour of His miracles, but still unable to understand the lowliness of His station, the humility and the free condescension of His life, the sincere zealots for the tradition of the elders like St. Paul afterwards, the timid hesitating good men whose very eminence was in their way,

[1] Acts vi. 7.

like Nicodemus or Gamaliel. All the diseases or infirmities of their souls lay open to the eyes of this Divine Teacher, on Whose lips the whole of this heterogeneous assemblage was for the moment hanging, and for all of them He felt the burning love of the Redeemer and the Good Shepherd, for the wants of each He could provide healing and strength in the words which fell alike on the ears of all. As when His Apostles spoke on the Day of Pentecost, as it seems, in one language, and their words reached the ears of the strangers from so many various lands, so that each one understood them for himself in his own tongue, so the power of the Lord, as St. Luke says, in this discourse was adapted so as to touch each soul at the point where it was most vulnerable and where it most needed relief. There was light for the ignorant, and the unravelling of entanglements for the perplexed, there was courage for the timid, and strength for those too weak to cast off the chains of sin, reproof for the haughty, comfort for the mourner, peace for the troubled, refreshment for the weary. Such is the power of the word of God, even in the mouths of the weakest of the ministers of the Church. A large crowd of the teachers of religion is always certain to contain the most varied forms of spiritual condition, and it is seldom without some among it who are most ready for the influences of grace, and some others with whom grace must have a hard battle not to plead in vain.

This seems perhaps to be the most natural interpretation of the words of St. Luke in this place. But a more common way of interpreting them is that which understands his language about the power of our Lord being there to heal them, as referring simply to the exercise of His miraculous power in curing diseases, which so constantly accompanied His teaching. It is at all events certain that one of these interpretations does not of necessity exclude the other. What may have been the special subject of our Lord's teaching on this occasion, we are not told by any of the Evangelists. It is quite possible that it may have had some reference to the last great miracle which had been wrought by Him, which had attracted to Him so much attention, and which had probably occasioned, in part at least, the great assemblage of doctors of the Law which is mentioned by St. Luke. The transition from the subject of the leprosy of the body to that of the leprosy of the soul, and to its other diseases, would be natural and easy, and thus it may have been that the minds of His audience were full of the subject of moral disease at the time when the discourse either came to an end, to be succeeded by the exercise of the miraculous and merciful power on the bodies of men, or was interrupted by the incident which now follows in the history.

'And behold men brought in a bed a man who had the palsy'—who was carried by four—'and they sought means to bring him in and lay him before Him. And when they could not find by what way they might bring him in, because of the multitude, they went up on the roof and let him down through the tiles, with his bed, into the midst before Him.' St. Mark says, 'They uncovered the roof where our Lord was, and opening it, let down the bed'—and we must gather from his description, which is, of course, that of St. Peter, that they did something more than merely let the bed down into the open middle court which was so commonly to be found in the houses of that time and country. Eastern travellers tell us that at the present day it is not uncommon to open a part of the roof in the manner which is suggested by the words of St. Mark. The resolute faith of the four bearers of this poor sufferer was too impatient for delay, and although there may have been many others waiting their turn for our Lord's attention, they forced their way to the front in the manner related, and the palsied man lay in his bed before our Lord's feet in the sight of all, and the eyes and thoughts of all the watchers and listeners were concentrated upon him.

The Gospels do not tell us anything of the interior dispositions of this poor man. He does not speak to make any prayer or request, nor do we know that when he allowed himself to be carried through the streets in his bed to the place where our Lord was teaching, he had any other thought than that of obtaining deliverance from his bodily malady. Nor is there anything to make us believe that the bearers themselves sought from our Lord for more than this. Their case is thus in some respects like that of the nobleman whose son seems to have been the first person whom our Lord healed in this same city of Capharnaum, for whom his father petitioned that He would come from Cana to heal him, when it was our Lord's intention to raise his faith to a higher level, and lead him to believe that He could work miraculous cures at a distance as well as when present by the side of the sufferers. Thus, on the present occasion, our Lord did not ask them what they desired, but turned at once to the palsied man. 'And when Jesus had seen their faith'—when He had witnessed the toil to which they had put themselves, which was evidence enough to outward eye of the faith which He also discerned in their hearts—' He saith to the sick of the palsy, Man, My son, be of good heart, thy sins are forgiven thee.'

Thus, as holy writers tell us, the faith of the bearers— for it is their faith which is directly mentioned as the cause which moved our Lord—won for the sufferer under their charge not only the benefit which they directly sought, but also, a far greater benefit, the healing of his soul. For it is the way of God to allow this power to faith, that it can obtain great boons for others as well as for itself. For an action of faith like that of which we are speaking was a silent but most forcible prayer to our Lord to exercise His merciful power in favour of the palsied man. Again, it is the way of God to give more than He is asked, and in a higher order, sometimes instead of in the order in which He is asked, —as when He gives the grace of resignation and patience when He is asked to remove some calamity, or the grace of strength and victory when He is asked to take away some temptation, and the like,—sometimes as well as in the order in which He is asked, as when He grants some temporal boon and at the same time some great spiritual gift. Nor is it beyond the power of faith to make Him combine these two favours, and grant to the prayers that are made for the temporal benefit of others, both that temporal benefit and also a spiritual boon of a higher grade. In this last case He does not, it is true, directly grant the spiritual gift to the prayer alone of others than the recipient, because another law of His dealings with moral agents, who are capable of cooperating with or resisting grace, requires that their own will should consent to the merciful design of God. But He then grants, to the prayers which are made for them by others, that they may have the graces which lead to the dispositions in themselves which are necessary for the reception of the spiritual boon.[2]

It is to be noted also that our Lord speaks as if the forgiveness were already complete—He does not promise it as something future. The forgiveness of sins is used in the language of Christian theology in two different senses, both of which concur in making up the full idea

---

[2] See Toletus, *in Luc.* cap. v. annot. 26.

of forgiveness. For sin, it need hardly be said, implies guiltiness and separation from God in consequence, and this guilt involves two distinct penalties—the penalty of eternal damnation or the loss of God, and the penalty of a certain amount of temporal punishment. As the essence of sin, in this case, is its guilt, so the essential meaning of forgiveness of sin is the removal of guilt, the restoration therefore of the soul to grace. This cannot be without at the same time containing and implying the removal of the penalty of eternal damnation, which belongs to all mortal sin, and corresponds to the banishment of grace from the soul. But when sin is forgiven as to its guilt and as to its eternal doom, the temporal punishment which is due to it may remain or may not remain according to the intensity of the contrition in the subject or other conditions. When this also is altogether forgiven and blotted out, the forgiveness of sins is perfect and, as we may say, adequate—all that has the character or that is the consequence of sin, has been removed. When this temporal punishment has not been cancelled along with the guilt which has incurred it, the sin may be said in one sense to be forgiven, and in another sense not to be completely forgiven. The guilt is gone, the temporal punishment remains. In this latter case, the process of forgiveness has not proceeded to its full limit, on account of certain causes, which may be called accidental, in so much as, in the design of God, they are not intended to prevail. Thus when our Lord uses the words, 'Thy sins are forgiven thee,' in this place, and again, to the blessed Magdalene, as we shall see a little further on in the history, we must understand Him to use the words in their largest sense, and to imply the remission of all pain as well as of all guilt, or of all pain alone that might be remaining, as in her case, and, perhaps, in that of this palsied man, after the guilt had been already cancelled by contrition. His words are equivalent to a declaration of all the remission which may have already taken place, and to a granting of all remission which yet remained to take place. There is the same fulness of meaning in His words when He confers on the Apostles[3] the power of forgiving sins, because it is His desire that the Sacrament of Penance should be received, by all who receive it, in the perfect fullness of the benefit it contains, and because He has also left in the Church the power of enjoining satisfactory penance and of granting Indulgences, by means of which the debt of punishment which may remain may be entirely cancelled.

This will help us to understand the connection between the boon which these bearers desired for the paralytic, and the boon which was actually, in the first instance, conferred by our Lord. Some writers consider that our Lord implied that the disease from which he was suffering was the direct consequence of some personal sins—that is, that it had either been produced by them, or had been inflicted on him, in the Providence of God, as a penalty for them. Thus to declare his sins forgiven would be the same as to tell him that the cause and source of his malady was removed, and that therefore the removal of that malady itself would immediately follow. Whether this be true or not, it is certain, as has already been said, that all human maladies and miseries are in a most true sense the penalties and consequences of sin, and that therefore the removal of guilt from the soul must involve a sort of title to the removal of such chastisement. But, even if there were no direct connection between the maladies of the body and the sin of the soul, the former are, in any case, the most perfect pictures and images of the latter, and it was for this

[3] St. John xx. 23.

reason, as we may suppose, that it pleased God to make so large a part of the evidence by which the mission and authority of the Saviour of souls were accredited and authenticated, consist in the exercise of the miraculous powers of healing. In this case the assertion of the power to forgive sins was a claim to something which could not be externally tested or proved. It might have been proved by any display of miraculous power whatever, such, for instance, as the stilling of the tempest, the multiplication of the loaves, the change of water into wine, or the withering of the fig-tree. But nothing was so like to the healing of the soul as the healing of the body, and thus the miracle on the body of the paralytic which our Lord was about to work, was naturally, and as it were congenially, the legitimate proof of the power which He claimed to have exercised over the soul.

'And there were some of the Scribes and Pharisees sitting there and thinking in their hearts, why doth this Man speak thus! He blasphemeth! Who can forgive sins, but God only?' In truth, the objection which these Pharisees made in their thoughts had a foundation. For sin being an offence against God, which cannot be done away with unless God restores to the offender His grace and favour, and removes the sentence of eternal damnation which He has passed upon it, there can be no forgiveness of sin except by an act of God's mercy. The very idea of sin as such rests upon the rights and the character of God, and upon nothing short of these. In a system of morality in which God is set aside and denied, there can be no true sin, and, in the same way, there can be no true forgiveness of sin except by God. Thus much was true, and the truth which was contained in their thoughts was wholesome and necessary for a right appreciation of sin. Thus the model of all penitents, the blessed David, had said in his great confession, 'Against Thee alone I have sinned'—my sin is nothing short of an attack on Thee, an insult and injury to Thee, a rebellion against Thee, a defiance of Thee, involving, if such were possible, Thy destruction and Thy murder. In the second place, it is clear that this power of forgiving sins, which is inherent in God alone, had not hitherto, in the dealings of God with man, been committed to others than Himself. There was no ordinance or commission in the Old Law by which priest, or saint, or prophet could forgive sins. But, at the same time, these Scribes must have known that many things which belong essentially to God can be and had been committed by Him to men. God alone is to be adored, but they honoured saints and prophets and angels, and, in an inferior sense, those who represent God on earth. God alone can know the future or the hearts of men; but He had committed the revelation of the whole scheme of His designs in the world, in the Incarnation and otherwise, and also the knowledge of men's thoughts, to His prophets and saints, though 'in part,' as St. Paul says, and at certain times, and in a certain measure, according to His own wisdom in each case. In the same way it belongs to God alone to work miracles, that is, to suspend or go beyond the laws of the natures which He has made, and yet this power of miracles, even the raising of the dead to life, had been sometimes communicated to His saints and prophets.

In the nature itself of the case, therefore, there could be nothing to prevent the communication even to man of the power of forgiving sins on the part of God, although there had not as yet been any instance of this communication in the history of His dealings with mankind. Nor had our Lord said in so many words, 'I forgive thee thy sins,' but only, 'Thy sins are forgiven thee,' using the more reserved and modest way of speaking of Himself which He usually followed. Our Lord's answer to the thoughts of the Scribes was in itself, apart from the words which He used, an explanation of their difficulty in grasping the truths which have just been set forth. For it does not seem that a word had passed their lips, or reached His ears, and yet He spoke as knowing the thoughts of their hearts. This is perhaps what He had done in the case of Nathanael, when He spoke to him about what had passed in his mind under the fig-tree. It was in itself an exercise of a power which belonged to no one but God Himself. Thus it implied an argument of the same kind as that which our Lord immediately went on to use from the exercise of miraculous power. It implied that, at least, God must be with Him, if it did not necessarily imply that He was Himself God. But if God was with Him, as was shown by His knowledge of their hearts and thoughts, then He could not have been acting without the authority of God when He had told the palsied man that his sins were forgiven him. It was not true that to say this was to blaspheme; it was true that to say it was either to blaspheme, or legitimately to claim Divine power. And the display of Divine power in reading their hearts was enough to show that the last of these two alternatives was true, and not the first.

And Jesus presently knowing in His spirit that they so thought in their hearts, answering, said to them, 'What is it you think in your hearts? Why think you these things in your hearts?' For, even if He had not gone on in any way to confirm by a display of supernatural knowledge or power the claim which had been implied in His words about the forgiveness of sin, still there was, as has been shown, an alternative open to them other than that condemnation of Him for blasphemy to which their thoughts inclined. They might at least have suspended their judgment, or they might have felt bound, from all that they already knew or had heard concerning Him, to think that it was the most probable supposition that He had any power of this kind which He claimed. They were, therefore, in danger of passing a rash and severe judgment, even if they did not express it. Then, having modestly reproved them for this, and also rebuked them by showing His knowledge of their hearts, which was enough to convince them as to His power, He went on to argue formally in the manner which has just been mentioned, 'Which is easier to say, Thy sins are forgiven thee, or to say, Arise, take up thy bed, and walk?' This is often understood as if our Lord had meant to urge on them, not so much the comparison between the powers which might be claimed in these two cases respectively, as the truth that in both cases the words implied a power which was altogether above man. He says, as it seems, that it is as easy to say one of these things, as to say the other, because the fault which had been found with Him in the hearts of His hearers was that of blasphemy, which consists in speech —in His claim to a power which belongs to God alone. As to the two things to which His power refers in these two cases, both are above man, though perhaps it might be said that the forgiveness of sins belongs to a higher order than the healing of a bodily disease or infirmity. There is, however, a contrast between the two cases, to which perhaps our Lord's words refer; for it is easier, in a certain sense, to claim a power our possession of which cannot be tested, than to claim a power as to which it can be immediately seen whether we possess it or not. In this sense it is easier to say, 'Thy sins are forgiven thee'—as a false teacher, or a pretended priest, may go through the form of absolution or of consecration in the sacred Mass, and the like, and no human power can discern his imposture—than to say to a man sick of the palsy, 'Arise, take up thy bed, and walk;' for in the latter case the result will not only not follow, but it will be clear to the eyes of all that it does not follow, and so the imposture will be detected.

This being the case, the force of the argument on which our Lord insists is easily apprehended. He had used words which claimed Divine power in the spiritual world, and now He uses words which claim the same power in the world of sense. 'But that you may know that the Son of Man hath power on earth to forgive sins (He saith to the sick of the palsy), Arise, take up thy bed, and go into thy house. And immediately rising up before them, he took up the bed or pallet on which he lay, and he went away to his own house, glorifying God.' The words of our Lord seem to have been chosen for the purpose of counteracting the false judgment which they had formed, not merely as to His supposed blasphemy, but as to the truths in which the doctrine of the forgiveness of sins consisted. That is, they had considered that the power of the forgiveness of sins was not only essentially and exclusively inherent in God Himself, but that it could not be communicated, as those other Divine powers of miracles, prophecy and the like, were communicated by God to man as He chose. This was false, and although this communication had never before been made, yet it was not only possible that it might be made, but also actually true that it had now been made. Our Lord was Himself God, but He was also Man, and in His Human Nature, as the Son of Man, He exercised this power on earth as

He exercised it as God in Heaven. This was one of the great boons which earth had gained by the Incarnation. The forgiveness of all sins was to be abundantly purchased by His Passion, and the fruits of His Passion in this respect were not to be stored up in His own Sacred Humanity alone, but were to spring from it for ever for the benefit of the whole human race, and to be administered, according to the ordinance and decree of God, by His Church after Him. He was to communicate this power of His Sacred Humanity in the most solemn way to His Apostles and the Church in them after His Passion and Resurrection were accomplished. No doubt, this was to be something new, of which these Scribes and Pharisees had never heard, and for this very reason, perhaps, it was that He took this first occasion of claiming the possession of this power at a time when so many of the teachers of the Synagogue were present, and of proving it by one of His most signal miracles in a manner which could not be gainsayed.

This great miracle, therefore, was far more than a simple act of compassion on the bodily sufferings of the palsied man. It was, in a most pointed and determinate manner, the proof of a great doctrine relating to the Sacred Humanity of our Lord. His words show that He did not so much set forth His Divine Nature by the miracle, and the argument which He founded on it. For He did not say that God could forgive sins on earth as well as in Heaven, but that the Son of Man had power on earth to forgive sins. It is clear also that He might have proved the possession of this power by any other external miracle, if He had chosen, such as might have had no relation or resemblance in any way to the internal miracle, as it may be called, in which the forgiveness of sin consists. But He chose to do this by means of a miracle which represented the act of spiritual mercy in proof of which it was wrought. For until sins are forgiven, the soul is either dead in the sight of God or palsied, unable to move or act in any healthful way towards salvation. But when the decree of pardon is given forth, and the precious Blood has been applied to it, the soul is full of life and strength, as the man who could at once take up his bed and go to his own house. Thus the internal cure of the soul was represented and evidenced by the new health conferred upon the body.

Something has already been said as to the connection of this miracle with that on the leper, which had preceded it at some little interval of time. If leprosy had been so especially marked, and, as it were, branded, by God, as the physical evil which most closely pictured the spiritual evil of the soul, in its loathsomeness, its incurable character, the sort of excommunication which it involved, and the like, it was natural that when our Lord had filled men's minds with the exhibition of His marvellous power in cleansing their physical corruption, He should go on to declare to the world the power of the Son of Man to forgive the far greater evil of sin. The leper had been forced by the Law to take a long journey to present himself to the Chief Priest in Jerusalem, and all along the road he must have declared the power of his benefactor. He had had to submit to a careful examination, and purifying rites and sacrifices, all of which required the intervention of the Levitical priesthood. The new power of cleansing from sin was exercised at a moment and by a few simple words, 'Thy sins are forgiven thee,' and the power of these words had been proved by the evident effects of other words quite as simple, 'I say unto thee, arise, take up thy bed, and go into thy house.' The first miracle had prepared for the second, and the second had shown the pre-eminent power and beauty and condescension and simplicity of the new kingdom of the Son of Man on earth.

'And the multitudes seeing it feared, and glorified God that gave such power to men.' This is the manner in which St. Matthew speaks of the miracle, which, as we shall see, had so much connection with his own call to follow our Lord more closely. The other Evangelists use more general terms, 'They wondered, and glorified God, saying, We never saw the like.' 'They were filled with fear, saying, We have seen wonderful things to-day.'

We hear nothing at all of any more objections on the part of the Scribes. The language of St. Mark and St. Luke might seem to leave it in doubt whether the fear and wonder which took possession of the multitude are to be attributed simply to the miracle which they had witnessed, which was great in its kind—though we can hardly suppose that our Lord had never before worked any so striking in that place—or whether we are to suppose that they took in the connection between the doctrine which our Lord had asserted as to His power on earth to forgive sins and the proof by which He had confirmed this assertion. The miracle in itself was marvellous enough, but still more marvellous was the truth in evidence of which it had been so professedly worked. But the words of St. Matthew seem distinctly to refer to the point of doctrine, as proved by the miracle, as the subject matter of the wonder and joy of the crowd. For he says, 'They glorified God, Who had given such power unto men,'—as if to refer to our Lord's own words, 'that you may know that the Son of Man hath power on earth to forgive sins.' The same word, signifying power or authority, is used in each sentence. And it would seem also that the first Evangelist meant to point to the further doctrine, that the power and authority of the Son of Man passed on to the Church after Him, for he speaks of power given to men and not only to one man or the Son of Man. Thus we have every reason for thinking that some at least of the audience to whom our Lord had been preaching, and some at least of the multitude who had gathered round the door when the time came for the sick to be brought to Him, were fully and deeply impressed with the great truth which had now been set forth. There is nothing said about their not understanding our Lord. Indeed, mankind in general are quick enough in grasping the force of the argument from miracles in proof of doctrine. That argument is not, of course, direct—that is, an exhibition of Divine power does not directly prove that a certain statement is true, for the force of the inference rests upon the principle that God will not exercise miraculous power in support of a statement which is not true. This principle forms a part of every right conception as to God. But, notwithstanding the indirectness, so to speak, of the theological force of the argument, men at once, in general, apprehend it without hesitation. This is the true reason for the hostility of all rationalists and Protestants, as well as of all infidels, against the miracles of the saints and especially of the modern Church. They know how unreasonable it is to deny the possibility of such miracles, and yet they will not look into the evidence on which each case in particular rests. They reject them at once as impossible, and deal with the particular evidence as proving nothing but fraud and delusion. On the other hand, the children of the Church rejoice over miracles which are vouchsafed in their own time, after the evidence has been established as sufficient in any particular case, not merely for the proof which they afford of the goodness and mercy of

God, of the power of our Blessed Lady or the Saints, but also because they show that He is still with the Church, and that He continually, generation after generation, furnishes her with fresh confirmation of the truth and holiness of her doctrine. It is not wonderful, therefore, if this simple multitude in Galilee glorified God after this great miracle, not only because a wonderful act of mercy had been wrought, but because it had been proved in the sight of all that henceforth men might be endowed by Him with the power of forgiving sins.

Thus it may well be said that this miracle takes its place by the side of those most conspicuous actions of our Lord, in which He foreshadowed or declared the greater marvels which were to become permanent in His Church after Him. Such was the miracle at Cana, or again that of the marvellous fishing, or again those of the multiplication of the loaves, in which the institution of the Blessed Sacrament was prefigured. If our Lord had chosen to subjoin on the present occasion a long discourse, in which He might have explained fully the whole doctrine of absolution and of the power of the keys as applied to sins, this miracle would have seemed to Christians in all ages quite as appropriate an introduction to that doctrinal exposition, as the miracle of the feeding of the five thousand to the great discourse on the Blessed Sacrament which St. John has added to his narrative of that miracle of the multiplication of the loaves. The poor people who rejoiced so heartily at this first announcement of the power which men were to receive as to the forgiveness of sins, could only anticipate in part and dimly what the exercise of that power was to be. Their marvel at the goodness of God could only touch it in general, and without experience of its practical application. It was to be left to Christians of all times and generations to thank God with a more full intelligence for His mercy in giving this power to men. Next to the marvellous power of offering the Divine Sacrifice, and so making present on the altar the very Body and Blood of our Lord, no greater boon has ever been conferred on earth, even as the fruit of the Passion and Death of the Incarnate Son. If our Lord had left nothing behind Him in the Church but the Sacrament of Penance, He would have left a gift worthy of the praises of all Heaven throughout all eternity. If it were allowed to Christians once in their lives, after a long and painful preparation, to approach this single sacrament, it might well seem as if God had exhausted the utmost largeness of indulgence and compassion for those who were in need of it. It might have seemed as if salvation had been made so secure and so easy of access, that no one could fail, without the most outrageous madness, to reap its full benefit. And this is one of the boons of God's love as to which there has been the greatest amount of negligence on the part of those who have known of it, and which have provoked the greatest amount of obloquy and calumny against the Church for proclaiming and using the power which God has bestowed upon her. It is common, even still, to hear Christians repeat the objection of the Scribes—'Who can forgive sins but God alone?' The confessional has been made the great point of attack against which heretics, especially of modern times, have directed their assaults, and, amid the whole range of the ordinances of our Lord, there is not one against which the father of lies, and the men who have sold themselves to be his instruments, have poured forth torrents of falsehood more persistent and more abominable.

It is true that the unregenerate mind revolts against almost every instance of the goodness of God in conferring, to any extent and in any way, supernatural power on men like ourselves. But there is something peculiarly furious about the hostility which has been so constantly aroused by the doctrine that the Son of Man hath power on earth to forgive sins, and that this power is perpetuated in the Church. No plain declarations of Scripture have been so violently dealt with as those texts of the New Testament which witness to this doctrine, no point to which the teaching of tradition bears so unmistakeable a witness has yet been so determinedly denied. It is a more wonderful thing, certainly, that men should have the power of consecrating the Blessed Sacrament, and of making our Lord's Body and Blood present on the altar by the words of his mouth. But men who can believe this, because our Lord has virtually said so, cannot believe in the power of absolution, of which our Lord had spoken even more directly. It may perhaps be, that the power of the forgiveness of sins, as it is spoken of by our Lord in this and other places, implies, in a manner which men instinctively recognize, the correlative duty of confession in those whose sins are to be forgiven. Whatever may be the cause of the rabid hatred with which this doctrine has been received, it is certain that it shows the extreme tenderness and consideration of God for our poor and weak nature, in a degree which is nowhere surpassed in the whole economy of redemption. It seems as if the sacred writer had almost intended to draw our thoughts to this immense condescension and considerateness in the words in which he has recorded the wonder of the crowd. They are said not merely to have glorified God for allowing sins to be forgiven on earth, but for having given the power to do this unto men. It is true that the whole arrangement of the kingdom of the Incarnation involves the commission of the chief spiritual powers which were to be permanent therein to men rather than to angels. For our Lord took on him the seed of Abraham, not the created nature of the angels. But the mercifulness of this dispensation is nowhere so conspicuous as in the selection of men as the ministers, especially of reconciliation and pardon. The greatest English writer of our time has drawn out this thought in a discourse of which it will be enough to quote only a part. 'It is almost the definition of a priest that he has sins of his own to atone for. "Every high priest," says the Apostle, "taken from among men, is appointed for men, in the things that appertain unto God, that he may offer gifts and sacrifices for sins; who can condole with those who are in ignorance and error, because he also himself is compassed with infirmity. And therefore he ought, as for the people, so also for himself, to offer for sins."[4] Most strange is this in itself, my brethren,' continues Cardinal Newman, 'but not strange, when you consider it is the appointment of an all-merciful God; not strange in Him, because the Apostle gives the reason of it in the passage I have quoted. The priests of the New Law are men, that they may "condole with those who are in ignorance and error, because they too are compassed with infirmity." Had angels been your priests, my brethren, they could not have condoled with you, sympathized with you, have had compassion on you, tenderly felt for you, and made allowances for you, as we can; they could not have been your patterns and guides, and have led you on from your old selves into a new life, as they can who come from the midst of you, who have been led on themselves as you are to be led, who know well your difficulties, who have had experience, at least, of your temptations, who know the strength of the flesh and the wiles of the devil, even though they

[4] Heb. v. 1—3.

have baffled them; who are already disposed to take your part, and be indulgent towards you, and can advise you most practically, and warn you most seasonably and prudently. Therefore did He send you men to be the ministers of reconciliation and intercession; as He Himself, though He could not sin, yet, by becoming Man, took on Him, as far as was possible to God, man's burthen of infirmity and trial in His own Person. He could not be a sinner, but He could be a man, and He took to Himself a man's heart, that we might intrust our hearts to Him, and "was tempted in all things, like as we are, yet without sin."[5]

In His discourse with the Jewish authorities at Jerusalem, after the miracle on the impotent man at the pool of Bethsaida, of which we shall have to speak in the present volume, our Lord tells us that the Father has committed the office of the judge of mankind to Himself in His human nature, because He is the Son of Man. It is a further carrying out of the same principle, that the priests of the New Covenant, who have to exercise the functions of judges with regard to the sins which are to be submitted to the sacred tribunal of penance in order to absolution, by virtue of this power of the Son of Man on earth to forgive sins, should also be men like the sinners whom they are to judge and to absolve after judgment. The reason given by St. Paul in the Epistle to the Hebrews contains many points which might be unfolded in pious meditation, and to this reason that other may be added, of which the same Apostle speaks in the Second Epistle to the Corinthians,[6] where he says of the Gospel ministry, that 'we have this treasure in earthen vessels, that the excellency may be of the power of God, and not of us.' For if the power of

---
[5] *Discourses to Mixed Congregations*, No. 3.
[6] iv. 2.

forgiving sins is so peculiarly the prerogative of God, it is greatly to His glory to commit it to a sinful and weak race, rather than to the Princes of His own heavenly Court, who have never known sin in themselves. The pardon of sin is a triumph over the enemies of God and man by which they are especially confounded, and by which their malice is in a certain true sense turned against themselves, for if they had not led man into sin, he could never have reaped the benefits of redemption. And thus the administration of this great fruit of our Lord's victory is more complete a defeat for them when it is committed to men, than if it had been intrusted to the blessed spirits like themselves in nature, who stood firm when they fell away from God.

CHAPTER V.

The call of St. Matthew.

St. Matt. ix. 9; St. Mark ii. 14; St. Luke v. 27, 28; *Vita Vitæ Nostræ,* § 39.

THE three historical Evangelists connect the miracle of which we have just been speaking with the call of St. Matthew to that close following of our Lord which already distinguished this chosen disciple, and out of which, soon after this time, the Apostolate itself issued. It is impossible to say whether St. Matthew had been present at the miracle of the healing of the paralytic man. That our Lord, passing from the scene of this miracle, found him already seated in his office by the shores of the lake, does not prove with absolute certainty that he had not himself seen the miracle. But it is more likely that he had heard of it, that the eager crowd had spread the news all over the city almost as soon as the miracle had been performed, and that in this way the future Apostle and Evangelist had learnt of the new manifestation of power on the part of our Lord. It was a manifestation which was by no means limited, either in our Lord's intention or in the minds of the people who witnessed it, to the external cure which had been wrought, wonderful as that might be. The miracle had been wrought with the express design of drawing attention to, and proving by the most tangible evidence, the claim, which our Lord now advanced, to the power of forgiving sins. It may be assumed that this feature in the miracle was the ground of the great astonishment and exultation with which the cure itself was received by the people at large, and that when it was announced to those who had not been present, as may have been the case with St. Matthew, this was the point on which particular stress was laid. Thus, even if St. Matthew had not been present at the working of the miracle, it is very likely that he may have heard, before our Lord addressed him, not of the miracle alone, but of the great point of doctrine which our Lord had so markedly connected with it. That it was so may be gathered from the manner in which he speaks of the impression produced by the miracle on the multitudes, who glorified God, Who had given such power unto men.

If we put together the accounts which are here given us by the three Evangelists, it appears that, after working the miracle in the house, which was in the middle of the town, our Lord went forth and began again to teach the people. There seems to be some contrast drawn between the crowds and the more limited audience who had gained admittance into the house, and whom, from the words of St. Luke, we may suppose to have been ecclesiastics, and scribes, and other persons of more or less authority and influence. Our Lord went, then, to the sea-shore, and there taught the people in the same way as on the occasion lately mentioned, before He worked the miracle of the wonderful draught of fishes. As on that occasion He may have led up in His teaching to the miracle which He was about to perform, and which was full of significance, especially to the future Apostles, St. Peter and the others, so now He may perhaps have made the forgiveness of sins, or at least that image of sin which is represented in the palsy from which the bedridden man had been delivered, the subject of His discourse. The teaching came to an end in due time, and, instead of launching out to sea as on the former day, our Lord passed homewards towards the house in which He usually dwelt. On His way, by the side of the lake, perhaps on some small pier or quay at which the vessels which plied on the lake discharged their cargoes, or at some spot near the gate at which some of the great roads which met at Capharnaum entered the city, He saw one on whom His thoughts had long rested, and who appears to have been already a disciple, although not yet in that close degree to which some were admitted. "He saw a man, Levi the son of Alphæus, or Matthew, sitting at the receipt of custom." He was a farmer of the public revenue, and was engaged in his ordinary office, taking toll on the merchandise or supplies which entered the city. 'Our Lord said to him, Follow Me, and he arose, left all, and followed Him.'

St. Jerome tells us, in the passage which is selected as a lesson in the Roman Breviary for the feast of this Blessed Evangelist,[1] that certain infidel writers had fastened on this incident as furnishing ground for a

[1] *St. Hier. in Matt.* c. v. (lib. i.).

charge either against the Evangelical narrator or against the persons concerned in the incident. Either St. Matthew must have had some more convincing reason for following our Lord than this simple call, and then the narrative is defective, or he must have acted foolishly, and then the incident discredits the whole cause of the Gospel kingdom. The holy Father remarks that St. Matthew, like the other Apostles, must have had abundant evidence, before the simple call of our Lord, to reveal to him Who He was Who thus called him. The call came at the end of a period of many months, during which the character, preaching, and miracles of our Lord must have been before the mind of a dweller in Capharnaum like St. Matthew. We have no account at all of his parentage or education, but it is fair to suppose that his selection from among the Apostolic band for the special office of the Evangelist of the Hebrew Christians, must have been made with some regard to qualities which he possessed by character or training. Thus it would have been natural for him to have been comparatively well acquainted with Greek, the language of commerce, Capharnaum being, as has been said, on some of the high roads of traffic between Syria and Egypt, passing through Galilee to the sea coast. It is a natural conjecture that he was trained for the position which he held, in which case he may have received it from his father or some other relation. It is certain that the character of his mind was simple and devotional, and that he was well acquainted with the Scriptures of the Jews, in every page of which he had learnt to see a prediction or anticipation of the great object of hope towards which all the pious minds of the holy nation were turned. His mind was full of the glories of the kingdom of the future Christ, the Son of David. There is a conciseness and summariness about the narrative in which he afterwards arranged so many of the actions and sayings of our Lord, which shows a certain masterful grasp of matter before his mind, and a habit of arranging it according to ideas and principles, rather than in the simple chronological or local connection. That he was large-hearted and open-handed, a man whom people were ready to like and love, even though his profession was in itself unpopular, and, to some extent, looked down upon,—like all callings which are supported on the laws or regulations imposed by conquerors or an alien Government upon a subject people—may be gathered from the readiness with which he opened his house to a great concourse of friends when he celebrated, as we might say, his vocation, by an ample entertainment to our Lord and His followers. It may have been the case that he was to some extent despised by the stricter Pharisees and Scribes, but we find that the objection raised on this occasion by the critics of our Lord's conduct referred rather to his company than to St. Matthew himself. He may have been thought of as the good publican, just as his neighbour the Centurion was in high esteem among the Jews, although a Gentile and an officer under the usurping power of the Cæsars.

If such were St. Matthew's character and antecedents, it is certain that he must have gathered much about our Lord from the many opportunities which had been afforded him at Capharnaum. Our Lord had now made the city His chief place of residence for nearly a year, and although He had during that time been often absent, and for long intervals, still He must have excited an amount of attention in the minds of all the more religiously disposed inhabitants which must have drawn them to Him with an irresistible force. How soon after His first appearance at Capharnaum St. Matthew may have become acquainted with our Lord it is impossible to tell. He may have been among the Galileans who had seen His wonderful works at the time of the first of the Paschal feasts after His baptism; at all events he must have heard of the marvellous cure of the nobleman's son at a distance, which followed so soon after His return to Galilee. He must have been present at the synagogue on that memorable Sabbath Day when our Lord cast the devil out of the possessed man in the course of the public service, and it is hard to suppose that he knew nothing of the subsequent healing of the mother-in-law of St. Peter, or, much less, of the almost numberless cures of all sorts which took place on the evening of that same day, before our Lord started on His first great missionary expedition. All these things would sink down into the heart of a man like St. Matthew, and during the long weeks which followed, when our Lord was absent from the city, news would come from time to time of the progress of the marvellous Preacher and worker of miracles through the various towns of Galilee.

The gainful calling of the future Evangelist was one which occupied him during the greater part of the day—perhaps he was like one of the busy servants of commerce in our own cities, who leave their homes in the morning to toil all the day in the accumulation of wealth, but who throw off the thoughts and interests of the day's labour as soon as it ceases to occupy them directly. Even in the intervals of his business the thought of the new teacher would grow more and more constantly in his mind. He probably became a believer in our Lord long before the moment of which we are now speaking. It is probably not safe, in a case like St. Matthew's, to assume that he was present at all the incidents and discourses which he describes. But it is very probable at least that he, who has left us the great authentic report of the

Sermon on the Mount, was one of the disciples who listened to that teaching. Meanwhile he had come to know that many of the disciples of our Lord were following Him about from place to place, that to many the attendance on His teaching had become the main business of life, and that some were even almost inseparable companions of His labours and journeyings. There had been many things in the Sermon on the Mount, and in the other teaching of our Lord, which had seemed to point to a life quite different from that in which even good Jews had been hitherto content to serve God—a life even above that of the virtuous holy home, the faithful discharge of domestic duties, the careful attention to justice and purity of conscience in the practice of a lawful calling in the world. Then, again, his own calling was full of danger. He had many opportunities of kindness and consideration for others, he could do many a good deed almost unknown therein, and he could use the wealth which it brought him for purposes of religion and piety. Still it was a dangerous calling, and if it had not been dangerous in itself it might still have come to seem very uncongenial to one who had heard our Lord preach, who had listened to the lofty teaching of the Beatitudes, who had heard the doctrine about laying up treasure in Heaven, about relying entirely on the providence of the Father, and whose heart had bounded within him as his ears caught the words about some who were to be the light of the world and the salt of the earth, some who were to have committed to them the precious pearls of Divine truth, which were not to be cast to the swine, some who were to keep even the least of the Commandments as well as the greatest, and then by teaching them to others to become great in the Kingdom of Heaven; some who were to be persecuted for the sake of the name of our

Lord, and whom He bade to rejoice and be exceeding glad thereat, because they were to have the same treatment at the hands of the world as the prophets of old had received.

It would not be easy to measure the force of these and other words of our Lord on a simple deep heart like that of this good publican, or to tell how the doctrine about the poverty of spirit and the hunger and thirst after justice, and the mourning for sin, his own or of others, which were to have so high rewards in the new kingdom, must have smitten him at times, as it were, to the ground, and made him yearn for an opportunity of putting in practice in his own case the counsels which made everything else seem worthless and vain in his sight? In such cases there is often a hard struggle. Even when the heart is not closely entangled in the meshes of some earthly love or interest, there is a time of darkness and doubt and mental distress, in which the soul seems for a moment to lose the clue to guide her onwards, the light which shines to show her where to set her feet. At such times temptations arise in unusual force, and external circumstances seem to combine with internal difficulties to make the onward path impossible. They are times of trouble without and storm within, of gloom and dryness, when prayer moves heavily, and the thoughts and affections are beaten back when they would fain soar to Heaven. The natural reason is that the soul is drawing near to the decision of a great issue, which has much in it that is repugnant to flesh and blood, and the instincts of the human spirit are arrayed against the change which threatens them with crucifixion. There is also often a preternatural cause at work, for God, Whose strength is made perfect in weakness, allows His poor creature to be tried and exposed to the malice and assaults of its enemies, that it may learn to rest entirely on Him, and to take courage for future conflicts from the experience of past victory. The evil powers are on the watch against the danger of losing for ever their prey, or at least of seeing the soul, which they have been able to play with by ordinary temptations, place itself in the citadel of a higher vocation, against which their assaults must be made at far greater disadvantage. And then in the midst of the darkness and the struggle there is a sudden peace, for the Master's voice is heard, 'Follow Me!'

The circumstances of the call of St. Matthew seem to sum up, as in a type, the methods which God so frequently uses for the calming of storms such as those of which we have been speaking, for the dissipation of doubts, and the sudden breathing into the soul of the courage which it requires for its great decision. It is sometimes an external incident which breaks down the last resistance of a struggling will, or sets the imprisoned soul free. Some great act of mercy, something that seems to bring God nearer to us than before, or a display of His masterful way in dealing with human affairs and human life, such as the death of a person by our side, or the sight of marvels such as those seen at the great places of pilgrimage, or even a sudden change in temporal matters which removes a score of minor difficulties—these, and other things like them, fall on the soul like the touch of spring on a winterbound plain. Thus the tidings that our Lord had taken on Himself, not only the power of healing diseases, but that far higher and more incommunicable power of forgiving sins, may have struck with a fresh weight of difficulty upon the heart of some Pharisee or teacher of the law, kept in slavery by the chains of human respect and ambition, for which our Lord soon after this time reproached the whole class to which such a man would belong. But to the humble simple publican, it might seem like a ray of heavenly light, dispelling in a moment the clouds which hang over His soul. There is an anecdote in the early annals of the Society of Jesus of a learned man who had for years been battling with himself as to his vocation to the Society, and could never overcome his difficulties, but who fell in of a sudden with the letters in which St. Francis Xavier described his work in India and the blessings with which God prospered it, and who at once gave way, crying out, 'This is something indeed, this is something indeed!' Such is the effect of tidings which waken up in us the consciousness that God is so much nearer to us than we thought, and that His mighty arm is being put forth in our time as in the days of old. And this is another reason why the enemies of the Church and of Christian perfection are always so unwilling to admit the truth of modern miracles, whether moral or material, because they feel that such manifestations on the part of God reduce their quibbles to dust. If St. Matthew had not been present at the miracle and at the teaching with which our Lord illustrated it, the mere tidings of what had passed must have sent a shock through his soul, and gone far to prepare him for the yet more cogent appeal that was soon to follow.

Our Lord, in the cases of which we are speaking, and of which we may well consider this call of St. Matthew to be a normal type, addresses Himself to the soul, internally and personally, as well as by the external incidents lately mentioned. In truth, every vocation involves a personal command or invitation, on the part of our Lord, addressed to the individual soul. It is couched, as this invitation to St. Matthew is couched, in the words of authority. There is here no promise, no suggestion, no counsel, but simply the words, 'Follow Me.' It is not that our Lord cannot sometimes add promises as inducements to those whom He may call to this or that work or life for Him, as when He said to the first called among the Apostles, on the shore of this same Lake of Galilee, 'I will make you fishers of men;' or as when He said to the rich young man who inquired after the conditions of salvation, and was not content with the way of the Commandments, that he should have treasure in Heaven if he gave all that he had to the poor. These instances show us that the spiritual gains of a lofty vocation are not to be set aside in our deliberations as to a choice, for example, of life, or in any other election that we may have to make. But they are to be considered as reasons for the conclusion which is the direct motive for the choices to which they point—that is, the conviction that it is the will of God that such or such a choice should be made in this particular case.

The truth on which the doctrine of vocation rests is that God is the Father and Lord of every human life, and that He has not only laid down certain laws for the freewill which is to guide our choices, laws which cannot be violated or neglected without positive sin, but that He has also a right to choose for His children this kind of life or that, this line of conduct or that, within the limits of the necessary commandments, and that an intimation of His pleasure in this respect has a direct claim on our obedience. We are His servants as well as His children: as a Lord He bids us do this or do that, as a Father He marks out for us the path in life along which He desires our service to take its course, for which He fits us by nature or by grace or by both, and along which He arranges the occasions and opportunities and graces and conflicts and victories on which He has made our crowns depend. To discover what is God's will in regard to this is the one important matter for each several soul, as St. Paul, immediately on his conversion, put himself at once at the absolute disposal of God, in the famous words, 'Lord, what wilt Thou have me to do?'[2] The will of God, in the case of St. Paul, was to call him to a very high and singular office in the Church, which involved a career of service altogether without parallel. But the will of God is the law of every single life—of that of the most ordinary Christian as well as of the Apostle of the Gentiles.

The answer which was given to the question of St. Paul, that it should be told him what he must do, implies the truth that this knowledge of the particular design of God over the soul is not always gained in the same way. It is sometimes imparted to us by the obvious import of the external circumstances and position in which we are born. It is sometimes imparted to us by the simple considerations of reason and prudence, balancing the advantages and disadvantages of this or that calling which may be open to us. It is sometimes pointed out by a strong impulse and interior desire, which may require to be tested by reason and submitted to the judgment of a spiritual guide, but which, as a motive influencing the choice, is so powerful as to sweep all obstacles before it. Sometimes again, our Lord, as in the case of St. Matthew and St. Paul, takes the matter, as it were, into His own Divine hands, and interferes almost personally and visibly in leading us up to the choice which He desires us to make. But all sound vocations must have as their foundation the conviction that this is the will of God, that He desires the particular soul in question to take the particular step or line in question, even though He may have left it to the simple considerations of spiritual prudence to formulate the conclusion. In whatever way, then, the will of God may be brought home to us, it

[2] Acts ix. 16.

amounts to a command, and it is an appeal to our personal duty to Him as well to the considerations of prudence, the desire of saving our souls most securely, the wish to be of use to the Church and our brethren in the most efficacious way, and the like.

In this respect, the moment at which a Divine vocation becomes clear to the soul is the most important in life, because it brings us to the point at which we are to choose God's designs or to reject them. It is not, indeed, to be thought of, that God will never repeat a call which He has once given, or, indeed, that He will abandon the soul which has turned away from His call. In the case of persons who have not closed with His Divine call, and have thrown themselves into another path of life—as, for instance, a person who having been called to religion has entered on the duties of the married state—God may let them feel all along their course the many difficulties and dangers and troubles to which they have exposed themselves, their own unfitness for the temptations and trials which beset them, and the comparative absence of special graces which they might have expected if they had walked along the path which He pointed out to them. But He will not abandon them, or deny them the graces which are enough to secure their salvation if they use them faithfully. In the case of persons who hesitate to obey the Divine call, it may sometimes pass on, never to return, as seems to have been the case with the rich young man, of whom mention is made at a later period of our Lord's Ministry, but it is also very true that God often waits long, and returns, as it were, over and over again, with infinite patience and condescension, until His refractory and reluctant child is forced by interior pressure and external miseries to throw itself absolutely into His loving arms. Still, in proportion to the clearness and force with which the call of our Lord falls on our ears, is the danger great of heedlessness or of delay in attending to it. It is an immense favour to the soul, when God thus addresses Himself to it, and, as it were, solicits it to make the surrender of its freedom, in order that that freedom might be used to its own infinite profit in the best and most secure way. Thus we often see vocations delayed, and the light which is required for them is only vouchsafed after long preparation and fervent prayer, and much suffering, for this reason, it may be, among others, that a very great grace is needed to enable the soul to close heartily and at once with the will of God.

Again, it is observable that the glorious vocations of which we have instances in the New Testament history are put into the form of a command to follow our Lord personally. Here we seem to touch the immense and indescribable advantage of the Gospel dispensation over all other forms of God's dealings with man. It is no longer a law or a counsel, but an example, that is to be followed. The law and the counsel remain as before—but beside them there is the example of our Blessed Lord, the perfect pattern of obedience, the one Son in Whom the Father is well pleased. This example, by a marvellous arrangement of Providence, is not withdrawn from the sight of the imitation of any one of the adopted children of God. It fits all classes of men, every line of life, every age, every condition. The highest saints cannot outsoar it, the common flock of men whose path lies along the ordinary road of the Commandments are not too low for its light to illuminate their footsteps. It gathers to itself, not only the obedience to a Divine precept, but the love called forth by the infinite condescensions of the Incarnation and humble daily life of our Lord. So it is in all cases, even in those in which there is no question of a distinctly apostolic vocation. Much more is the value of the change infinite, when the call is something higher than the ordinary path of the children of God. The more arduous is the path, the more need is there that every step should be set in the right place and taken in due order and time. The more abundant is the harvest of good works which is to be reaped, the more need is there for the powerful impulse of personal example and personal love to secure that the work be done while yet there is time. The greater are the dangers, the greater the need for the feeling of loyalty to a Master Who bears Himself the most terrible of the pains and dishonours and disappointments which have to be braved. If the call, 'Follow Me,' stirs the hearts even of the ordinary Christian more than a thousand commands and threats and promises, much more must its effect be irresistible when it is addressed to those whom it invites to the closest companionship with Him Who utters it! This is the spiritual truth on which St. Ignatius has founded what is called the 'second week' of his Exercises, the introductory meditation being the 'Kingdom of Christ' —the invitation of the Incarnate Son of God to all His subjects to follow Him, and be His companions, in the war which he desires to wage for the glory of His Father.

CHAPTER VI.

The Feast at St. Matthew's house.

St. Matt. ix. 10—13; St. Mark ii. 15—22; St. Luke v. 29—39; *Vita Vitæ Nostræ*, § 40.

THE bright and simple character of St. Matthew is shown in a very beautiful way in the incident which is selected by the three historical Evangelists—himself one of them —immediately after the account which they give of his vocation to the more close following of our Lord. It may not have happened immediately and without any interval upon that call; but it is hardly likely that there should have been any great distance between the two. 'Levi,' says St. Luke, who delights to give to his brother Evangelist the more honourable of the names by which he was known among the Jews, 'made Him a great feast in his own house, and there was a great company of publicans and of others that were at table with them.' Many publicans and sinners came and sat down with Jesus and His disciples. 'For they were many,' adds St. Mark, 'who also followed Him.' That is, there were already a large number of men of this class attracted to our Lord. We have already seen that the publicans formed a sufficiently numerous body among those who flocked to the baptism of St. John to receive some special instructions from him. Our Lord, at a later point in His Public Ministry, reproached the priests and scribes for their neglect of the opportunity of repentance which was offered to them by St. John, and told them that the publicans and harlots went before them into the Kingdom of Heaven. If the austere preaching of St. John had so much attraction for men of this kind, on account of the appeal which it made to their consciences, and the abundant grace with which that appeal was accompanied, it is certainly not surprising that the winning and gentle teaching of our Lord should have drawn them to Him in large numbers. Thus we get a picture of the extent to which our Lord's preaching had already penetrated the various classes of which the society of Galilee was composed. On the occasion of the miracle of the healing of the paralytic, the audience to which He was addressing Himself was made up in large measure of ecclesiastics, teachers of the law, and the like, who had come even from a great distance to hear Him. Now we see Him in a very different company, less honourable in the eyes of the world, even of what is called the religious world, but not less dear to His Sacred Heart, not less precious in the eyes of His Eternal Father.

St. Matthew's joy needed, as it seems, some outlet, and he could express it in no more natural way than by a great feast in his house, to which our Lord and His near disciples were the most honoured guests, but to which he also invited his friends of his own class, and a multitude of others who had already begun to be followers of our Lord. He was like a man who had found a great treasure, or attained the greatest success in life for which he could hope, or which he could desire, or who had received the greatest boon that could be bestowed upon him, as one who has won a long-sought bride, or had a firstborn child born to him, or recovered from a most dangerous sickness, or been raised to a throne. No doubt there were other ways in which he could and did show his gratitude to God, in alms to the poor, or offerings for the maintenance of divine worship, and the like; but that particular manner of manifesting his gratitude and joy, which consists in 'calling his friends and his neighbours together to rejoice with him' was not to be omitted. For the blessings which we receive, if they can be shared by others, are to be imparted to them, and, even if they are in themselves incommunicable, it is at all events natural and right to make those who love us and whom we love have that much of companionship in them which they can receive, by being called upon to rejoice and make merry with us. Thus our Lord, when He draws the picture of Himself in His love for souls in the parables of the lost sheep, the lost piece of money, and the Prodigal Son, always insists upon this part of the similitude, which indeed is the point of all others to which He seems to wish to draw the attention of His critics. The Good Shepherd and the woman who has found her piece of money call together their neighbours and friends to share their joy, and, by sharing it, to increase it. The father of the Prodigal incurs the censure of his eldest son by his rejoicing over the return of the younger. 'There shall be joy in Heaven over one sinner doing penance, more than over ninety and nine just persons who do not need penance.' 'Rejoice with me, for I have found my sheep which was lost,' or 'my groat which was lost.' 'It was meet that we should be merry and make glad, for this thy brother was dead and is alive again, he was lost and is found.' All this witnesses to the fitness of the holy joy which vents itself in celebrations of the kind which took place on this occasion in the house of St. Matthew. Not that the children of God are to rejoice after the fashion of worldlings, but that they are not to avoid the usual human ways of showing their gladness at the reception of spiritual benefits, and that by so doing they make religion more amiable and attractive. For there is nothing which more forcibly witnesses to its Divine authorship than its power to flood the human heart with intense and pure joy.

We have already seen our Lord taking part in the holy happiness of a wedding feast, and selecting that occasion for the beginning of the marvellous cycle of His miracles of love and mercy. And now He is to be found celebrating the spiritual nuptials—for so they may indeed be called—of the soul of one who was henceforth to belong to Him alone. St. Matthew, in his glorious innocence and simplicity of heart, could not but call his neighbours and friends to his banquet, and it was only natural that they should be men of the same class with himself. Indeed, we may gather from the criticisms made on our Lord at this time, that the more seemingly religious of the Jews would not have been found in his house. No doubt the crowd was promiscuous in character. No class, at least no set of men devoted to any lawful calling, however much it may approach the limits of entire worldliness, is ever without at least some few good among its members. The majority of the guests may have been like St. Matthew himself to some extent,—that is, they may have been to some measure disciples of our Lord, who had not abandoned their gainful calling. There may have been among them some souls very dear to our Lord; but it is very likely that some, at least, may have been unconverted. Some may have come out of curiosity, to see Who the Teacher was Who exercised so marvellous an influence over their own former companion. To others the occasion may have been simply one of merry-making and good cheer. Amidst all this crowd our Lord took His place like one of themselves, and gladdened the heart of His future Evangelist by the sweet condescension and cordiality of His manner, mixing freely with the other guests, and raising their hearts to high truths by the way in which He spoke of the most ordinary subjects. Nor can we doubt that many a publican went away from that banquet with the seeds of future good sown in his heart. Many a sinner was forced by some secret influence of the Divine Presence to which he had unwittingly drawn near, to curb his thoughts, his eyes, or his tongue, to refrain from the evil or violent words, or the self-indulgence in the satisfaction of his appetite, with which he might otherwise have still further degraded his soul.

It must be remembered that one of the great faults of the religious people of that time and country, as we learn from the words of our Lord about the Pharisees, was their hypocrisy. Since the return of the Jews from the Babylonian captivity, we hear little of the open apostacies and abandonments of religious profession of which their ancestors had so frequently been guilty. The preservation of their nationality came to be entwined, as it were, with their profession of the true religion. The enemies of the independence of the Jews as a nation endeavoured to force on them absorption in the Greek civilization and culture all around them, and, although there were times when the persecution seemed almost triumphant, still the nation, as such, survived the storm, and emerged from its sufferings with an intense feeling of tenacity for its peculiar faith, now its only distinction in the world. The Romans were too sagacious to interfere with any peculiarities in their subjects which did not clash with their own position as masters of the world. We see the same policy pursued by the wisest princes of the house of Herod, as by Herod himself, who, although he seems to have hated the Jews and to have delighted in occasional insults to their religion and their rulers, nevertheless rebuilt the Temple with the utmost magnificence. At the time when our Lord appeared, religious observance was in the highest esteem among the Jews, and the credit of being a strict follower of the Law was likely to bring to those who possessed it great opportunities of worldly advancement. All this naturally led to an immense prevalence of hypocrisy, such as has been sometimes seen in Christian Courts, when absolute sovereigns —men, themselves, of notorious profligacy—have insisted on patronizing religion as an engine of statecraft, or in sectarian communities, which have aimed at exhibiting something like a counterpart of the visible theocracy of Judaism.

Under such circumstances, it was likely that our Lord would act in a way which would run counter to the fashion, or, rather, that the way of acting which was natural to Him would be very much in contradiction with that fashion. Everything of this kind was most deliberately and thoughtfully adopted by Him—and we shall find that, at the time of His teaching on which we are now occupied, there were many occasions on which He chose to contradict the maxims of conduct common with persons who made profession of religion. He must have known what the remarks were that would be made on His presence at a banquet of this kind, and He must have chosen deliberately to brave them. So He afterwards chose to brave the common maxims as to the observance of the Sabbath Day, at the cost of alienating from Himself the rulers at Jerusalem, or, if they were already alienated, giving them a pretext, which they were not slow to use, of acting against Him as a violator of the law. He must have seen, therefore, some great mischief in the maxims which enforced so wide and continual a separation, in the matter of social intercourse, between those who made a special profession of strictness and religious observance and those who were considered worldlings. He must have intended to leave behind Him an example, as well as to protest in the most pointed manner against the exclusiveness of the religious world of the time. He must have looked forward to the manner in which so many of His chief saints would follow His example. He may have thought of the beautiful incidents in the lives of men like St. Francis Xavier, who thought it worth his while to make a voyage on purpose to keep company with a man of bad life, that he might win his love and confidence, and lead him at last to confession and a perfect change of life. He must have had in His Heart the same saint, at the time when he was criticized by those who knew little of him for mixing with the soldiers and mariners and merchants at their games, looking on as they gambled, rejoicing if they won and mourning if they lost, sometimes even blessing their cards, that they might have good luck. He must have thought on St. Symeon Salus, paying the poor victims of debauchery in order that they might not sin, and exposing himself to the danger of the foulest charges by his friendship for the wicked. This example of our Lord has been the sanction for a thousand such actions, and numberless souls would have lost their only chance of repentance and conversion, if the saints could not have remembered how He condescended to sit at meat in the house of St. Matthew, in company with a crowd of publicans and sinners.

This and other similar actions of our Blessed Lord, even when the company in which He placed Himself was less likely to expose Him to criticism than on the occasion before us, must be considered as the foundation, in His own Divine Life upon earth, of all that large branch, so to speak, of the work of His saints and ministers after Him which may be called by the name of 'Apostolical conversation.' This is in many respects a part of the general work of preaching the Gospel, to which is committed, in the providence of the Father, the conversion of the world. But it differs in many more respects from preaching and instruction, in the stricter sense of the terms. If it has not all the security, all the authority, all the power, all the promise and blessing, of the preaching of the Word of God in its highest sense, it has still some advantages, and a direct mission of its own. For private conversation can be carried on at any time and in any place; it can address itself to the wants and condition of each individual person one by one; it can reach hundreds of persons who can never be persuaded to take their place in a public church and listen to a formal sermon. It is a weapon of grace, the power of which depends in a very particular manner on the character and qualities of the person who uses it, and it requires great dexterity and great union with God to use it well. At the same time, it must not be supposed that the successful use of this weapon requires high sanctity, for God can often bless the chance word of a child, or the passing observation of a Christian of ordinary virtue, nay, even of those who are not virtuous, to enlighten the darkness of some one who is struggling towards the truth, or to loosen the chains of some prisoner of sin. In this case the effect follows from the state of the heart and soul of the person to whom the word is addressed, rather than from the state of the person from whom it comes. So that it may be said that all Christians may have some part in the work of Apostolical conversation. Not all, indeed, are fit to undertake this work, and especially, it must require a special grace of sanctity and a special direction of obedience or of the inspiration of the Holy Ghost before it can be safe for a Christian to mix freely with those whose lives are either lax or bad for the purpose of winning their confidence and then converting them. The danger will always be great that the self-constituted Apostle may lose more than he may gain, and that spiritual persons may become worldly while they are undertaking to make worldly persons spiritual. Apostolical conversation is not confined to that intercourse with sinners, in the common sense of the term, of which we have the example, the sanction, and the blessing in this action of our Lord. This is but one, and one most difficult branch of Apostolical conversation. The truth is, that the whole conversation of Christians is in a certain sense meant to be Apostolical, for it is all to be edifying, and the gains and losses to the soul of others among whom he may move which may result from the habitual intercourse and conversation of any one are, in truth, immense. This holds true of the conversation of the strictest religious persons among themselves, as well as of the intercourse with the world at large, or with a special circle of friends, which any one may carry on whose direct vocation or purpose it is to glorify God in all things.

Holy writers have given some rules for this conversation in general, to which all Christians are more or less called, but which naturally belongs to the special range of duty of those who have the definite Apostolic calling. The first rule that may be mentioned is that to which allusion has already been made, namely, that we must undertake a work of this kind only after the direction of some kind of authority, such as that of religious or ecclesiastical superiors in the case of their subjects. This must be understood as an ordinary rule, to which there may nevertheless be exceptions. For it is clear also that there is a general obligation of charity in this respect, and as we are already bound to converse kindly and openly with our neighbours, so we are bound, in regard to this particular matter, to endeavour humbly to advance the cause of God and of religion in their souls by what we say and what we do not say. It may often be altogether imprudent to wait for a special mission when the opportunity is presented to us and when we are prompted to exert ourselves by strong interior inspirations. But there may be delusion as to this in certain persons, whose zeal is altogether indiscreet and imprudent, and who precipitate themselves into controversy or into religious conversation when they are not even able to control their own temper or to refrain from exaggerations. Any great love for this sort of enterprize, any great desire to get ourselves employed upon it, are marks of a soul which may easily be deluded in the matter, and which may really seek its own satisfaction in what appears to be undertaken for the glory of God.

Again, a work of this kind must not only be undertaken by obedience of some sort, in the way that has been explained, but it must be directed aright by a special intention of God's glory and elevation of the mind to Him. This should be made at the beginning of the action, that it may not be done at haphazard or for any lower motive, and the intention should be renewed from time to time, as occasion may serve, during the action itself. Few works that can be undertaken by a servant of God need this intention and elevation of the mind more than it is needed in this Apostolic conversation. This is the way to secure an abundance of the grace which is needed, for then we may hope for the fulfilment of our Lord's promise, 'He that abideth in Me, and I in him, the same beareth much fruit.'[1] The same holy precaution secures us a great alacrity and zeal in the work which we undertake, which, to really spiritual men, is certainly distasteful, and it will also wing our zeal with fresh strength when the persons with whom we have to converse are such as to discourage us or present great difficulties in any other way. Lastly, other benefits which may be gained by carefulness as to our intention and the raising of our mind and heart to God, are the security that we shall not be too much discouraged or put out by our own failure, if that is the issue of our enterprize, and that, after the work is over for the time, we shall find it comparatively easy to return to our normal state of calm recollection with God.

Another rule of the same kind is that which bids any one who undertakes work of this kind for God to be very careful lest he lose his own fervour while he is attempting to communicate fervour to others. This is the order of charity, and in this subject matter also our Lord's words hold true, 'What shall it profit a man to gain the whole world, and suffer injury on his own soul?' Our Lord's our example of retirement and prayer, His taking the Apostles into the desert after their short course of preaching, which is mentioned in the Gospels,[2] and the prudence of the Apostles in the Acts, when they determined to free themselves from the external occupations of charity in order to give themselves to prayer and to preaching,[3] may be quoted as illustrating this precept. The practical fruit of this is to make us unwilling to undertake too much intercourse with many persons at once, to be in a hurry to catch at every such work the moment it presents itself, to act without consideration for our health and strength, which may easily

---

[1] St. John xv. 5.
[2] St. Mark vi. 31.   [3] Acts vi. 4.

suffer and thus render us incapable of doing any good at all in this way, and above all, to neglect, under the pretext of charity to others, our own essential and regular spiritual exercises. In cases where this kind of mixing with the world has been undertaken foolishly and, consequently, without profit, there will almost certainly be some of these signs of imprudence and precipitancy. Other things that are to be avoided are such as these —rivalry with others and interference with work of this sort which has been committed to them, in which case positive mischief may be done, and much disedification given—or again, 'acceptance of persons,' a preference for those who are more distinguished in position, and, what is almost certain to follow, a loss of Christian liberty in dealing with such persons, and taking our own tone from them, instead of forcing on them higher principles, higher maxims, and more spiritual views. The persons who are the most fitted to receive benefit from this kind of conversation may thus often come to be neglected— the poor, the sick, the ignorant, children, and the weak or suffering in any way whatsoever. It is here that we see the difference between the perfect exercise of this Apostolical function, as we may call it, and its exercise by those who are actuated by imperfect motives, or not guided by the consummate prudence of the saints.

But perhaps the most important rules for the use of this weapon of charity are those which relate to the manner in which it is to be employed. In the office of the preacher there is much room for vanity and display, and for imprudence of various kinds. But in the conversation of which we are speaking, which is conducted with far more familiarity than can be allowed in ordinary preaching, and in which there is an opportunity for question and answer, argument and objection, not only *is* the speaker more off his guard, less able to prepare and consider beforehand what he is to say and what he is to leave unsaid, but there is also more opportunity for the natural character of each person to display itself, as it were, in undress, and for the betrayal of any hardness, severity, impatience of contradiction, or rigorism, which may belong to that character. On the other hand, the pulpit is the place for declamation, for the denouncing of vice in strong language, for the objurgation of the sinner, for the threats of Divine judgment, and the like. All these things are alien from the kind of conversation of which we are speaking. Conversation of itself implies courtesy, gentleness, consideration, affability; and, if it may now and then be necessary to speak plainly and strongly, it must even then be remembered that we are on the same level with those to whom we are speaking, and not above them, as is the case when we are preaching the Christian doctrine and the Word of God. Thus it is that all exhibition of temper, or anything that has an overbearing character, any severity of language or harshness of demeanour, are out of place in the exercise of this part of the Apostolical office. It was on these occasions in particular that our Lord displayed His immense meekness and gentleness. He could, as we know, speak with extreme majesty and authority, and He could, as we learn from other parts of His ministry, use severe language, and denounce in the strongest terms the hypocrisy and malice of His enemies, even when He had at the same time to tell the people that the Scribes and Pharisees sat for them in the seat of Moses, and were therefore to be obeyed. It is on these occasions, therefore, that the servants of our Lord must be especially careful in the practice of the virtues of meekness and gentleness. They are to lead people on sweetly and lovingly, without bitterness or severity, to the practice of virtue, especially to the frequentation of the sacraments, and the use of the means of grace which unite the soul to God. Thus we find it said in the contemplations of St. Mary Magdalene of Pazzi, that the spirit of St. John the Evangelist and that of St. Ignatius of Loyola were greatly pleasing to God, because each of those Saints strove to lead men to Him by the way of love. And, it was added, this pleasure of God was renewed as often as the children of St. Ignatius used the same method for the same purpose.

A slight consideration of these rules, and others which may be suggested by them, will show us at once that the most perfect exercise of this function of the Christian Apostolate requires a great and consummate virtue. It requires much familiarity with God, and much prayer for the persons with whom we have to deal, as well as with ourselves. It requires above all things an exquisite prudence, lest, as St. Ignatius used to say, we may be among the number of those who not only build up but also pull down, who do good, as it were, with one hand and mischief with the other. Thus he himself, and his disciple and brother saint, St. Francis Xavier, were both remarkable for the great use which they made of consideration before they undertook any work of this kind for the good of souls. They examined the condition and character of persons with whom they were to deal, they found out how to approach them, what works of piety or religion to recommend to them, what motives to urge on them for their conversion, and the like. The long letter of St. Francis Xavier to Father Gaspar Baertz[4] is a treasure-house of the wisest counsels for this holy prudence. Again, it is evident that a work of this kind requires all the spiritual power which holiness of life can alone give, and that it must be exercised with the most

---

[4] See *Life and Letters of St. Francis Xavier*, vol. ii. p. 109.

perfect benevolence and goodwill towards those with whom we have to deal.

It is also plain, that the opportunities for the kind of service to God of which we are speaking may be more frequent and ordinary under certain external conditions of society than under others. There may be times when there is hardly any other means of bringing home to many classes of persons the truths of the Gospel, or at all events, no other means so easily available. The Christians in many of the towns and cities in the Roman Empire in the early ages must have had a very distinct and universal mission, so to speak, of this kind. Those were days when there could not be much preaching to the heathen from the pulpit, and when personal influence and private conversation must have played a large part in the enlargement of the Christian flock. The same may be said in a measure of states of society in which there is a great deal of intercourse among persons of different religions, and in which matters of controversy are constantly introduced in promiscuous conversation. The bringing back of heretics and those who are involuntarily outside the pale of the visible Church, is a work as pleasing to God as the conversion of sinners in the more ordinary sense of the term. But it may often be almost impossible to reach such persons in any other way than by means of social intercourse. In all such cases the practice of the most prudent Christian charity is the duty of those who are endeavouring to walk in the footsteps of our Lord and His saints in this respect. There are many reasons, for instance, connected with our own spiritual well-being, for acquiring an intellectual knowledge of the doctrines which we believe, and the history of our religion. It is almost shameful to be learned about anything else, and comparatively ignorant about these, even for our own sakes.

Much more is it prudent to acquaint ourselves with these subjects, for the sake of being able to 'satisfy every one that asks of us a reason of that hope which is in us, with modesty and fear,' as St. Peter tells us,[5] and thus not only defend ourselves, but perhaps help on some soul that is in good faith, but under false impressions as to the truths of the Catholic religion. And if the saints just now mentioned made it a point to study the dispositions and tastes of the men across whom they came, in order to be the better able to help them, rather than harm them, it may well be a study for Catholics to make themselves in some degree acquainted with the intellectual position and characteristics of those among whom they live, in order to prepare themselves for their questions, and for the opportunities which may occur of delivering them from popular misconceptions. The present days are times in which religious subjects are very generally talked of in promiscuous society, and in which the servants of the Church have as much to do with those who are under the bondage of false doctrines, as with those who are in the toils of sin.

It is not easy to lay down any rules for such cases which may be of universal application, on account of the very great difference which prevails between one instance and another. For there are many persons with whom it is useless to convince the intellect as to the truths of the faith, on account of the moral state of their souls, which is the real obstacle to their conversion. Others, on the other hand, are in a state of perfect moral rectitude and innocence of life, while their minds are full of false maxims and erroneous impressions concerning the Catholic doctrine and the practices habitual to Catholics generally. It may be said with regard to those who are in good faith and good lives, that it is a work of

---

[5] 1 Ep. iii. 15, 16.

immense charity to deliver their minds from any misconception or intellectual error as to the faith or the Church. With regard to others, whose moral state is in truth their chief difficulty, it is better to gain their affection and regard by kindness and charity and then to endeavour to lead them to amend their lives before entering on controversy in the proper sense of the word. The first companion of St. Ignatius, the Blessed Peter Favre, has left a beautiful letter on this subject, addressed to his friend Father James Laynez.[6] The experience of Father Favre led him chiefly to speak of the Lutheran heretics with whom he had so much to do in Germany. The main principle on which he insists, in the letter of which we speak, is that after their affection has been won by kindness, they are to be induced to resume the practice of virtue and the ordinary Christian devotions which they have abandoned, before they are led on to the rejection of the false doctrines which they have taken up.

[6] *Life of B. Peter Favre*, ch. xiii.

CHAPTER VII.

'*Mercy and not sacrifice.*'

St. Matt. ix. 11—13; St. Mark ii. 16, 17; St. Luke v. 30, 32; *Vita Vitæ Nostræ*, § 40.

THE foregoing considerations may serve to show the importance, in the Divine scheme of the Kingdom of the New Testament, of the principle on which our Lord had acted in His condescension in sharing the feast given by St. Matthew with so many publicans and sinners. They may also guide our thoughts to the rules which ought to be observed when those who have in any way or degree the commission to carry on the work which our Lord began, find themselves called to undertake to imitate Him in this particular office of Christian conversation. It was hardly to be expected that His conduct would pass without remark from those who were usually looked up to as patterns of strictness and religious acts, and whose own rules of conduct were altogether different from those on which He had acted. As has already been said, we have no reason for thinking that at this particular time there was among these Scribes and Pharisees in general any fixed determination to find fault with and oppose our Lord. The difference between them and Him was, in truth, a difference of system, and we shall see this still more forcibly illustrated as time flowed on. The good that He had in view when He accepted the invitation of St. Matthew was too important to be left aside, even if it might to some extent scandalize those who had been accustomed to far stricter rules as to the intercourse between religious teachers and the poor children of the world who were despised as publicans and sinners. In many respects and on many occasions our Lord guided His own conduct by the motive of avoiding scandal. On this occasion He did not do so. A principle was at stake, and He had the deliberate purpose of innovating in many respects on the established usages and maxims of the religious people of the day. It was but natural that His conduct, therefore, should incur criticism, though as yet the criticism appears to have been respectful, and not addressed to Himself.

We must, in the first place, remember that it is not quite clear from the narratives of the Evangelists who precisely those persons were who are here spoken of as sinners. It is well known that, in several places of the Gospel history, including many in which the narrative is a report of our Lord's own words, the word 'sinners' is used as synonymous with the other word 'heathen.' In the present place, the word is used by St. Matthew and St. Mark in their description of the company assembled at the feast of the former, but St. Luke, in his account, uses the softer word 'others,' in the place of the word 'sinners.' This does not seem to come from any reluctance on the part of this blessed Evangelist to speak of sinners as the objects of the special condescension of our Lord, but, as St. Luke is the special Evangelist of the heathen, he sometimes drops the word 'sinners' when it has been applied to them by others. From this circumstance it might seem as if we might conclude, in the present instance, that the 'sinners' spoken of by the Evangelists included some heathen, and that this is what was objected to by the critics of whom we are now speaking. Nor would there be any improbability, in the nature of the case, if the fact were supposed so to be. The occupation of St. Matthew and the other publicans must have brought them very much into contact with heathens of various classes. There would be many traders, on the great roads of commerce which passed through Galilee, who were Gentiles, and with these the publicans must have had much to do. There would also be officers of the Roman Government, or under the tetrarch Herod, who would probably be Greeks or Italians, or at least foreigners by extraction. Many of the publicans themselves may not have been Jews. And if St. Matthew had a large acquaintance with such persons, it is not unlikely that he would invite them on an occasion like the present. It would be a different thing for even a strict Jew to bid a Gentile to his own table, and for the same person to accept the meats which the Gentile might offer him in return.

If this were so—if it could be thought with any degree of certainty that there were some Gentiles among the guests at this banquet of St. Matthew, our Lord's conduct, and His defence of that conduct, would have a new and special interest to us, because we should then be able to see in it a precedent which might have strengthened the courage of the Apostles, St. Paul and others, in their contention against the exclusiveness of many of the Jewish converts, in this very respect. Our Lord was at this time, as we have already seen, very mainly occupied in laying down the principles on which His Church was to act, as well as in asserting the powers which He was to leave behind Him in her. One of the difficulties of the apostolic age was the fusion between the two races of Christians, those of the Circumcision and those of the Gentiles, and this difficulty was felt in nothing more constantly and powerfully than in the question as to eating and drinking together, on account of the prescriptions of the Mosaic law concerning clean and unclean meats. The example of our Lord in eating and drinking at the same table with Gentiles — even though the meats at the table were strictly clean in the Jewish sense of the word,—would go far to throw the weight of His authority on the side of indulgence and largeness. But the fact, as we have said, must remain uncertain. The word which is translated 'sinners' in the English versions is used of others besides the Gentiles, and even when it appears as if it were meant to designate a particular class, it seems safer to understand it in the sense in which the word 'worldling,' or 'person of the world,' is sometimes used in certain circles which are composed of the direct professors of religion. But we do not on this account lose the support of our Lord's authority for indulgence, in the sense in which it had to be pleaded for by the Apostles, as to the admission of the Gentiles to perfect social intimacy and equality with the Jewish converts. On the contrary, it seems safe, here also, to understand that our Lord was deliberately looking forward, that one of His motives for going against the common Jewish prejudice in this respect was that He might lay the foundation, by this tolerance of the presence of worldly people at the table at which He ate, of the wider tolerance which was to be established in His Church in the matter of merely external principles of separation. For it was in truth a far greater condescension on His part to eat and drink with sinners, however strict they may have been as to the outward observances of legal prescriptions, than for any of His children afterwards to admit Gentiles, whose heart God had cleansed, to their table, or to go and eat and drink with them as social guests, after having been made partakers with them of the privileges of the Gospel, and even of the heavenly banquet of the Body and Blood of our Lord Himself. Having said thus much on the question as to the possibility of the presence of Gentiles at this feast of St. Matthew, we shall continue our comment on the passage of the Evangelists before us without reference to that particular possibility.

'The Scribes and Pharisees, seeing that He ate with publicans and sinners, said to His disciples, Why doth your Master eat and drink with publicans and sinners? Jesus hearing this, said to them, They that are well have no need of a physician, but they that are sick. Go then and learn what this meaneth, I will have mercy, and not sacrifice. For I am not come to call the just, but sinners, to penance.' Thus our Lord, as we may say, justified His conduct on three different grounds. In the first place, on the ground of reason. He was the physician of souls, and the souls that needed Him most were those to whom He ought to pay attention. 'They that are well have no need of a physician, but they that are sick.' In the second place, He was acting on a general principle of the government of God. He had laid down by the mouth of His prophet that He would rather have mercy than sacrifice, that is, that the works of mercy were more acceptable to Him than even that worship of Himself which He had ordained. But if mercy was to take the precedence of sacrifice, it was certainly better to do what was a work of mercy in itself than to refrain from it on the motive of strictness, even if that motive might be traced up to a love of the honour of God Himself. This was a general rule for the servants of God, which they might apply, as occasion arose, and which we shall find our Lord applying Himself to another question. But besides this, there was a third and special reason for the conduct which He had adopted, which rested on the character of His own personal mission. For He was not come, He had not been sent, to call the just, but to call sinners to penance. That is, He was sent more for the conversion of sinners than for that of the just, although, in truth, all were sinners in the sight of God, all were in need of conversion, and the just themselves, as they deemed themselves, must acknowledge themselves sinners, and be led by Him along the path of penance. These seem to be the three grounds on which our Lord, very gently and considerately, justifies His conduct, taking the men who were finding fault with Him on their own grounds, so to speak, acknowledging the difference between the just and the sinners, allowing the state of the facts to be as they supposed them, appealing to the authority of Scripture which they acknowledged, and passing no censure at all on their own different manner of acting, much less implying that there was anything of hypocrisy in the way in which they viewed and spoke of others, or of malice in their criticism of Himself.

The first part of our Lord's answer, 'They that are well need not a physician, but they that are sick,' is cast in the form of a parable or proverb, such as our Lord was so fond of using. It is full of significance, as well as of that humble gentle consideration for those with whom He had to do which was characteristic of Him. It implies that His great object in going among the sinners whom He met at St. Matthew's table was to heal their souls. A long and beautiful meditation might be drawn out, on the character of the physician of souls which is here assumed by our Lord. The physician's art is in many respects among the most God-like and compassionate of all human employments, and there are in this image many features which are scarcely to be found elsewhere. It belongs to the duty of a physician to endeavour to alleviate where he cannot cure, and prolong life which he cannot save. Indeed, his struggle is always one which, in the long run and at last, must end in defeat. He can never altogether avert death, he can delay its approach and palliate the pains which are its heralds. We see in this an image of the very deep compassion of our Lord, and especially of that tender consideration which is spoken of a little later on by the Evangelist St. Matthew, when he observes on our Lord's yielding to the persecution which was raised against Him by retirement, that He might fulfil the prophetic description about not breaking the bruised reed or quenching the smoking flax. It is a gain to the physician if he can for a day stop the onward march of disease, or deliver his patient from even a single malady out of several which may be afflicting him. Thus, the use of this image represents our Lord's work in its humblest condescension. Again, He does not speak of Himself as a rich man supplying the needs of the poor, or as a teacher enlightening the ignorant, though He might have used images of that kind—nor does He here describe Himself as the Shepherd Who has lost His sheep, and is determined not to rest until He recover it, nor as the woman who has lost a piece of money and sweeps the house diligently until she find it. Perhaps all these other images convey the idea of comparative ease in the execution of what is undertaken, for they represent our Lord as engaged on acts of mercy, laborious indeed and even dangerous, but still as requiring devotion and love, rather than skill and art. Whereas the exercise of the profession of a physician is one to which skill is everything for success, and in which even the greatest skill may be defeated by the obstinacy and hostility of those in whose favour it is enlisted. Moreover, the poverty, or the ignorance, or the wandering from home, in the other cases, are all palpable and obvious, whereas the physician has to deal with subtle evils, which are often hidden and even unsuspected, and he may find as much room for the exercise of his art on those who think themselves to be in good health as on those who acknowledge their sickly state. He can do little for them against their will. He must prevail on them to put themselves into his hands and to submit to his discipline, before he can administer his remedies or even probe their wounds and examine their sores. Again, the physician must go to his patients, he must, if it be necessary, expose himself to the danger of infection, he must breathe the bad air of the sick room or the hospital, he must handle the wounded limbs and touch what he is to heal.

In this way the image which our Lord chose was one which expressed better than any other the reasons which prompted Him in this act of condescension. The mere statement that He is the physician of the souls of men, is sufficient to account for all the humiliations and inconveniences to which He was exposed in the work of our redemption. Nor could any image describe more forcibly or more truly the state of the souls of men for the sake of whom our Lord came, especially as to all the variety of spiritual miseries which called for His Incarnation. The whole range of the maladies and afflictions to which the bodies of men are liable is not too large to picture the immense multitude of these spiritual afflictions—and when we find a little later on in the Gospel history the account of the many 'sick, blind, lame, and withered,' who lay waiting for cure at the pool of Bethsaida, or of the many blind and lame and lepers and deaf persons who were cured before the eyes of the disciples of St. John Baptist, we have only the faint outlines of a picture of suffering of a great variety of kinds, for the whole of which the art of the physician of souls has to provide some kind of remedy. And again, it has been already said that the diseases of the body are not only the images and representations, but in many cases the direct, in others the indirect, consequences of sin, either original or personal, and on this account also the image used by our Lord had its deep significance. The weakness of the body, the languor and utter want of power which is sometimes the chief feature in a dangerous state, the paralysis of limbs, the inability to take or assimilate food, or the loss of the use of some of the senses, the eyesight, the hearing, or the others, or again, great disfiguring maladies, leprosy, and others, which make men loathsome to their fellows, the infectious diseases such as fever, or the plague, or those in which the sufferer is covered with wounds and sores and ulcers, or those which partake of the character of frenzy and violence, dangerous to those about the person afflicted—even those extreme cases in which our Lord had to chase the evil spirits from the bodies of which they had possessed themselves by the permission of God —all these maladies have their counterpart in the various degrees of spiritual disease, which is probably far more multiform and various, as well as more dreadful, than anything that the body can suffer. In the multitude of the sinners across whom our Lord might be brought in the course of a day's preaching, or of intercourse with men in mixed society, He might find almost all the varieties of disease spiritually represented, and the one perfect and adequate remedy for them all would be in Him.

There is a bright and beautiful courtesy about the answer of our Lord to His critics in this place, for His words seem to imply a sort of apology, and at the same time He seeks to give a reason why He has, as it were, left them for others who had more need of Him than they. Moreover, He seems to ask their compassion for the sinners on whom He was spending so much time and condescension. It is as if He had said, 'You and others like you do not need Me, and these need Me very much : they are, you see, very much afflicted by various maladies of the soul, of which you have not the experience, and they are objects of compassion to you as well as to Me.' There is, as has been said, no occupation more full of opportunities of compassion and mercy than that of the physician. But our Lord is a physician like no other; for He not only can cure all diseases, if His patients will allow themselves to be cured, but He is Himself the medicine of all, and He heals all by shedding His own Precious Blood for the remedy of the diseases, of which He has allowed Himself to have all the personal experience which He can have, being tempted in all things as we are, only without sin. 'With His stripes we are healed,'[1] says the Prophet of Him; and He takes away our maladies by suffering Himself all the pain and misery which they involve.

The next part of our Lord's reply consists, as has been said, of an appeal to Sacred Scripture, which of course was familiar to those whom He was now answering. 'Go then and learn what this meaneth : " I will have mercy and not sacrifice."' The words seem to imply that they were to study the passage of Scripture to which He referred them, as if its sense were not obvious at first sight, or at least as if study were required to understand it in all its fulness of meaning. The passage of which He speaks is indeed one which sums up a great deal of Scripture teaching. It occurs in a passage of the Prophet Osee,[2] in which God remonstrates with His people for the scarcity of their mercy, by which He seems to mean, charity to our neighbour in the

[1] Isaias liii. 5.   [2] Osee vi. 6.

widest sense and extent—which mercy, He says, is like a morning cloud and as the dew that goeth away in the morning,—that is, it is very inadequate and transient. 'For this reason I have hewed them by the prophets, and I have slain them by the words of My mouth, and thy judgments shall go forth as the light, for I desired mercy and not sacrifice'—that is, mercy rather than sacrifice, 'and the knowledge of God more than holocausts.' The words seem to refer to other passages of Scripture, in which obedience and mercy are preferred before sacrifice. The idea occurs first in the reproof of Samuel to Saul, when the King had not fulfilled the commandment of God as to the utter destruction of the Amalekites and their goods. 'Doth the Lord desire holocausts and victims, and not rather that the voice of the Lord should be obeyed? For obedience is better than sacrifice, and to hearken rather than to offer the fat of rams.'[3] The same idea is found in the Book of Ecclesiastes: 'Keep thy foot when thou goest into the House of God, and draw near to hear. For much better is obedience than the victims of fools,' that is, of sinners, 'who know not what evil they do.'[4] The thought is greatly expanded in the Prophet Micheas, where he makes the people inquire, 'What shall I offer to the Lord that is worthy? Wherewith shall I kneel before the High God? Shall I offer holocausts to Him, and calves of a year old? May the Lord be appeased with thousands of rams, or with many thousands of he-goats? Shall I give my firstborn for my wickedness, the fruit of my body for the sin of my soul?'[5] And then comes the Divine answer: 'I will show thee, O man, what is good, and what the Lord requireth of thee; verily to do judgment and to love mercy and to walk solicitous with thy God.'

[3] 1 Kings xv. 22.   [4] Ecclesiastes iv. 17.   [5] Micheas vi. 6—8.

In all these passages of the prophets we find the idea that the spiritual service of God is more pleasing to Him than external worship, however costly and precious. And in the passage of Micheas, at least, as in that of Osee, the further idea is involved, that the faithful and charitable exercise of the virtues enjoined in the second table of the law, which deal with our duties to one another, is more acceptable to God than the direct service of sacrifice and worship. For sacrifice and worship may be offered without charity, and in that case they are worthless, and even, in a certain sense, a mockery of God, Who requires that the heart which draws near to Him should be pure and free from bitterness, according to the doctrine of St. John in his Epistle, where he says, 'He that doth not love his brother whom he seeth, how can he love God Whom he seeth not?'[6] But we cannot be truly charitable and merciful, and at the same time have a heart alien from God. Sacrifice is well as a testification of the supreme homage which is owing to God, and of our sense of our own dependence on Him, the gratitude which we owe to Him, the need we have of His mercy, and of the pardon of our offences, and, as has often been said, it expressed the faith of those who offered it in the redemption which was to be consummated on the Cross. But God could do without this testification, and His 'are the cattle on the hills and the oxen,' as the Psalmist speaks.[7] It could add nothing to God: it was but a protestation of the truths already mentioned. On the other hand, the interests of God were directly engaged, so to speak, in the exercise of charity and compassion to our neighbour. For it is to these that He has committed a great part of the administration of His providence, inasmuch as when He permitted so much human misery in the world, He did so,

[6] 1 St. John iv. 20,   [7] Psalm xlix. 10.

as it were, on a kind of understanding that it was to be the office of those who had it in their power to do so, to relieve the wants of their brethren, and inasmuch as the whole condition of His kingdom in this world would be lowered and hardened beyond endurance, if the law of mutual charity did not rule society. The noblest thing in God's creation, as far as it is visible to us, is man himself, the image of God. He is raised to a dignity by his resemblance to his Maker, and more by his brotherhood to Jesus Christ, the incarnate Son of God, which places him above even the temple and the altar in his nearness to God, and so, in case of necessity, it might be that the service of the temple might be neglected for that of the visible and spiritual temples, the children of men.

This is the great principle which our Lord now urges on those religious minded persons who objected to His conduct on the occasion of which we are speaking. It may be remarked that He does not give it absolutely as the reason of His action, as if there never could be times when sacrifice and not external mercy might be the rule for Him and His disciples to follow. For He gives as a reason for the application of the principle in the present case the fact that His mission was especially to the sinners. 'For,' He says, 'I am not come to call the just, but sinners, to penance.' Such is the general character and purpose of the present mission of our Lord and the Church. He was to say afterwards, in defence of the Blessed Magdalene, that they had the poor always with them, but not always Himself, and that was to be the reason why Magdalene was right in spending all her ointment upon Him, although it might have been sold for a large sum and given to the poor. If it had been so spent, it would have been spent in mercy rather than in sacrifice, and thus there would have been an instance in which the application of this principle would not have been the most perfect thing. Magdalene acted on another great principle, which is the foundation of a thousand glorious acts of homage and of the devotion of large sums and treasures on the direct service of God, the altar, the sanctuary, and the like. We shall have to speak of this other principle in its proper place and time. For the present it is enough to see that our Lord does not deny the duty of honouring God in the many various ways to which the name of sacrifice may be applied. And it is remarkable, that He refers to the principle expressed in the words of the Prophet as one which His critics had not understood, as if it required meditation and consideration of the ways of God to understand it completely and adequately. It is as if He had said to them, 'You do not take in the full import of these words, with which you are nevertheless familiar, and they are words which are not at once understood.' And indeed these words are the explanation of many things in the government of the world and of the human race by God. And they are words which are not to be taken by themselves, as it were, but coupled with others, in which other rules of the Divine government are conveyed. And at the moment at which our Lord was speaking, they were words which it was very important that the Jews, and especially their ecclesiastical rulers, should understand; for our Lord was about to act upon them in other instances besides that before Him at the time. We shall soon find Him using them again in vindication of His conduct, and again He will imply that they were not understood by the persons who were finding fault with Him; just as He would say to the Sadducees, that one of the reasons why they held the miserable doctrines which they did hold was their ignorance of the Scriptures.

The principle which our Lord was so earnest in urging on the consideration of His critics, has been one of the most fruitful rules of Christian practice in all ages of the Church. It has prompted the labours and self-sacrifice of the apostolical ministry in the evangelization of the heathen, it has sent the saints from their cells or their prayers to the conversion of souls or the vindication of orthodoxy, it has broken up the chalices themselves, used in the Divine Mysteries, that their fragments may be sold to feed the poor, it has torn religious from their cloisters or contemplatives from the intimate enjoyment of God in prayer, in order that the plague-stricken may be tended or the dying sinner assisted with the sacraments. It has become the principle on which countless holy organizations have been founded, for the single purpose of consecrating the whole of human lives to the works of mercy, corporal or spiritual. Here, again, our Lord is looking far beyond the occasion before Him, and His Sacred Heart is drinking in with delight the contemplation of the thousand beautiful creations of grace which were to spring from His words as from a seed. Like others of His sayings, this also was not to escape misrepresentation and perversion. But the Church was to be guided in its application by the infallible teaching of the Holy Ghost, and the possible mischiefs which might result from false interpretations were to be far more than compensated by the glories which the truth was to produce.

The last words of our Lord, 'I am not come to call the just, but sinners, to penance,' are to be understood according to the idiom of the language in which He spoke, as meaning that His mission was more, and more primarily, to sinners, or to those who felt themselves sinners, than to the just, or to those who felt themselves just. For the Gospel is essentially a mission and a message to sinners, the whole race to whom it is addressed lying under the ban of God's justice on account of sin, and the Divine purpose in sending our Lord being one of redemption. It is conceivable that God might take a created nature, for the sake of uniting Himself to His creation, and so raising it and securing His own greater glory thereby. He might have taken on Him the nature of angels, as St. Paul speaks, and then His mission might not have been one of redemption, but simply one of elevation. The humility which He would perhaps have required as a condition of the enjoyment of the benefits of such a condescension, would have been the humility of a created nature in its utter dependence on God, not the humility which manifests itself, among other ways, in the acknowledgment of sin. But this is not the character of the Incarnation as it has actually taken place. It begins its work by the cancelling of original sin, and it carries on its work as one of healing and restoration unto the very end of its effects on mankind. To those who are capable of hearing its call, it is a call, in the first instance, to repentance. So true is this, that the reception of the Forerunner of our Lord, whose mission did not go beyond the baptism of penance, was the test by which it was decided, in the case of different classes of men among the Jews, whether they were fit for the Gospel or not. The classes who rejected or despised the preaching of the Baptist, did this because they did not feel the necessity of repentance, and in consequence they did not close with the offers of the Gospel. The words of our Lord, on the present occasion, may be considered not only as setting forth this truth, that the whole of our Lord's dealings with men were regulated by the motive of gaining sinners, but also as implying a warning to those who found fault with Him for His condescension. To do this was not only to set themselves up as critics, where they ought to have been humble and grateful disciples. It showed further a self-righteousness, a contempt for others as sinners, and so as below themselves in the spiritual level, and a hardness and rigidity and formalism, which, if not inconsistent altogether with true religiousness, might at least make all virtue unprofitable and vain, because of the admixture of pride and uncharitableness which seems inevitable in such cases. It seems to imply that if they are so just as they think themselves, or rather if they think themselves so just as to have the right to despise others as sinners, they will have no part in the sweet visitations of our Lord. He is not come for them. That is, He is not come for them, as long as they remain as they are—not that His mission is not to them, as well as to other sinners, but that they must first of all acknowledge themselves sinners, if their hearts are to be in any way open to the influence of His grace. It is the same now as then. There are scores of men in every educated and intelligent community with whom the difficulty of conversion does not lie in any want of completeness in the Catholic argument, or in any want of power on their part to appreciate that completeness. The difficulty lies deeper—in the self-sufficiency and want of self-knowledge and self-measurement by a high and pure standard, which prevents them from feeling the want of our Lord's redemption, because they do not acknowledge the sinfulness of their own hearts and their deplorable impotence to rise without the aid of redeeming grace.

CHAPTER VIII.

The Children of the Marriage.

St. Mark ii. 18—21 ; St. Luke v. 33—35 ; *Vita Vitæ Nostræ*, § 40.

IT appears that, after the banquet in St. Matthew's house, which gave occasion to the criticism of our Lord's conduct in eating and drinking with publicans and sinners of which we have been speaking, a further question of the same sort was put to Him, implying another similar criticism. In both cases the remark that was suggested by the critics bore upon the appearance of laxity and indulgence which characterized the system of our Lord, when compared to those of other teachers. St. Mark tells us that the disciples of St. John and of the Pharisees 'were fasting.' The words seem to mean, not only that it was customary for these persons to fast often, which is certainly true, but also that, at the time of which the Evangelist is speaking, they were actually observing some fast. For there were many periods or days in the year on which the stricter among the Jews observed such fasts. Some of these fasts are mentioned in the Prophet Zacharias [1]—the fast of the fourth month, on the day when Nabuchadonosor took 'Jerusalem ; of the fifth month, on the day on which the Temple was burnt ; of the seventh month, on the day of the murder of Godolias ; and of the tenth month, on the day on which the Chaldeans laid siege to Jerusalem. We also learn from St. John,[2] that it was the custom of the Jews to

[1] Zach. vii. 35 ; viii. 19.   [2] St. John xi. 55.

go up to Jerusalem a little before the days of the great feasts, in order to purify themselves by certain ceremonial observances, of which fasting was probably a part. In many cases it may have been more convenient for those who lived at a distance, and who could not afford to spend a longer time than was absolutely necessary at the holy city, to perform at least some of these observances before they left their own homes. In this way there must have been many occasions during the year at which it was customary for the more devout and observant of the Galileans to practise public fasts. The time of which we are speaking may have been one of these occasions, and it is very likely that it was just before the time for the caravans of pilgrims from Galilee to start for the celebration of the Pasch at Jerusalem. The disciples of the Pharisees and the disciples of St. John—by whom the Evangelist seems to mean the persons who had not only received the baptism of our Lord's forerunner, but had also taken from him a rule of life of the stricter sort, although they were not any longer able to devote their whole time to listening to his teaching, which indeed must have been interrupted for many months past by his imprisonment—may have been conspicuous, for the rigid manner in which they performed these penitential exercises. It is most likely that some actual and visible contrast, which forced the difference upon the eyes of men, may have occasioned the question of which we are now to speak; but even if this were not so, the contrast certainly existed, and a difference of this kind between our Lord's rule, as far as it could be gathered from the practice of His many disciples, and that of the recognized teachers of the Jews and also of His own special forerunner, was one of those things as to which many surmises and conjectures would naturally be formed.

St. Luke, who deals with the incidents of our Lord's life more in the historical and general manner than the other Evangelists, puts the question in the form of a general complaint—'Why do the disciples of John fast often and make supplications'—that is, formal and collective prayers—'and likewise the disciples of the Pharisees, but Thine eat and drink?' The mere fact that the question was put to our Lord, and not to His disciples themselves, is enough to show that the criticism which it implied was directed against the Master rather than against the disciples. It is clear that these questioners made Him responsible for not having taught His disciples what, in their opinion, He ought to have taught them—for not training His followers in the same school of outward austerity with the Pharisees and St. John. And there is even an attempt to set up a contradiction between Him and His precursor. It might have been more easily understood if He had opposed Himself to the traditional teaching and rule of the Pharisees, who were in possession, as it were, before the appearance of either St. John or Himself. But it was less easy to explain why He departed from a custom which had been followed by one with whose teaching His own was in complete harmony.

There was undoubtedly a contrast, and an intentional contrast, between our Lord's method, so to speak, and the method of St. John. Our Lord referred to this contrast a little later, when he said that the generation, to which He and St. John had both preached, was inexcusable, and, to use His own image, like the children in the market-place, whom nothing could please.[3] They had found fault both with our Lord and with St. John on different and opposite grounds. They said St. John had a devil, and they said that our Lord was a gluttonous

[3] St. Matt. xi. 16.

man, a drinker of wine, and a friend of publicans and sinners. This remark of our Lord proves the conspicuous character of the contrast which existed between Himself and St. John in their manner of acting on the people. It was certain that it would be observed, and it was meant that people should observe it. It is not therefore necessary to see in the proposal of this question any direct or bitter hostility to our Lord. It was a question to which His own line of conduct naturally led. It gave Him the opportunity to put forward, in His own sweet and beautiful way, a point of doctrine or principle which was to be of great importance and fruitfulness in the kingdom of the Church; and it is probably to this that we owe the record of this question and of His answer by the Evangelists.

Our Lord's answer is couched in words almost of apology and excuse, and there is no severity or reproof in His tone towards the questioners, who may have been men of simple and good, though narrow minds, unable to understand the fundamental principles of difference between the Law and the Gospel, the Synagogue and the Church, unable to take in the character of the new dispensation, the wide liberty of its spirit as well as the loftiness of the sanctity to which it was to raise mankind. 'To whom He said, Can the children of the marriage fast, or can you force them to fast, as long as they have the Bridegroom with them? As long as the Bridegroom is with them, they cannot fast. But the days will come when the Bridegroom shall be taken away from them, and then in those days they shall fast.' As to this answer, we may make some few general remarks before considering the words in particular. In the first place, our Lord does not deny the advantages or the duty of fasting, nor does He say that it is not for a religious teacher to enjoin it on his followers, nor that the Pharisees or St. John were wrong in training their disciples in that holy practice. On the contrary, His language implies that, but for some special circumstance, which He speaks of under the image of the presence of the Bridegroom with the children of the bridal, that is, with his friends celebrating his joy, He would Himself have done as St. John had done, and as the Pharisees were wont to do. In the second place, our Lord neither admits nor positively denies the truth of the supposed fact on which the question was founded. The persons who asked the question may have supposed that there was no such thing in the system of our Lord as the observance of fasting, whereas He had, as we know, given instructions, in the Sermon on the Mount, as to the manner in which that holy practice was to be observed, especially as to fasts which were not of public obligation. He had especially inculcated the duty of the concealment of any such works of devotion or satisfaction. If He had been strictly obeyed, as it is most probable that He was obeyed, as to these injunctions, it would have been out of keeping, perhaps, with the spirit in which He had given them, to reveal, in answer to these objectors, the great amount of secret austerity which was practised by the Apostles and others of His followers generally. All that was to be addressed to the Father in Heaven, the Father in secret, and it was not our Lord's will to open it to the gaze of the public, even in defence of His system or its followers. He had Himself drawn the veil over those delicate virtues, and He would not now lift it. Again, it may be remarked that our Lord speaks in the most guarded and veiled way of His own separation from His disciples by His cruel Passion and Death—for this it is which, as it seems, must have been in His mind when He used the words about the days which were to come, when the Bridegroom should be taken away from the children of the marriage. Here, again, there is no reproach or complaint against those who were to be the instruments of that separation. It is spoken of as something natural and inevitable. The joyous days of the marriage feast, during which the children of the marriage could not be asked to fast without a certain impropriety and violence, could not last long. They were days which, in the nature of things, were exceptional and transitory. At the same time, the language of our Lord seems to hint at something more than ordinary separation. People do not usually fast merely for the ending of the happy bridal season, but this time is to be one of real mourning, as if the Bridegroom were not only absent, but torn away by some sudden calamity or catastrophe.

It is further to be noticed, that our Lord here uses, as far as we know for the first time, the image of the Bridegroom and of the children of the marriage or of the bridal chamber, which had been employed, as we know from the Evangelist St. John, by the blessed Baptist himself, on the last recorded occasion on which he had born his loving testimony to our Lord. Thus, as it seems, this graceful, tender, and pregnant image, which gathers into itself, so to speak, so many details concerning the intimate relations between our Lord on the one hand, and the Church or the Christian soul on the other, and which enfolds those relations in the poetical garb of the Canticles and other similar parts of Sacred Scripture, is owing, in the use which the Church has made of it, to the tender and pure devotion of the holy Baptist. We know that it was our Lord's way, in quoting Holy Scripture, to refer to more than the particular words which He quoted; He constantly meant to direct the attention or memory of those who heard Him, to the whole passage, or even to more than one passage, when He cited a few words only. In the same way, we may see a reference, in the use of the image employed concerning him by St. John, to the whole teaching of the Baptist on the occasion on which He had so employed it. It is not certain that the question, on the occasion of which we are now speaking, came directly from the disciples of the Baptist themselves. The Evangelists do not say this. It was perfectly natural that such a question should be asked, and there is nothing in the account before us to specify the disciples of the Baptist any more than those of the Pharisees. But if we are to suppose that on this occasion, as on the other similar occasion mentioned later on by St. Matthew,[4] the disciples of the Baptist were either the questioners themselves, or were present when the question was put, it is clear that any one of them who may have remembered, or heard of the testimony which their master had borne to our Lord when he used this image of the Bridegroom and the friend of the Bridegroom, must have been reminded, by our Lord's adoption of that image, not merely of the use of it by St. John, but also of the whole body of doctrine concerning the Incarnate Son of God which St. John had then poured forth. But, if this had been the case, nothing more would have been needed to make them certain that their question was already answered—so far, at least, as it implied any censure on our Lord—for any One of Whom those things could be true which St. John had then said of our Lord, must certainly have the best and wisest reasons for any course which He might take, and any line which He might adopt as to the discipline to which He subjected those who became His disciples. Thus we may see here something analogous to the manner in

---

[4] St. Matt. ix. 14. For the reasons for supposing this to have been another occasion, see the *Life of our Life*, vol. i. p. 177.

which our Lord satisfied the mental question, which had occurred to so many of those who had been present when He told the paralytic man that his sins were forgiven him. On that occasion He silently proved to them that He must have reason on His side, by showing them that He had the power of reading the thoughts of their hearts. On the present occasion He at once placed Himself before the minds of the disciples of St. John as a Divine Teacher. 'What He hath heard and seen, that He testifieth. . . . He Whom God hath sent, speaketh the words of God. . . . The Father loveth the Son, and hath given all things into His hand. He that believeth in the Son, hath life everlasting, but He that believeth not the Son shall not see life, but the wrath of God abideth upon him.'[5] One of Whom these things were true, was not only above criticism—it was dangerous, not merely to doubt whether He could be right, but to consider His decision, on points of practice or religion, as anything short of the judgment of ineffable wisdom, to be revered and adored, instead of to be cavilled at. This would be enough to silence anything that there was, if there was anything, of captiousness in the questioners before us, and to prepare them for the further teaching which was to be contained in what our Lord went on to add, expressed parabolically, about the new wine and the new bottles, and the old and new pieces of cloth.

It is clear that the true and full explanation of the difficulty, which seemed so great to these questioners, is to be found, not simply in this answer of our Lord's about the children of the marriage, but in that answer taken in conjunction with the other heads of doctrine to which we have just now referred. The answer about the children of the marriage was enough for the time, but it

[5] St. John iii. 31—36.

pleased our Lord to go beyond the needs of that particular moment, and of the persons who were immediately before Him, and to lay down a principle which was to have a great variety of applications and illustrations in His Divine Kingdom. The words about the children of the marriage are in themselves a perfect image, though not exactly what we call a parable. Our Lord went on to use another pair of images which may be said to constitute a parable in the stricter sense, the actual and formal application of the words as such being alone wanting. It was His custom afterwards, when it came to be inevitable that among those who listened to Him there should be men whose hearts were in many various states in relation to the truth—some honestly faithful to grace, others struggling with self-interest and worldliness, and so less fit for the reception of Divine truth, others again almost entirely alien, turned away from light, and hearing Him only for the sake of finding fault—to veil the truths which He taught in the form of parables, which might convey His meaning to those whose hearts were fit for it without unfolding it to those who were not fit. Thus those who were intelligent were instructed, and those who were dull to spiritual things were not offended. If, as has been said, we take the whole passage together, we shall see that our Lord has set forth the truth relating to this subject in two different ways, according to the powers of intelligence of those with whom He was dealing. Thus we owe much indeed to these questioners about the fasting of the disciples of St. John. Our Lord has satisfied them directly in the first part of His answer, and He has also gone on, in the second part, to make their question the occasion for the setting forth of a great principle of His Kingdom in a manner intelligible to us—a principle which has been constantly used by the Church from the very beginning, which is of daily use in her dealings with various classes of her children, with those who are being from time to time brought into her fold from without, and with difficulties and questions which are constantly arising.

The whole answer of our Lord, then, may be divided into three separate heads. The first part is that of which we have hitherto been speaking in the present chapter—about the Bridegroom and the children of the marriage. The second is contained in the double parable or similitude which next follows. 'He spake also a similitude unto them,' says St. Luke, whose statement is also found in St. Mark, 'that no man putteth a piece from a new garment upon an old garment, otherwise the new piece taketh away from the old, and there is made a greater rent, and he both rendeth the new, and the piece taken from the new agreeth not with the old. And no man putteth new wine into old bottles, otherwise the new wine will break the bottles, and it will be spilled, and the bottles will be lost. But new wine must be put into new bottles, and both are preserved.' This is the second part of our Lord's answer. The third is contained in the few words which are added here by St. Luke alone, and which must not be confounded with the parable of which we have been speaking. 'And no man drinking old, hath presently a mind to new, for he saith, the old is better.'

We have already said something about the doctrine contained in the first part of this answer of our Lord. He says, in effect, 'The state in which My disciples are at present, is like that of the friends of the bridegroom while the marriage festivities are being celebrated.' Such festivities were continued among the Jews for many days after the wedding. 'The bridegroom is yet with them, and it is no time for them to fast and mourn, or for him to suggest it to them so to do.' Our Lord adds, as has been said, that it will not always be so. The time will come when the days of rejoicing and welcome will be over, and then there will be no lack of penitential observances, even of such as are of general precept, and much more of counsel, among His followers. This answer implies a sort of appeal to natural indulgence and gentleness in judgment, as if our Lord desired, in the first instance, to disarm His critics rather than to confute them. The fastings and supplications of which they spoke were excellent in their way and at the proper time, but, in the case of the disciples in general, that time had not yet come. It was to come, He added prophetically; the present stage of joyous delight would cease, and then the Christian society would be organized by regular laws, among which would be all those which relate to the matter of public and solemn seasons of mortification. It is clear that the reason here given is not precisely the same with that which follows, in the passage about the new wine and the old bottles. Each therefore may be considered by itself. The one is founded on the peculiar circumstances of the time as regards the disciples, the other is based on the new character of the dispensation which our Lord came to introduce.

Of this last we may speak presently. In the meanwhile there is much to be learnt from our Lord's words in the first of these points. It is as it were an assurance that is here conveyed to us by our Lord Himself, of the happiness and joyousness which at this time characterized the community which had already gathered around Him, varying, no doubt, in degrees of nearness and intimacy with Him, as in the grades of virtue which individuals had attained, but still all alike in this feature of intense and glowing delight. The same joyousness breathes through all the descriptions of the early Christian communities, which are scattered over the history of the Acts of the Apostles, and it is evidenced by those parts of the Epistles of St. Paul and the other Apostles, in which the sacred writers insist the most on practical precepts and recommendations, and which reveal to us the sort of life which was led in those first churches of our Lord. The state of joy, in a most true sense, may be said to be the state which God means to be habitual in the Christian soul and in the Christian people, and it could hardly be otherwise, when consciences are so pure, faith so bright and keen, and the will entirely united to God as a Father, whatever may be the external condition in which the providence of God may place His children. But there are periods in the Christian life, whether of particular souls or of communities, in which joy is more predominant, in which it comes more to the surface, in which it seems legitimately to guide the whole conduct, and to overflow even to the exterior, and to light up all around. Such are the times after a conversion from sin, after the first finding our Lord in the Catholic Church, in the case of those who have been brought up outside the true fold, or again, the blessed hours after a First Communion, or confession, or any reception of the Blessed Sacrament, or the celebration of a first Mass, or the admission into a religious Order, or the consecration of a life to God by the vows of religion. Such are the times when a new pastor has been given to the Christian people, or when a new sanctuary has been raised and dedicated to the Divine service, or when some schism has been healed, or the Church delivered from some persecution or tyranny. In all these cases the soul, or the Church at large, may be said to have found her Spouse and to have been united to Him in some more special way. And it is natural that at such times we should be flooded with joy, like the friends and companions of a bridegroom in an ordinary marriage, who are here spoken of by our Lord as the 'children' of the marriage. These are times when God allows the soul to taste His sweetness without alloy. He leaves her in consolation, and lets her have her fill, though afterwards He intends her to undergo the discipline of adversity or trial or desolation, or persecution from without, for which the time of consolation, which is first granted, is meant by Him as a preparation. In any case, such times and occasions are fitted for joy, not for mourning, and fasting has always something of the character of affliction about it, holy though that affliction may be. We find this often the case, in the history of Christian societies, when a large body of people have been converted to the faith, or when the founder of a religious Order has gathered round him his first followers, and they live together under no law but that of charity, in intense happiness, half intoxicated with the sweetness of the spiritual delights which are vouchsafed to them. God orders all things sweetly, as the son of Sirach tells us, and it is a part of the beautiful benignity and condescension with which He deals with His children, that such times as these should be arranged for the feeding and strengthening of the soul, or of the community, by the enjoyment of the first-fruits of spiritual freedom and the admission to great privileges, while for a time the establishment of the discipline of penance and the regulation of public observances are postponed. It is the time of the marriage festival, it will soon pass, and then the work of discipline will begin.

The whole time of the public teaching of our Lord may be considered as included in this figure of the marriage feast. He had taken upon Him our nature and was celebrating His nuptials, so to speak, with His

Church and with the human souls who came to Him to give themselves to Him, and it would not have been much that such a time should have been celebrated with universal rejoicing and festivity on earth as well as in Heaven. It would not have been incongruous if the whole world had broken out into joy at the appearance of our Lord. It would not have been unseemly if all the external marks of rejoicing had been seen everywhere on such an occasion. It was not unseemly for the Blessed Matthew, as we have seen, to celebrate his own vocation by a solemn banquet, and if Matthew might have done this, so might Magdalene on her conversion, as Zaccheus on his, or any other of our Lord's disciples. The ordinance of festivals and times of rejoicing is as holy as that of times of penance and humiliation—though in our present condition, the latter ordinance is more in harmony with our ordinary condition than the former—and, at such times, severity is out of place. The outward demeanour must follow the state of the soul and of the heart.

Moreover, there was another Divine reason contained in our Lord's words about the presence of the Bridegroom. It was the design of God that our Lord in His earthly course should lead a common life, free from all hardness or austerity, that He might so make Himself all things to all men, and drive away from Himself no single sinner by the appearance of severity. But it would have been incongruous if He had led this common life Himself, and had at the same time enjoined on His followers public and conspicuous practices of austerity. It was ever His way to do first and to teach afterwards, and He never laid on the necks of those who came to Him a yoke which He had not Himself borne before them. For this reason also, therefore, He could not do as St. John or as the Pharisees, even if on other grounds there had been no motive for His acting in a different manner. His own life was indeed a perpetual cross, even as to those very matters regarding which He left so much liberty to His disciples. He had fasted as no one of them was to be required to fast. He had no home, nowhere to lay His Head, and if His followers were so hungry as to be fain to rub the ears of corn in their hands and eat them, it is not probable that their Master was better provided than they. Hard and austere His life was in truth, but this did not meet the eyes of men. He was going about as a Bridegroom from one place to another, everywhere, as it were, taking possession of His bride, and His followers were always rejoicing to hear His voice. This is what men saw, and this being so, He could not lay upon them a burthen which was out of keeping with the joyousness of the time as well as unauthorized by His own example, as far as His manner of living was known to the world at large. There were also, as has been said, other grave reasons for this method of our Lord with His disciples of which we may proceed to speak in the next chapter.

CHAPTER IX.

New Wine and New Bottles.

St. Mark ii. 21, 22; St. Luke v. 36—39; *Vita Vitæ Nostræ*, § 40.

WE have seen that the first part of the answer which our Lord made to the question about the apparent neglect of certain ceremonial or ascetic observances on the part of His disciples, is framed so as to be a defence and apology for them, as well as an explanation of His own method of guiding them. For it was ever our Lord's way to speak in defence of those with whom fault was found. Certainly if any occasions of spiritual joy and consolation could be considered as times when any unusual rigour of mortification would be out of place, the circumstances of our Lord's disciples in these first few months of the Galilæan preaching must have made that an acceptable reason. The ineffable delights with which those who gave themselves up to that teaching must have been visited, must be measured by the extreme beauty of that teaching itself, by the heavenly attractiveness of our Lord's character, by the sweetness and tenderness of His condescension, the prodigality with which miracles of mercy and power were showered by Him on all who needed them, the indescribable enthusiasm of the people, the power by which all hearts were drawn to love and honour Him, all tongues to praise Him and welcome Him as the long-promised and long-expected Messias, in Whom all the prophecies were fulfilled, all the glorious dreams of the fathers of the holy nation accomplished, and Heaven itself laid open to mankind. The holy and infectious joy of such seasons is reflected to us in some of the services of the Church on her great festivals, as in the *Exultet* and other parts of the Easter Office, or as when we sing at Christmas of the true peace which has come from Heaven, 'the dawn of redemption, of ancient restoration, and of eternal felicity,' *Hodie per totum mundum melliflui facti sunt cœli*. This, then, was the first part of the answer of our Lord, so full of instruction to us on many different points.

It has already been said that there is more contained in the whole answer of our Lord than this. He took occasion, in explaining the method which He had adopted as to the matter immediately in question, to shed a great light on the whole line of conduct or policy of which that method was but a part. For the institution of a certain system of rule, in such a matter as public fasts and supplications, at certain stated times, could be but a part of a whole religious and ascetical discipline, to be enacted for a community such as that which our Lord came to found. We know that, in fact, it was so to be. Our Lord was acting as to other even more distinctive parts of the system of the Christian kingdom as He was acting in this matter of fasting. That is, He had in His heart a whole body of legislation which He did not produce in the course of His public ministry, and which He afterwards confided to His Apostles to enact in His name. The Christian sacraments, the Christian priesthood, the hierarchical and liturgical arrangements which were to prevail in the Church, the form of worship, the sacrifices, the ritual of the new kingdom, all were to come. The details of this system were to penetrate the whole of human life, and it was to rule the actions of the children of the Church from their cradles to their graves. Some of the sacraments were to be necessary as matters of obligation, all were to be necessary to the society of the Church as such. We do not know, even as to the most necessary of all, the Sacrament of Baptism, that it was imposed as matter of precept till after our Lord's Ascension. At all events, it is clear that our Lord kept back this great system as a whole. His words at the opening of His teaching were the same as those in which St. John the Baptist had expressed his own mission, that is, He insisted on the necessity of repentance and of faith. The practical rule of life for the future Christian community, as far as it was dependent on the external laws of that community, was not yet given, notwithstanding the very lofty precepts of interior perfection which had been promulgated in the Sermon on the Mount. There were the most stringent and Divine reasons why this should be so, and all the weight of those reasons bore against the enactment of any part of the system without the rest. To introduce a system of fasting and other such observances without the rest of the Christian system would be just this, it would be introducing a part when the whole was kept back. But, if it was not in our Lord's counsels to introduce a part of His system without the whole, it was much less natural for Him to introduce the whole prematurely. It was to be a living system, the parts of which depended one on the other, like the limbs of a body, or the root and trunk and branches and leaves and fruits of some glorious tree, and time must be given for its natural growth and maturity. To introduce the whole system would be to anticipate the workings of the interior spirit, without which outward ordinances are valueless, and to bring in what was new before the old had died away. Further, the old system now in possession was to be allowed to expire of itself, and not by any violent substitution of the new. And this, among other reasons, on account of the hold which the ancient system had upon the hearts of men, a hold so great as to make those under its influence indisposed to see the beauties and appreciate the excellencies of the new. Time was to be allowed for this affection to die out. This last reason virtually contains another motive for not insisting on the old observances where they were not of themselves obligatory. To do this would be giving the children of the new kingdom motives for entwining their affections around what belonged to the old, and thus increasing the difficulty of the ultimate substitution of the new. This is, in brief, the sum of the further answer given by our Lord to His questioners on this occasion.

This will explain how the further answer of our Lord of which we speak is to be divided into more than one head. First, we have the two similitudes of the new and old cloth, and the new and old wine. There is a difference observed by the commentators on this place between these two similitudes. The difference is this. The first similitude is that of the piecing on of a portion of a new cloth or garment on to an old one. This results, our Lord says, in the tearing of the new to furnish the piece for the old, in injury to the old, and in the obvious and visible inconvenience of the disagreement between the two. This is the first objection made by our Lord to the system which His critics would have wished Him to pursue as to the formation of His disciples. It is, in truth, the objection to joining a part of the new system on to the old. The second similitude differs from the former in this respect, that it no longer speaks of a piece or of a part, but simply of new wine or of old wine. Our Lord says that new wine cannot be poured into old bottles without the double loss of the bursting of the bottles and of the spilling of the wine. This, then, is another head of objection—the objection against introducing a system for which men are not yet prepared. The short passage added by St. Luke contains a third head of argument. Our Lord says, in the third place, that new wine is not at once and immediately to be set before people accustomed to old, whether the new is better than the old or the old better than the new is of little consequence. In any case, custom makes the old seem better. This is an objection to anything like haste or precipitancy in forcing new observances, the expression of a new spirit, upon persons as yet wedded to old practices, representing an older and a different spirit and system.

There can be little difficulty, after what has been said, in understanding the threefold reason which our Lord here gives for the manner in which He had acted as to the matter before us. The last reason is at once clear. Men's minds must not be at once and violently turned to a new system. It must grow on them by degrees. They must first learn its spirit and principles, and when these have taken possession of them they will find no difficulty in adopting the external and detailed system which is the natural expression and application of that spirit and those principles. The other two heads of teaching differ in this respect; the first is the principle of not forcing a part of a new system on men till the whole can be introduced. The second is the principle, more or less like that of which we have spoken as the third, of not forcing on a new system as a whole before men are ready for it, that is, on men who are not as yet imbued with its spirit. These are general principles of Divine prudence, and of human prudence also. They might have been at once recognized as such by the persons to whom our Lord was speaking, and they were based upon the character of the dispensation which our Lord came to introduce. But, like all the parabolic teaching of our Lord, they are full of Divine light to us who can trace the working out of these principles in the history of the Christian Church, who can understand what its system was to be because we live under it, and who can to some extent appreciate the difficulties which were avoided by this heavenly prudence of our Lord, and the lessons which He thereby meant to give His Church after Him.

In the case of the first principle, which in effect condemns anything that can have the character of patchwork in what concerns religion, internal or external, we can see at once that its application extends far beyond the particular matter which was before our Lord at the moment. In the case of religious systems it applies to all attempts to mix up together heterogeneous elements, whether the attempt be to foist what is old upon what is new, or what is new upon what is old. This principle is constantly violated in our own day, by persons who endeavour to make a patchwork of Protestantism and Catholicism, or, to use another image, to engraft Catholic practices, ritual, or systems of life, upon the uncongenial stock of Anglicanism. The fasts of the Pharisees and of the disciples of St. John were, after all, practices of natural religion, specified as to time and occasion by the days of which commemoration was made in the Jewish calendar, as we should say, and connected, as it seems, with the dealings of Providence with the synagogue and the holy nation as such. This was but a very small and most unobjectionable part of the system in possession, and yet our Lord was looking forward to a far more sweeping abandonment of the traditions of Judaism than that with which He was taxed. He was intending that the whole sacrificial and liturgical system of the Old Law should be done away with, not as bad in itself, but as belonging to a dispensation of

God which had passed away. The fasts of pious people among the Jews were like the particular or local devotions, as we call them, of Catholics, as compared with the fundamental laws and ordinances of their religion, but they grew out of the Jewish system, and expressed its spirit. They were its developments. Our Lord, therefore, would have none of them. He never told His disciples not to be circumcised, not to offer sacrifices at Jerusalem, not to observe the law as to purifications, and the like. Yet He meant all these things to cease, and to be supplanted. The Christian Law was to have its regulations about all these things—regulations in many respects parallel to those which He would not impose. There were to be seasons of fasting and humiliation, times of public supplication, a whole array of special devotions and religious and ascetic practices, as large as any that existed in the old dispensation. But all these things were to spring from the Christian Church herself, naturally and spontaneously, and as far as they were connected with events and great public mercies of God, they were to commemorate nothing which belonged to the older dispensation. Even the greatest feasts of the Law were to be forgotten in the Christian mysteries which took their place. The Exodus and the sparing of the firstborn were to be swallowed up in Easter, and the Day of Pentecost was to commemorate the descent of the Holy Ghost. Our Lord's own life, and the mysteries of His Death, Resurrection, and Ascension, were to furnish the subject-matter, so to speak, of the great chain of the festivals of His Church. In the same way, the fasts of Christians were to spring from the mournful commemorations of the new kingdom. Lent was to honour our Lord's fast, and to prepare for the celebration of Passion-tide and Easter. Advent was to go before Christmas, and the day in each week which revived the memory of Gethsemani and Calvary was to become the continual day of abstinence. All these things belonged to the Gospel kingdom, as a piece of a new garment belongs to that garment, and it would have been poor patchwork indeed to enjoin these celebrations before the mysteries themselves had taken place, while as yet the older dispensation had not been superseded, or to enjoin the parallel celebrations of that elder dispensation on those whose life was being formed in the spirit of the new. The events had not even yet taken place, except in part, on which the system of public observances in the Church was to be founded. And when these great mysteries had happened, and when the time came for the gradual development of the Christian order of festivals and fasts and devotions, the incongruity between these and the commemorations of the events of the sieges of Jerusalem, and the like, would have been exactly that of the obvious discrepancy between new cloth and old in the same garment.

Moreover, the danger against which our Lord was guarding was not only that of incongruity. It is a characteristic of religious, but narrow-minded, people, to endeavour to force their own observances and even their own tastes in devotion on others. They are lynx-eyed in detecting any independence, for example, on the part of new converts, any deviation in a religious Order from the precedents to which their own prejudices are wedded. They suspect whatever is not precisely in accordance with their own education or habits. If this is so common as to matters of confessedly lighter importance, it is naturally much more dangerous when the points as to which there is an appearance of novelty are of real moment. It was a matter of vital importance that the Church should be free at her outset from the influence of all traditions but her own. Especially was she to be altogether exempt from all particularism. She was to be the mother of the Gentiles no less than of the Jews; she was to adapt her system to the fierce barbarians of the North, when their time came to be brought into her fold, and she was to be equally large in her reception of those who had been nurtured in the corrupt civilizations of Greece and Rome. She was to penetrate further than the armies of Alexander or of the Roman Empire, towards the almost unknown regions of the East and South, and in due course of time she was to send her teachers to nations and continents of which neither Greek nor Roman had ever heard. Everywhere she was to bear the same truths and the same spirit, the same teaching, the same priesthood and sacraments and means of grace. But her law of unity in all things essential was not to be fettered by the weight of obligations which were not founded on her interior spirit. It was most necessary that her freedom from precedent should be at once proclaimed by her Divine founder Himself, that He should not leave behind Him any precedent which might be turned against the rulers of the Church, when they came to legislate for her children over the whole world, in the face of all the jealousies of Judaism, whether without or within her own fold.

We may see, in truth, in these questioners of our Lord, the forerunners of the many narrow-minded or even heretically-tempered men who have created difficulties as to the perfect exercise of Christian liberty in successive ages of the Church. We think at once of the first Judaizing teachers, who caused so much pain to the Apostles by their love and zeal for the Jewish law, as well as other intolerant men among Christians of later days,—more narrow-minded than the Judaizers, because they have not the excuse of a supposed point of doctrine to explain their dogmatizing spirit against customs of devotion or styles of architecture or music which are different from their own liking. We seem to see that our Lord had in His mind many a difficulty of the Church which might have been enhanced if He could have acted more in harmony with the prejudices of His critics. The whole case of the Gentile Christians in the apostolic age is founded on the principle which is here asserted. 'Let no man judge you,' says St. Paul to the Colossians, 'in meat or drink, or in respect of a festival day, or a new moon, or of the Sabbath—which are a shadow of things to come, but the body,' or substance, 'is of Christ.'[1] The question between St. Paul and the Judaizing teachers was one of doctrine, and so of vital importance. But there may have been many good but unenlightened Christians, who might have wished to see the Gentile converts bound to the legal observances, without thinking them necessary, and the resistance which the Apostle would make to such persons would be founded on the principle of our Lord about the new wine and the new bottles. He would tolerate, as we know he did tolerate, the strictest observance of the law in the Jewish Christians themselves, so long as it was not held that the law was of necessity. But when he came to legislate for the new Churches among the Gentiles, he would form them entirely and exclusively on the Gospel spirit. That is, he would resist the conjunction of the old bottles and the new wine.

It is a principle of the method according to which God deals with us, founded upon His knowledge of the nature which He has given to us, that every thing that has real life in the way of a religious system, and even of a political system or a social system, has a spirit of its own, and that the external laws and dominant features of its institutions and customs are the expressions of

[1] Coloss. ii. 16, 17.

this spirit. So true is this, that few things are more remarkable in the gentle government of the Church, than her careful regard for the spirit of any institute which springs up among Christians, and has to be sanctioned by the authorities which rule them. There have sometimes been foolish attempts made to force uniformity on religious Orders, or to introduce into them new customs and lines of work or of devotion, as when Cardinal de Berulle endeavoured to make the nuns of St. Teresa's Reform in France adopt the Perpetual Adoration of the Blessed Sacrament. All these efforts fail, because they produce incongruity with the original spirit of the institutes which are thus tampered with, and not from any other cause, as if Trappist monks were sent out to preach retreats, or Sisters of Charity bound to silence and to the spending of long hours in contemplation. These things are holy and beautiful, but not equally fitted for all. One of the beauties of the Kingdom of God, as we see it in the Catholic Church on earth, is the endless variety, so to speak, of colour and feature, which the Holy Spirit produces in Christians of different characters, different generations, different vocations. The fertility of the Church in this respect is as multifarious as the fertility of nature in her trees or her flowers. But all this variety is founded on delicate but most true diversities of spirit, which make religious institutes, or the various saints of God, or masses of Catholic population in various countries, alike, each to each, as the members of the same family, yet each one different, in some slight but individual characteristics, from the rest. All this beautiful arrangement of God is set aside or ignored by those who would have every one stamped with the same pattern and moulded in precisely the same mould.

This is enough to illustrate the principle of the

Kingdom of God which is expressed in the image of the new wine and the bottles. The true history of the dealings of our Lord in His Church is made up of the application of all the various principles which are contained in the whole answer which is here given by the Evangelists, rather than of the application of any one exclusively. We have to trace not only the careful abstinence from the patching of old cloth with new, and the patience with which the new wine was allowed to wait for the bottles which were fit for it—or, as we may put it in other words, the reverent manner in which the system of the Church was allowed to unfold itself, like some beautiful but slow growing flower—but also the working of the principle which is enunciated in the few closing words of St. Luke's report of our Lord's answer, that 'No man drinking old wine, hath presently,' or at once, 'a mind to new, for he saith, The old is better.' This principle differs from, and is the counterpart of, the first of which we have spoken. It is the principle of the tolerance of old systems as far as they do not contain what is wrong or contrary to Christian truth, and of the abstinence on the part of those who represent our Lord in the Church, from all violent destruction or proscription of rites or ceremonies or religious customs, consistent with truth, in which those who come into her fold are brought up. The Church of the Apostolic age will supply us with abundance of illustration of this principle of our Lord. Judaism was the old wine to which the earliest converts and the earliest churches were accustomed. They were wedded, almost in proportion to the depth of their religiousness and devotion, to the rites and ordinances which had had so much Divine sanction, and which had prepared the holy nation for its coming King. No doubt the Apostles could have taught the first converts, on the day of Pentecost and afterwards, that the glory had departed from the Temple, that the sacrifices of the old law had ceased to have any meaning, that circumcision was an empty rite, and that the Sabbath was transferred to the Christian Sunday. They did nothing of this kind. The Apostles in Jerusalem observed the law themselves, they even waited for the Divine command to admit the Gentiles into the Church. Even the minor observances of the Mosaic system were held by them in scrupulous honour. They still clung to the old wine. We find St. Peter himself, before the admission of the Gentiles into the Church, abstaining from all the kinds of food which were forbidden in Leviticus, and, long afterwards, afraid to eat publicly with the Gentile Christians at Antioch, on the occasion mentioned by St. Paul in the Epistle to the Galatians. On the other hand, St. Paul himself, the great champion of Christian liberty in all things unessential, caused St. Timothy, the offspring of a mixed marriage of a Jewess with a Gentile, to be circumcized, and he went himself through the ceremonial purifications of the Nazarites at the time of his last visit to Jerusalem, in order to conciliate to himself the many thousands of Jews who believed, as St. James advised him.[2]

These points of conduct on the part of the chief Apostles testify to the recognition, by the rulers of His Church, of this principle laid down by our Lord. They are based on that tender consideration for human character which is everywhere exemplified in the dealings of God with man. They are other developments of the principle on which our Lord acted when He retired before His enemies, that He might not break the bruised reed or quench the smoking flax. It seems strange to us sometimes that the Church should have tolerated the observance of the Jewish law so long as she did, while

[2] Acts x. 14; Galat. ii. 14; Acts xvi. 3; xxi. 26.

the Gentile Christians had to be defended in the use of the liberty which she had secured for them. But she has acted on the same principle in a thousand cases since the Apostolic age, and she acts on it continually in our own as well as then. It is on this that she acts in tolerating so many diversities of ritual, of discipline, of religious rule, in communities which either submit to her unity after long times of separation, or have inherited from antiquity the peculiarities to which their members are attached. It is on this principle that she deals so tenderly even with populations converted from Paganism, so long as she is asked to tolerate nothing that is in itself wrong. This principle has actuated her saints in a thousand instances of condescension to customs and habits and prejudices, which have long been deeply rooted among those for whose salvation they have had to labour—often at the cost of leading themselves lives of the utmost mortification, for the sake of winning the confidence of new converts or of those who may possibly be led to the truth, when it is presented to them in a form as like as possible to what they have been in the habit of venerating. When all these principles are taken together, we see that our Lord was laying down laws of action for all times and for all nations, when He seemed to be simply uttering a few proverbial sayings to meet the especial difficulties of the good, but not large-minded, people, who came to Him with their objections about His manner of training the future members of His Church.

CHAPTER X.

The Miracle at the Probatic Pool.

St. John v. 1—15; *Vita Vitæ Nostræ*, § 41.

THE miracles and discourses of our Lord on which we have been dwelling, since the time of the Sermon on the Mount, may all be considered as belonging, not only to the same period in point of time, but as linked together by one general purpose of our Lord in working them or uttering them. We have endeavoured to trace this unity of purpose in the miraculous fishing on the Lake of Galilee, after the discourse to the crowd on the shore from the boat of St. Peter, in the healing of the leper and the injunction to him to show himself to the high priest, in the miracle on the paralytic man, connected, by our Lord's own declaration, with His power as the Son of man to forgive sins, and in the principles which He laid down in answer to His critics, when He had eaten and drunk with publicans and sinners, in the house of His disciple, St. Matthew, and when He explained parabolically, and, so far, enigmatically, His reasons for not as yet ordaining a system of public penances and times of humiliation in the community which already followed Him so closely. In all these things we seem to see that our Lord was looking forward to the Church which He came on earth to found, laying down her foundations, and preparing the minds of the disciples, as well as of others, for the novelties which were to distinguish her from the Synagogue and for the great powers which were to be intrusted to her. He foretold her fertility in the miracle of the fishing, He prefigured her power to heal the soul in the miracle on the leper, He foreshadowed her authority to loose and to bind in the miracle on the paralytic, and He hinted at her large liberty and tolerance, as well as at other of her distinctive principles, in all that passed at the feast of St. Matthew or after that feast.

In all this, our Lord had already given some blows at the rigid system of the Jews of the day, and more than obscurely hinted at the entire independence of the kingdom which He had come to found. We now shall see Him following the same line of conduct still further, on a more conspicuous field of action, and with reference to a point which involved the right interpretation of one of the ten commandments, braving in Jerusalem itself the authorities of the holy nation, not yet pledged to hostility towards Him. We are thus brought to the point of the sacred history at which it may be said to turn decisively in one direction, as far as concerns the relations of our Lord to the Jewish rulers. There can be little doubt as to the perfect continuity of the history, however the particular details which belong to this time may be arranged. Hitherto we have had nothing in our Lord's actions or words which has seemed in any way to run counter to the ordinary ideas of the Jews as to the observance of the Sabbath. The first Sabbath that is specially mentioned in the sacred history is that memorable day at Nazareth, when our Lord was treated so barbarously by His fellow-townsfolk, because He would not satisfy their pride and curiosity by working miracles for them as well as for others who, as they thought, had less claim upon Him than themselves. It is clear that they, at least, would not have been scandalized if He had wrought miracles of mercy on the Sabbath. The next Sabbath Day that is particularly mentioned, is that which so soon followed on the other, when in the synagogue at Capharnaum, He cast the devil out of the demoniac, when He healed the mother-in-law of St. Peter, and, after the sun had set, worked an immense number of miracles of healing and mercy. There we come across the observance of the Sabbath, inasmuch as the reason why the sick who were then cured were not brought to Him earlier in the day, was that the rest of the Sabbath endured till sunset. But at that time our Lord in no way protested against this common belief as to the Sabbath. His other miracles were not wrought on the Sabbath, and the discourses of our Lord say nothing about it. We are now to enter on a series of actions and teachings of our Lord, which seem to have had the direct and specific aim of correcting the common idea on this most important point, and so of preparing the way for the Christian method of observing the Sabbath, and even for that transference of the weekly solemnity to the Sunday, which was effected by the Church.

'After these things,' says St. John, 'there was a festival day of the Jews, and Jesus went up to Jerusalem.' The question as to the particular festival has been hotly discussed, but in truth there is nothing in the words of St. John to favour the supposition that it was one feast of a certain class rather than another, and much less to exclude any of the great feasts. His words imply that it was one of the greater festivals, on which the attendance at Jerusalem was obligatory. For he seems to tell us that our Lord went up to Jerusalem to be present at it. The question is sufficiently discussed elsewhere, and we assume in this chapter that it was the feast of the Pasch—the second, therefore, of the

The Miracle at the Probatic Pool. 159

four Paschs of our Lord's teaching. It was the fact that it was on a Sabbath Day that the miracle of which we are now to speak occurred, and not that it took place at a festival, that was the important matter in the mind of the Evangelist, and thus it is that he has not mentioned that it was the Pasch. 'Now there is at Jerusalem a pool, called Probatica, which in Hebrew is named Bethsaida, having five porches. In these lay a great multitude of sick, of blind, of lame, of withered, waiting for the moving of the waters. And an angel of the Lord descended at certain times into the pond, and the water was moved. And he that went down first into the pond after the motion of the water, was made whole of whatsoever infirmity he lay under.'

The critical questions connected with this passage will be found sufficiently treated at the end of this chapter. Taking the sacred text as we find it, there can be no doubt as to the character of the cures which were wrought at this Probatic Pool, any more than of the agency by which they were wrought. The narrative, even as it stands in the parts of the passage which are unassailed by criticism, implies quite clearly that only the first person was healed who entered the waters after they had been stirred, and that the preternatural character of the cure was shown by the fact that there was no difference between one form of disease or infirmity and another. These features in the circumstances of the cure are entirely in harmony with the obvious purpose of our Lord in working the miracle. It was an unsolicited and unexpected favour, granted, not for the sake of the man himself who was to be healed, but for that of the truth which our Lord desired to set forth in the most prominent light and in such a way as to attract public attention immediately. In this respect the miracle resembles that on the paralytic, of which we have so lately spoken, which our Lord evidently wrought in a manner purposely chosen in order to put forward, most publicly and solemnly, His authority to forgive sins. This could not have been promulgated in a manner more certain to attract attention and to secure for it the greatest publicity, than in the presence of so distinguished an assembly. This miracle at the Pool has the same obvious characteristics. Our Lord seems to have gone to this Pool for the very purpose of finding the occasion for the miracle He desired to work in order to create the sensation which followed about the apparent breach of the Sabbath which He enjoined. Without this last circumstance, the miracle might have passed almost unperceived and unnoticed. With this circumstance, besides being a striking evidence of our Lord's Divine mission, it became the foundation of a new revelation as to the Christian doctrine of the Sabbath, as the miracle on the paralytic involved the revelation of a new doctrine about the absolution of sins, in consequence of our Lord's words to the paralytic, which took the Jews so much by surprise.

'And there was a certain man there, that had been eight and thirty years under his infirmity. Him when Jesus had seen lying, and knew that he had been now a long time, He saith to him, Wilt thou be made whole? The infirm man answered Him, Sir, I have no man, when the water is troubled, to put me into the pond. For while I am coming, another goeth down before me. Jesus saith to him, Arise, take up thy bed, and walk. And immediately the man was made whole, and he took up his bed, and walked.' It is not necessary to conclude that this poor sufferer had been lying at the Probatic Pool for the thirty-eight years successively during which he had been infirm. The multitude of the sick persons who lay in the porches would collect there at certain times only, and men do not ordinarily seek miraculous cures till after they have exhausted natural means of recovery. This poor man may only have dragged himself to the Pool from time to time as he despaired more and more of human help. Our Lord's question was put, as it seems, for the purpose of drawing from him a statement of his own impotence, and further of exciting in him that hope and faith which were requisite for the cure, according to the usual rule followed by our Lord in the working of such miracles. For the infirm man does not answer the question directly. It was plain enough to any one who saw him there that he desired to be made whole. His answer implies that the desire was there, but that it was far from enough, for he had no man to help him. Again, the manner in which he addresses our Lord shows humility and respect, though he could not have known Who He was that spoke to him. His faith was made powerful enough to make him obey our Lord's command to rise up and take up his bed, and thus the condition on his part for the working of the miracle was fulfilled. Thus the word of our Lord fell on his ears, and did not merely convey the command which it embodied, but also gave strength to his limbs enabling him to obey. The command to take up the bed, or pallet, was probably added for the full proof of the miracle, as well as for the purpose of which mention has already been made. It was fit that the man who had been healed should do something unusual and conspicuous, in order to attract the attention of the people about him. He was made the witness or herald of the power displayed by our Lord, as the leper before him, who had made Him known wherever he went, and had also a special mission of making it known to the authorities of Jerusalem, that our Lord had taken on Himself to cure the disease which was considered as so particularly the infliction of God. So now this well known sufferer, who, from the long time during which he had been patiently waiting for his turn at the pool of healing, must have been most readily accepted as a witness, was a herald to the whole population among whom he walked, bearing his bed, of the fact that our Lord had exercised in his favour a power which proved Him to be a messenger from God. If he had simply been seen walking, he might have been known to those only, though they may have been many, who were aware of the affliction under which he had been labouring. But when he was seen doing a thing which was in contravention to the letter of the law of the Sabbath, no one who saw him and who was aware of that law could help being struck with what he saw, and so being led to interrogate him as to his conduct.

Our Lord could hardly have intended any other result from His injunction than that which actually, in the first place, followed. The singularity of the action which He had commanded attracted at once the attention of the people who saw it. 'The Jews therefore said to him that was healed, It is the Sabbath, it is not lawful for thee to carry thy bed.' St. John speaks at once of 'the Jews.' The language used is that of persons in authority, and it is well known that, in the Gospel of St. John, the general term 'the Jews' is used to signify the particular class of the ecclesiastical rulers. The action of the man who had been healed would first of all attract the attention of the by-standers and of the crowd collected round the pool. In a city like Jerusalem it would at once get abroad, and would very soon be brought to the knowledge of the authorities. It seems that the poor man was summoned before them, whether formally or not. Their language to him is not such as to surprise us. It was the criticism natural at the sight of such an action. It was, in fact, true, according to the received rules as to the observance of the Sabbath, unless the carrying of burthens was to be excused on account of some higher law or necessity. This is exactly the answer which was pleaded by the poor man who had been healed. He spoke with theological accuracy in the reply which he made. 'He answered them, He that made me whole, He said to me, Take up thy bed.' And his words imply that any one, to whom God could grant the power to make him suddenly and perfectly whole, after so many years of infirmity, must be so dear to God as not to be capable of giving a command which was contrary to the law of God. He knew that there was a legal prohibition, which had been renewed so lately as in the time of the Prophet Jeremias,[1] against bearing burthens on the Sabbath. But he could understand, in the first place, that a prophet or worker of miracles might be safely obeyed without fear of transgression of the true law, and in the second place, that the bearing such a burthen on the Sabbath in his own case, as an evidence of the mercy which God had showed to him, would be an action altogether different from the ordinary burthen-bearing which was forbidden— an act of religion, like the labour of the priests and levites in the Temple on the Sabbath Day. This was the conclusion to which a simple humble soul would naturally come. It could not be denied that there were positive precepts which forbade the action which was blamed by the Jews, but, on the other hand, it was not possible that One Whose mission God had authenticated by a great miracle of mercy could enjoin what was really in contravention of the Law of God.

The Jews to whom this answer was made were in

[1] Jerem. xvii. 24.

precisely the same position as those scribes and doctors of the law lately mentioned, to whom our Lord had seemed to speak blasphemy, when He had said to the paralytic man, 'Thy sins are forgiven thee.' That is, they had before them two facts, from which they might conclude rightly or wrongly, according to the state of their hearts. In the former case, the scribes in Galilee had the fact before them, that our Lord claimed a power which had never before been imparted by God, the power of forgiving sins, and the other fact, that He knew their thoughts, and that He proved His authority by the miracle on the paralytic. The right conclusion from these facts was formed by the people—that He had the power of forgiveness which He claimed, but which was incapable of visible and direct proof, because He exercised the other power which He also claimed, which also was beyond the reach of human nature, and yet was capable of visible and direct proof, the power of healing the paralytic by a word. In the second case, the Jews who were now confronted by the man who had been so wonderfully cured at the pool, had the fact before them that the person, whoever he was, that had done this miracle, claimed the power of enjoining a work which was forbidden on the Sabbath, and so, apparently, was in opposition to God's law, and also the other fact, that he had wrought a marvellous miracle, of which the action which he enjoined was the visible witness. The right conclusion for them to form was, that this person had power to dispense, for some purposes of God's glory of which he was the judge, with the positive regulations as to the observance of the Sabbath. This is the test to which our Lord put them deliberately, and for the purpose, as we cannot doubt, of drawing their attention to the evidences with which, by the providence of His Father, His mission was accredited. The circumstances of the miracle were all selected by our Lord with this intention—the publicity of the place where the miracle was wrought, the choice of one single person, and one whose cure was most clearly impossible to human means, and even His own swift withdrawal from the spot, which seems to have been arranged so as to avoid a disturbance at the moment, and also for the purpose of presenting the facts to the authorities, in the first instance, simply by themselves and unconnected with His own name, against which they may already have had some secret prejudice. As it was, the miracle came before them as a simple matter of evidence, concerning some unnamed person who had wrought a marvellous cure, and then given an order which was in contravention of the positive law. But, when they came to the knowledge that it was our Lord Who had worked the miracle, then it became one more link in the great chain of evidences in favour of His Divine mission, and could no longer be considered as apart from the rest. Thus, we shall see our Lord taking occasion, from the discussion now raised, to speak to them of the combined and accumulated force of all these evidences.

'They asked him therefore, Who is that man who said to thee, Take up thy bed and walk? But he who was healed knew not who it was, for Jesus went aside from the multitude standing in the place.' It seems clear that the miracle might have escaped without notice but for the action of the man who had been healed in carrying his bed. We are not now told of any sharp reproof administered to the poor man by the authorities. It is not easy to think that they admitted his answer, but the reasons for our thinking this are not drawn from the words of the narrative. The man was at least free to go on his way, and he went, as it seems, at once, to the Temple to give thanks to God for his cure. There the watchful eye of the Good Shepherd was upon him. His disease had been removed, but before it, or during its long pressure upon him, he had been a sinner, and perhaps we may even suppose that the infliction itself had not been unconnected with his sin. It may have been its physical result, or it may have been its providential chastisement. 'Afterwards Jesus findeth him in the Temple, and saith to him, Behold thou art made whole; sin no more, lest some worse thing happen to thee.' For the temporal chastisements with which God sometimes visits sin are not the worst things that can befall the sinner. They are mercies, which give him the opportunity of repentance, which withdraw him from the occasions of further transgressions, and, if they are borne with humility and patience, they may serve as the expiation of the sin for which they are sent. Worse things, then, may come on the sinner after his deliverance from them. He may relapse, and commit other sins, for which God will not chastise him here in mercy, but hereafter in justice and wrath, or He may send some more fatal and terrible visitation. In either case, the thing that happens to such sinners is worse, as they deserve worse.

'The man went his way, and told the Jews that it was Jesus Who had made him whole.' It is not necessary to imagine any malice or, as some people think, meanness, in this action of the man who had been healed by our Lord. The action is quite consistent with a simple faith and a desire to proclaim the name of his benefactor. We must be careful not to confuse different times, in our estimate of the state of mind of the authorities at Jerusalem with regard to our Lord, and, much more, as to the common ideas of the people concerning the attitude of their rulers. That attitude had hitherto been, mainly, neutral. Our Lord had been but very little in the Holy

City, and had carefully given very little occasion for any pronouncement concerning Him on the part of the Chief Priests. But He was now determined to force on them the consideration of the evidences of His mission, and it is difficult to account for the miracle of which we have been speaking on any other supposition as to His intention. It was His desire, therefore, that they should know Who it was that had worked this miracle and followed it up by a claim of authority so new to them. He gave no injunction, in this case, that He should not be made known. It would have been easy for Him to do this, as it would have been easy for Him to warn the man who had been healed against carelessness for the future, without revealing to him Who his Deliverer was. But it was in the counsels of His wisdom that the hearts of the Chief Priests should now be tested by this trial, and that He should have the opportunity of placing before them, in the solemn discourse which St. John immediately subjoins, the variety and cogency of the evidences with which it had been His Father's will to authenticate His teaching and His claims.

Once before, a year before this time, He had challenged their attention by an action with which they could find no fault, the cleansing His Father's Temple. Then they had questioned Him concerning His authority, and He had answered them enigmatically with a prophetic reference to His Passion which they were to bring about. Then He had retired from the neighbourhood, and they had seen no more of Him. It is very likely that the question as to His claims was one which they would have been glad to put aside and forget. Now, however, He had once more deliberately challenged their attention, by an act of authority not less sovereign than when He had taken on Himself to purge the Temple. It was impossible that the matter should be ignored, and the discussion which must now ensue was the most important in its issues of any that had ever been held in that Holy City.

NOTE I.

On the Feast mentioned in St. John v.

As St. John has not specified the particular feast at which the miracle on the man at the pool took place, many conjectures have been made to supply the omission. In the first place, some writers have assumed that the feast in question cannot have been the Pasch of the second year of our Lord's Public Ministry, for the simple reason that, if it had been so, St. John would not have failed to specify the fact. This is a weak argument. For the reason, as has already been said, for the mention of the feast at all, lies in the fact that our Lord healed the impotent man on the Sabbath Day. This is the important point in the narrative, not the fact that the miracle took place at a feast. This other fact seems to be naturally mentioned, as supplying the reason why our Lord should have been present at Jerusalem. The words, 'there was a feast of the Jews, and Jesus went up to Jerusalem,' imply that it was one of the feasts to which people 'went up' in obedience to the Law. This would apply to any one of the three great feasts.

On the same grounds, it may be said that St. John's language seems to exclude the minor feasts, such as that of Purim, which certainly was not a feast likely to draw our Lord to Jerusalem at its celebration. But, as we find afterwards that our Lord, in the last winter of His Ministry, was at Jerusalem at the feast of the Dedication,[1] which was one of the minor feasts, it is of course not certain that He might not accidentally be at Jerusalem for any one of these, although He might not go up on purpose. But, in truth, the only reason for supposing this feast to have been the feast of Purim is a chronological one, founded on a mistaken interpretation of our Lord's saying about the four months before

[1] St. John x. 23. It is not said our Lord 'went up' for this feast.

harvest in St. John iv.² This mistake has been already explained in the proper place in this work.

Putting aside the supposition of any decisive data by which this question may be settled beyond all controversy, it yet seems by far the most probable hypothesis that this feast was the second Pasch. In the first place, it is mentioned by St. John in a manner which shows that he is here, as elsewhere, supplying what has been omitted by the earlier Evangelists, for the reason for which most of the circumstances which he thus supplies have been omitted by them—that is, because they did not take place in Galilee. But St. John has a further purpose, almost as evident as the other—that of giving our Lord's discourse on the question raised by the miracle, and also of explaining the enmity borne by the Jewish rulers to Him. The incident of the miracle belongs to a series of incidents of the same kind, all of which have reference to the difference between our Lord and the Jews as to the observance of the Sabbath. The first incident of this kind, to be found elsewhere, which is related by all three of the historical Evangelists, is that of the attack made on our Lord because He allowed His disciples to pluck the ears of corn on the Sabbath Day.³ This is immediately followed by another incident of the same sort, when, on another Sabbath, our Lord cured the man with a withered hand in the synagogue, and by doing this gave occasion to the conspiracy of the Pharisees and Herodians to bring about His death.⁴ The narrative of the first incident fixes it to a time when the harvest was nearly ready, that is, to the week or two just after Easter. It is also very probable, from the words of the three Evangelists, that they mean us to understand that our Lord was on a journey when He 'passed through' the cornfields. Some writers, indeed, consider this to be quite clear, and the best interpretation of the unusual word by which St. Luke designates that particular Sabbath—'the second-first'—seems to be that which fixes it to a Sabbath after Easter. But if our Lord was travelling towards Galilee, in which country the incidents which next follow seem to have taken

---

² St. John iv. 35. See the *Ministry of St. John Baptist*, note vii. p. 329.
³ St. Matt. xii. 1, seq.; St. Mark ii. 23; St. Luke vi. 1, seq.
⁴ St. Matt. xii. 10, seq.; St. Mark iii. 1, seq.; St. Luke vi. 6, seq.

place, and in which He must have been when the Pharisees conspired with the Herodians, it is probable that the journey was from Jerusalem, and that He had just been at that city for the celebration of a feast, which, from the incident about the ears of corn, must have been the Pasch.

Moreover, the attitude of the Pharisees in both these incidents, that of the cornfields and of the miracle of the man with a withered hand, is far more decidedly hostile than ever before. In the latter case, indeed, it is distinctly said that the Scribes and Pharisees 'watched Him,' as if they expected that He might heal on the Sabbath, and as if they were prepared to find fault with Him if He did so. But such an expectation could not have been naturally produced merely by the fact that our Lord had allowed the disciples to pluck the ears of corn on the preceding Sabbath, much less if He had really been travelling in the intervening week, for in that case He would have been in a different part of the country. The 'watching' thus mentioned needs some explanation. It must have been occasioned by something which had previously taken place. But there is nothing of the kind in the history of the three first Evangelists, nothing at all in the Gospels, unless we suppose that the miracle on the man at the pool had occurred just before at Jerusalem itself, and had been made the subject of a serious and public charge against our Lord. It is clear, from the earlier history, that at the beginning of our Lord's preaching in Galilee there was no objection, in that part of the country, to His healing on the Sabbath in the synagogue, though it is not likely that the people thought it lawful to bring the sick to Him on the Sabbath Day. This is proved by the history of the first Sabbath at Capharnaum,[5] not to speak of the previous Sabbath at Nazareth, when it seems that our Lord gave offence by not working miracles on that day.[6] But all is explained, if we suppose that the miracle at the pool roused the strict and rigorous observers of the Law at Jerusalem to indignation, and thus was the signal for the cavilling and watching to which He was immediately subjected. It was natural that the authorities of Jerusalem

---

[5] St. Mark i. 23—34; St. Luke iv. 33; St. Matt. viii. 14; St. Luke iv. 41.

[6] St. Luke iv. 16.

should give the tone to the Scribes and Pharisees all over the country, and thus we see the full purport of St. John's mention of this miracle, as well as of his remark that this was the reason why the Jews, that is, the people at Jerusalem, sought to kill our Lord, 'because He did these things on the Sabbath Day.' We have had already other instances in which St. John has silently supplied what was wanting to the full explanation of the history as given by the former Evangelists. Such an instance is to be found in his mention of our Lord's words at the first Pasch, when He had told the Jews, in answer to their demand for a sign of the authority which He assumed in cleansing the Temple, 'Destroy this Temple, and in three days I will raise it up.'[7] These words were brought up against Him, as the other Gospels tell us, at the time of His Passion, and yet they are recorded by no one but St. John, as having been said at the time when they were said. Another instance in which St. John has supplied an explanation of what has been related by others, is to be found in his account of the miracle on the ruler's son at Capharnaum—when our Lord was Himself at Cana—which is wanted to explain the words of the people of Nazareth in St. Luke iv. 23. These instances illustrate one at least of the purposes of St. John in inserting this narrative of the miracle at the pool. It explains what was, in truth, a remarkable change of attitude towards our Lord on the part of the Scribes and Pharisees, not only at Jerusalem, but all over the country. Considered in this light, the incidents at this feast at Jerusalem, which are here supplied by St. John, are not less important in the Evangelical history than any others which St. John has supplied—not even than the miracle of the raising of Lazarus. The same Evangelist afterwards mentions[8] that on account of this danger our Lord did not go for some time into Judea. As a matter of fact, He does not seem to have been present at Jerusalem for any of the feasts after this, until the feast of Tabernacles in the following year—after an interval of eighteen months. Thus this miracle becomes, as has been said, a very important turning-point in the history of our Lord's preaching.

There is one apparent difficulty in this, which seems the most natural hypothesis on the question as to this feast, to

[7] St. John ii. 19.   [8] St. John vii. 1.

which it may be as well to devote a few lines. The difficulty is that, in the long discourse to the Jews at Jerusalem which is subjoined by St. John in this place, our Lord enumerates the various witnesses to His mission which the providence of the Father had furnished, and that when speaking of St. John Baptist, He uses the past tense, and this is understood as if the blessed Precursor were no longer alive. If this interpretation of the words of our Lord had any certainty, the difficulty would be great in fixing this feast at the Pasch of the second year of His Ministry. For it seems clear that at that time the Baptist was not yet put to death. But the fact that our Lord speaks of him as if he were dead is very far from certain. His words are, 'There *is another "witnessing"* to Me, and I know that the testimony is true which *he beareth* to Me. You sent unto John'—our Lord here alludes to the solemn deputation to the Baptist from the authorities at Jerusalem, mentioned by St. John the Evangelist in the first chapter of his Gospel[9]—'you sent unto John, and he bare witness to the truth. . . . He was a light, burning and shining, and you were willing for an hour to rejoice in his light.' If St. John were still alive at the time at which these words were spoken, that would not prevent our Lord from using the past tense about his testimony—though He uses the present tense in the earlier part of the passage—for at the time of the second Pasch the burning and shining light no longer burned and shone as before, since St. John had been many months before that put into prison, and the time when the priests and Pharisees were willing for a moment to rejoice in him was altogether past. In the same way when our Lord speaks to the multitude about St. John Baptist, after the mission of the two disciples of the latter to Himself with their master's question, 'Art Thou He that is to come?' the language used is that of the past, although it is certain that St. John was then alive.[10] There is therefore no reason, in this passage of our Lord's discourse, for supposing that the blessed Baptist had already received his crown when the words in question were spoken.

[9] St. John i. 19.
[10] St. Matt. xi. 7—12; St. Luke vii. 24—28.

NOTE II.

On the genuineness of the fourth verse of St. John v.

It is well known that there is considerable doubt, on merely critical grounds, as to the genuineness of the fourth verse of this chapter of St. John—the verse which contains the statement that an angel went down at certain times into the Pool of Bethsaida, and stirred the water, and that the first person who entered the water after that movement was cured of whatever disease it was that he was suffering from. There is great authority, as far as manuscripts and ancient versions are concerned, against the passage. There is also against it the apparent fact that it may be a gloss inserted to explain the remainder of the text—especially the statement implied in the words of the poor sufferer,[1] which shows that not all who entered the pool were cured, but only the one who was first to enter it. It is, however, highly probable that we should have heard little about the want of authority for the verse in question, if it had not implied the agency of an angel, and so what may be considered a recurrent miracle. This is the true reason why, as has lately been said by a Protestant commentator on this Gospel, 'the Biblical critic is glad that he can remove these words from the record, and that he cannot be called on to explain them." As Catholics will have little sympathy with 'the Biblical critic' of whom this writer speaks, it may be worth while to say a few words as to the reasons which may be found on the other side of the question.

It would require a considerable space to enter on the whole subject of the principles which should guide any reasonable person in forming an opinion on a controverted text of Scripture. But it may be safely asserted, without much fear of contradiction, that such a person will assuredly value the positive testimony in favour of a given text, when such exists, at a far higher rate than the merely negative authority against it, arising from its omission in a certain number of manuscripts or versions. It is easy to imagine accidents, or even reasons of prudence, which may have led to the absence of certain words from such documents, but it

[1] St. John v. 7.

is not so easy to allow that glosses could be inserted in the text with impunity, or without detection. In this respect, the Scriptures stand on a ground which no other writings share. It is therefore far more easy to think that a true portion of a Gospel may have been omitted in certain copies, than that a spurious insertion has gained possession in a great many. This principle makes a single affirmative voice, so to speak, countervail a good many silences in such a matter.

Moreover, Biblical critics, if they are worthy of their name, have by this time discovered that there is often a great fallacy lurking under the counting of manuscripts on one side or on the other, which is sometimes thought of so great importance. It is well known, for instance, that St. Jerome, when he edited the Vulgate, had possession of many manuscripts older and more precious than any that have come down to us. Supposing St. Jerome, therefore, as fit for his work as any modern critic, it would follow that his deliberate insertion or retention of a passage in the Vulgate is practically the witness to that passage of the manuscripts and versions which St. Jerome used, and which modern critics would gladly use if they had them. Now, the manuscripts available in the fourth century are worth ten times as much as those available in the nineteenth. The practical question for the critic ought to be whether there is sufficient positive evidence for any particular text to justify him, all things considered, in retaining it. He is not bound to explain all difficulties, or to account for all omissions. In the present case, the answer cannot be otherwise than in the affirmative. The writer just now quoted says: 'We meet with it'—the passage in question—'very early. It is found in the Alexandrian manuscript and in the Latin and early Syrian versions. Tertullian refers to it.' Against this he sets the fact that the passage is omitted by most of the oldest manuscripts, the oldest, that is, that we happen in the nineteenth century to possess, 'including the Sinaitic and the Vatican, and is judged to be no part of the original text by a consensus of modern editors, including Tischendorf, Tregelles, Alford, and Westcott, and Hort." The 'modern editors,' unfortunately, may share this gentleman's feeling and be 'glad to remove these words from the record, but such a question is not to be settled by the gladness or sorrows of editors, especially Protestants.

It may also be remarked, that the suggestion that these words are 'a gloss inserted in harmony with a popular interpretation,' and with 'a wide acceptance from the second century downwards,' is not very satisfactory. It remains to be proved that a popular interpretation all over the Church would agree in fixing upon the descent of an angel at a particular time into this pool—which, as the writer we are quoting tells us, has been lately thought to be the same as the Pool of Siloam, mentioned in ch. x. 7. of this same Gospel—as the specific cause of its occasional healing power. Again, some explanation of the text of St. John, as it would stand with this passage omitted, is certainly required. It is not like this Evangelist to leave a point like this unexplained. But if these words are not his, it seems tolerably certain that some words which were his have been omitted. The seventh verse proves that it was the first person only who entered the water after the motion who was healed, and it implies that it was indifferent what was his disease. But St. John has not said this in his account of the pool, unless we suppose him to have said it in the words to which objection is made. The text without these words is obviously imperfect, and we must suppose a mutilation first and an interpolation afterwards, if these words are not genuine.

CHAPTER XI.

Our Lord and the Chief Priests.

St. John v. 16—30; *Vita Vitæ Nostræ*, § 42.

THE Gospel of the blessed Evangelist St. John supplies us with a number of our Lord's discourses, with the Jewish authorities at Jerusalem, and with others, which have a character and an importance of their own. We need not now dwell on the theological and doctrinal purpose of this Divine Book, the construction of which is so remarkably simple and yet so constantly misunderstood. It is enough to say here that it is the practice of St. John to subjoin to any mention which he makes of the miracles of our Lord—miracles which, except in the case of the great action of the multiplication of the loaves for the feeding of the five thousand, are ordinarily such as have been omitted by the previous Evangelists —discourses or disputations of our Lord which contain high and difficult doctrine. It should, perhaps, rather be said that, except in some few instances, St. John makes his accounts of the miracles to serve as prefaces to these discourses, and that the miracles are mentioned for the sake of the discourses, rather than the discourses introduced as commentaries on the miracles. We have already had to speak of one discourse of our Lord, held at Jerusalem at the time of the first Pasch at which He was present after His Baptism by St. John. This is the conversation with Nicodemus, in which our Lord laid down the doctrine of the new birth, of the necessity and privileges of faith, of His own future Passion and His Divine Filiation. In that discourse there is nothing of severity, though our Lord complains of the dulness of His hearer, and marvels at his difficulty in comprehending the more easy portions of the doctrines which He came to deliver. We are now to speak of the second of these great discourses of our Lord preserved to us by St. John, a discourse occasioned by the miracle lately spoken of, on the poor man at the Probatic Pool, or rather by the injunction which our Lord had laid on him of carrying his bed on the Sabbath Day. We have seen that this man told the Jews—that is, the authorities —that it was Jesus Who had made him whole. This seems to have been enough to arouse against our Lord the enmity of these authorities. St. John does not tell us the particular steps which were taken against Him at this time. He seems rather to be giving a reason for the well-known fact of the persecution which now followed, when he says, 'Therefore did the Jews persecute Jesus, because He did these things on the Sabbath Day.' As if to say, this was the beginning of the persecution which afterwards led them so far; it was because our Lord did these things on the Sabbath. The things which our Lord did on the Sabbath were His miracles, and also the consequences of His miracles, for which He was made responsible, such as the enjoining of a servile work on this man who had been healed, and any other work of the kind which might have been occasioned in other cases, as if any people who were sick were brought to Him in beds, or in any other way which involved labour.

It need not, however, be supposed that this feature in our Lord's conduct was the sole reason on which their opposition against Him was founded. It was the reason more or less sincere, and also more or less of a pretext, for the outbreak of hostility which had been gradually growing, or which, at all events, was natural, and, as it were, inevitable, in persons under their circumstances, unless they were prepared to become His disciples. The Jewish Hierarchy, under many humiliations and degradations, was at that time in a position of much worldly comfort and consideration. The nation itself was prosperous over the whole Roman Empire, it was tolerated in the observance of its laws, it was treated as a community which lived by its own discipline, and its ecclesiastical chiefs at Jerusalem, the only chiefs which now remained to it, were the heads of a vast organization which loyally recognized their authority, and contributed with large liberality to their support, and to the maintenance of the worship of which they were the ministers. They were liable to occasional insults and acts of violence, either from the Princes of the House of Herod, or from the Roman Governors. But they had learnt to make themselves heard at Rome, and the masters of the world were too politic not to allow them all possible liberty, and not to secure their allegiance for the future by listening to their just complaints. They were not a very large body of men, but they were numerous enough to constitute a little world of their own, with its ambitions and rivalries and cliques, with its *esprit de corps*, with its keen sense of its own interests, any assault on which would at once unite its various parties, with its self-importance, its mutual courtesies and hypocrisies, its prizes and its traditions. Among the members of this body, as among the members of any established body of a similar kind, there were probably many very good and pious men, as well as many simply worldly and unscrupulous persons. But all were more or less in bondage in the interests and traditions of the body, except such as those whose hearts

God had specially touched. There would be certain acknowledged maxims and principles, all founded on devotion to the body itself as such, which devotion would wear the appearance of a virtue, much as patriotism, in the Pagan sense, in which the State is made supreme and its interests paramount over those of conscience and of God and of the Church, is considered in many even Christian countries as the first of duties at the present day.

In the providential designs of God the Synagogue was a means, not an end; in the hearts of its priests it was an end. These men, nevertheless, were the trusted rulers of the chosen people of God. They sat, as our Lord told the people, in the chair of Moses. They were the heirs of the prophets and saints of the Old Covenant. They were the guardians of those 'oracles of God' of which St. Paul speaks, the possession of which was the chiefest glory and blessing of the House of Israel. Thus they were bound, beyond all others, to be looking forward for the accomplishment of the prophecies, for the fulfilment of the shadows of the Old Law, for the spiritual kingdom which the Messias was to found. They ought to have been our Lord's first disciples, and His most eager partisans. They ought to have prepared the people for His coming, and attested His mission when He came. Humanly speaking, nothing more would have been wanting to the complete conversion of the Jewish nation and of the world by its means. But worldly policy and considerations of self-interest would naturally oppose this. The Chief Priests at Jerusalem knew very well the Roman power, and the Roman jealousy of anything like independence of the Empire. They knew how irresistible were the arms of Rome, and how on the other hand they were equally able either to secure peace and well-being to the nations who lived quietly under their sway, or to destroy the rebellious. 'The Romans will come and take away our place and nation.' This was the daily fear of that great part of the rulers of Jerusalem who were politicians, and, on the other hand, they had themselves everything to lose by any great change in the existing state of things. It was very well with them as things were. In our Lord and the movement, as we should say, of which He was the leader, they instinctively recognized a danger to the whole system under which they lived and thrived, with all its intrigues and ambitions and comforts and emoluments. The first principle of their practical creed was that Jerusalem should go on as it was and that they should be its rulers. All this was threatened by the new preaching.

Moreover, it was a first principle with these men, not only that the existing state of things at Jerusalem should continue, but also that they should continue to be the leaders of the people. Jealousy is the priestly failing, and it is more and more powerful in particular cases according to the state of the souls of those whom its temptations beset. These men, with their external show of devotion, not answered to by the interior feelings of their hearts, with their profession far above their practice, with their worldly aims or personal ambitions, were not likely to rise superior to the subtle assaults of a passion which has often affected the whole lives and conduct of men very far their superiors in all these respects. Nothing intoxicates more than the breath of popularity and the consciousness of influence, and nothing is more torturing to narrow and petty minds than to hear applause given to others and to see others more influential than themselves. Nor was it influence or moral power alone that was in question in their cases.

We gather from the descriptions of these ecclesiastical rulers given by the Evangelists that they were fond of money, and that their position gave them many opportunities of enriching themselves and, perhaps, satisfying passions even still more ignoble than that of avarice, on account of the immense confidence which was placed in them by pious persons of all classes and kinds. It is easy to see how all these motives would work on them, and even how they might half delude themselves into thinking that they were acting on high principles. No doubt many of these men would say to themselves that it was a danger to the people to follow so devotedly a Leader, Who did not belong to the official hierarchy, and that it would be a service to God to eclipse His influence. Self-love would find a thousand pretexts for their antagonism to One Whose real crime is that He cast them into the shade. It was this jealousy which at last drove them to use the whole of their ecclesiastical power and authority to crush our Lord, when they saw how hopeless it had become to think of turning the people away from Him, except by His judicial murder. But the same evil passions, which wrought that great crime two years after this time, were already brooding in the hearts of these Jewish priests, and, as we shall see, the design of bringing about our Lord's death was conceived soon after the date of this miracle.

Besides these reasons for their opposition, there were others still deeper. These men, as we gather from the Gospel history, were proud, and worldly, and hypocritical, and covetous, and morally corrupt. Their lives and hearts were, in many cases, bad. They had that most miserable part to play, the part of great outward profession and appearance of religiousness, while their thoughts and desires and secret practices were licentious. Moreover, a considerable number of them, and those, as it seems, in particular, who were about this time often in power, belonged to the unbelieving sect of the Sadducees, who denied the existence of the soul as distinct from the body, and disbelieved the dogma of the Resurrection. Thus the pernicious effect of a false doctrine was added, in their case, to the blinding and hardening influence of a sensual life. Men of this sort could hardly have felt any check on the indulgence of their passions, except the restraints of expediency. The very foundations of the moral code were sapped to them. It is difficult to see how the Sadducees, except from motives of human policy, can have been much better in their lives and hearts than the priests of some of the degraded religions of the far East. They were certainly not likely to meet the approach of our Lord, the promised Messias, the Redeemer of the world, the ineffable Purity and Truth, with anything but fear and revulsion. Of all the worldly members of the ecclesiastical aristocracy at Jerusalem, they were the most worldly, and the least likely to be restrained, in any opposition which it was their interest to offer to our Lord, by any motives of religion or any principles of faith.

The history, whether of the propagation of Christianity among the heathen, especially among those nations who have a civilization and established polity of their own, on which the Church has to work, or of the progress of Catholicism among communities which have in past generations fallen away from the centre of unity, is full of illustrations of this part of the life of our Divine Lord. Wherever there exists any body that can in any way be compared in its position to this body of the Jewish priests, there the Church has to contend with opposition of this special character of which we are now speaking.

Every one of the evil motives which have been here noticed as influencing the Jewish priesthood, may be expected to operate on the members of analogous bodies in producing resistance to the introduction of the Christian religion or to the enlargement of the frontiers of Catholic unity. Thus does our Lord bear in His own Person, from these priests and rulers of His own chosen nation, that special cross of opposition from persons of the same class which all His followers, under like circumstances, must expect. Something even further than this may be said on this subject. It would be a grievous mistake to think that such persons, either those who became the opponents or the persecutors of our Lord, or who in later days oppose the advance of His Church and His religion, are the only instances in whose case the play of the bad passions and elements of which we have been speaking is possible. The evil may infect and has infected the Christian sanctuary itself. The same motives which had so much power in determining the attitude of the priests as a body towards our Lord and the Apostles after Him, may operate, in a different degree indeed, but still, powerfully, in creating rivalries and jealousies among the various members of a hierarchy anywhere, or among various classes of the ministers of the altar. Experience has shown that the priesthood has furnished its contribution of victims to the passions of avarice, of sensuality, of gluttony, and the like, and to worldliness in all its various manifestations and developments. To say this is only to say in other words, that ambition, and envy, and jealousy, the love of popularity, of prominence in the eyes of the public, of external brilliancy even in labours for God, are dangers against which the Christian priesthood is no more safe than was the Jewish, dangers as rife in our time as in the days of Annas, Caiaphas, and their colleagues.

There is something very appalling in the thought of the trial to which this motley community was now to be subjected in the Providence of God. Our Lord had hitherto, as has been said, kept Himself very much aloof from the Holy City. He had appeared there for a few days, as it seems, on the occasion of the first Pasch, and He had then signalized His presence by the act of authority already mentioned, cleansing the house of His Father from the pollution of the traffic which was there carried on, under the eyes of these chosen guardians of its sanctity, and perhaps to their own profit. He had then, after a short time spent in the neighbourhood, left them to themselves, and betaken Himself to the simple and guileless people of Galilee, among whom He had taught for the greater part of a year, illustrating His teaching by a thousand marvellous miracles, and from whom He had gathered to Himself a large crowd of devoted followers. From time to time the fame of His doings had reached the capital—it had heard of His beautiful condescension, of His humility and affability, of His Divine teaching, of His miracles of mercy and power. His name was on the lips of the pilgrims who came up to the feasts, and it was evident to the rulers that He was already a power in the land, with which they must some day have to reckon. The leper had not long before brought the tidings of the Divine majesty with which He had, by a word or touch, delivered him in a moment from the sacred disease, and the scribes who had been present at the miracle on the paralytic had spoken of His claim to pardon sins. And now He had suddenly appeared among them, and had worked a stupendous miracle, at the same time giving an injunction that seemed to strike at the received law concerning a point so important and sacred as the observance of the Sabbath.

If the mere presence of our Lord, the Incarnate Son of God, among these priests and rulers of the holy people, who were in so many cases altogether unfit to receive the light and to welcome the graces of His coming, is in itself appalling, it is still more so to consider the language which He held to them and the topics on which He condescended to speak to them. It was no call to repentance, for they had already heard and despised the call of His forerunner. It was no announcement of beatitudes or of counsels of perfection, or of higher interpretations of the Mosaic code or the Decalogue, no invitation to purity of intention and gentleness in judging, to absolute confidence in God their Father. The language which He uses is at once the language of Divine authority. When the theologians of the Church endeavour to build up the fabric of dogmatic statement as to the relations of the several Persons of the ever-blessed Trinity one to the other, and to form, in some sort of way, into a whole, the various Scriptural declarations on these sublime subjects, they have recourse to this and to other discourses of St. John's Gospel as among their most definite sources of knowledge. Our Lord always spoke as God, though He constantly used language more in harmony with the humiliation of His Divine Person in His human nature, in order both to set forth the truth of His Incarnation and not to frighten those who saw Him only in the weakness of His Manhood. Even when His teaching was confined, or almost confined, to the precepts of Christian morality, He taught as One Who had authority, and not as any merely human teacher. But in this and other discourses to these men, who more than any others may be called His enemies, our Lord speaks at once in words which implied, and which were understood to imply, the Divinity of His Person. This it is which makes these disputations, so to call them, with the Jewish authorities, so terrible in their majesty to the Catholic reader. His faith tells him Who it was Who was thus reasoning concerning His own Divine nature with men who were so unprepared to throw themselves at His feet and adore Him. The eternal God condescends to argue as to His own Divinity, to meet objections, to suggest considerations, to quote texts. Of all the instances of our Lord's condescension, we can find none more wonderful than this.

CHAPTER XII.

The work of the Father and of the Son.

St. John v. 16—18; *Vita Vitæ Nostræ*, § 42.

IT must be remembered, in dealing with the discourse of our Lord of which St. John here furnishes us with the report, that, if the conflict into which He was now brought with the ecclesiastical authorities was deliberately sought by Him, for the purpose, as it seems, of drawing their attention most forcibly to the claims which He advanced, and to the providential evidence by which those claims were supported, it is not less clear that He must have chosen, for reasons of His own Divine prudence, the particular issue on which the question was raised. That is, our Lord must have chosen the question of the observance and obligation of the Sabbath as the point on which He determined to touch, in order to arouse the attention of the Jewish authorities, rather than any other question as to which He might have brought about a discussion with them. He was about to set forth in very strong language the doctrine about His own Divine Filiation, and His Equality and Oneness with His Father, and He chose to do this by taking His occasion from a question about the Sabbath and its obligation. It thus becomes important to say a few words on the general question of the Sabbath, and of our Lord's position with relation thereto.

The observance of the Sabbath was enjoined on the Jews by Moses, and forms a part of the Decalogue. But it seems indisputable that, like circumcision, it was not, as our Lord said once to the Jews, 'of Moses, but of the Fathers;'[1] that is, it was a traditional law handed down from the very earliest ages. Thus, even in the Decalogue, it is spoken of as a precept which requires remembrance, rather than any new enactment—'Remember that thou keep holy the Sabbath Day.' The reason for the enactment there given carries us back to the very origin of the world—'For in six days the Lord made Heaven and earth, and the sea, and all things that are in them, and rested the seventh day, therefore the Lord blessed the seventh day and sanctified it.'[2] It was therefore, and was meant to be, a perpetual remembrance of the act of creation of all things by God. It kept up, among the chosen people, that most necessary article of faith, which is placed at the beginning of the Christian Creed, that God is 'the Creator of heaven and earth.' If it had had no other purpose, it would have preserved the great truth which was to be the foundation, in a certain sense, of the whole Creed, and the denial of which involves the denial of the whole Creed. What effect forgetfulness as to this truth produced in the heathen we see, among other places, in the description of the Gentile world given by St. Paul in the famous passage at the opening of the Epistle to the Romans. The want of this truth makes Polytheism, Pantheism, idolatry, and all

[1] St. John vii. 22.   [2] Exodus xx. 8, 11.

their attendant train of corruptions and degradations of the foulest kind, possible, and as a matter of fact, it leads to them. The modern sophists, who have raised so many doubts as to the Christian doctrine of the creation of the world, are confronted by the practical commemoration of the truth Sunday after Sunday—for in this respect the Sabbath still remains in the Church, though she has now, as will be seen, a still more glorious act of God to commemorate and to honour.

The resting from external and laborious works, which was a part of the observance of the Sabbath as enjoined in the Law, was, in the first place, necessary, if the people were to have time and leisure to devote themselves to the service and worship of God on that day. Moreover, it was a continual witness to several most important truths. By interrupting the continued succession of days which had to be spent in the toils and cares of temporal concerns, it not only relieved the people from the endless and most wearisome strain of drudgery, both of body and mind, which would otherwise have deadened in them all sense of spiritual things, but it kept alive their faith in a future, the one thing worth toiling for and looking forward to, it witnessed to the emptiness of earthly goods and temporal treasures, all cares for which were to be laid aside, as of no moment in comparison to the obligations of the Sabbath. It helped them to conceive heavenly desires, to realize the truth that the present state of our existence is a penal and a passing state, and one of preparation for a better life hereafter. The Sabbath is also spoken of in the Old Testament as having been enforced on the Jews as a memorial of the particular blessings which they had received in the special providence of God over them, as His own people—at least, in the passage of Deuteronomy in which the Decalogue is repeated, there is added to this commandment, in special reference to the injunction, 'That thy man servant and thy maid servant may rest even as thyself,' 'Remember that thou also didst serve in Egypt, and the Lord thy God brought thee out from thence with a strong hand and a stretched-out arm. Therefore hath He commanded that thou shouldest observe the Sabbath Day.'[3]

It may perhaps be considered that this last injunction means that the gratitude, which was due to God for the deliverance from Egypt, should be a special reason to the Jews for the observance of the Sabbath, not that the Sabbath was instituted on that account. Looking forward, however, to the fulfilment of all Old Testament types and institutions in our Lord, we find it said by some of the Fathers that the Sabbatical rest was a foreshadowing of the rest of our Lord in the grave, during the Sabbath which intervened between His Passion and His Resurrection. But He was to be, in His own words, 'The Lord of the Sabbath,' in another and a deeper signification. If the great work of God in the creation of the world was to be commemorated by the observance of a day in each week, specially set apart for the worship and service of God, it was fitting that the second great work of God, in the new creation of all things through the Incarnation, should be commemorated in like manner, and this by the translation of the weekly festival, so to speak, to the day on which this new creation was commenced by the Resurrection of our Lord from the grave. This consideration explains the great reason, in the counsels of God, for the change which was to be made under the new Kingdom in the manner and time of the celebration of which we are speaking. And it also contains the sufficient account of our Lord's insisting on the works of mercy and charity

[3] Deut. v. 13.

by which He chose to solemnize the Sabbath. These works were a part of the formation of the new creation. And this creation was to take the place of the former creation in the tribute of devout thanksgiving and worship which the Church has to pay to God week after week. But, apart from this consideration, the works themselves were not violations of the Law, as our Lord on other occasions explained. For on the Sabbath Day the Jews themselves allowed of certain classes of works, besides, of course, those which were distinctly Divine, or ordered by God at particular times, such as the carrying the Ark round the walls of Jericho for seven days, which in itself was more than would have been allowed on a Sabbath, and the like. Other works which were not forbidden were all that related to the external worship and service of God; again, those that were necessary for the health and safety of the body; and lastly, the works which benefited the souls of men. But our Lord did not choose, on this occasion, to argue in this way.

Our Lord's first words in answer to the objections or charges which were now made against Him, differ from the answers which He made at other times, of which we shall have to speak hereafter, in putting the matter in dispute, so to say, on the highest possible ground. At other times He spoke of the example of the saints, or of the permissions of the Law in derogation of the strict duty of resting from all work on the Sabbath Day, or of the natural obligations of charity or necessity which might supersede that or any other positive law. Now He speaks at once of His Eternal Father. God must be above all such laws, which were only given by Him to remind the people who observed them of some mysteries of their faith or some events in the providential history of the world, or of their own nation, such as the Creation in six days, or the deliverance from Egypt, and the like. It was true that the Creation was finished in the six days, but this did not make any pause in the infinite activity and life of God Himself. The Father is always at work in His own creation. He is always active in the preservation and continuation of the existences which He has called into being, and which would fall to nothing unless He supported them. He assists in all the operations of their natures, which would not be without Him. He governs all things by His laws and by His special providence; He presides over their propagation and increase according to the laws of those natures. His creative power is always at work even for men, for He is continually creating new souls for successive generations. He is ever active in enlightening them with the lights of reason and of grace, He is justifying them from sin and increasing their graces and virtues, He pleads with them when they go astray and resist His will or His call, He conducts them through the struggles of their time of probation to the glory which He has prepared for them. His dealings with His creatures require His special activity, and, in a thousand ways, He is always toiling for them, if such a word may be used of God, according to the ordinary rules of His government. And then, besides all these ways in which He is at work, He has others which override and go beyond His usual operations, such as miracles and everything that is extraordinary in His administration of His kingdom. This is the rule of God's action in regard of His creatures. If the heavenly bodies hold on their appointed ways in the universe, if the sun shines, and the winds blow, and the earth continues to nourish plant and tree and the races of animals that move upon her; in a word, if life, animate and inanimate, goes on without resting at night or on the Sabbath Day, it is because God is always working. To stop this would be to stop the whole course of nature, of life, of mind, of grace. The work of the Incarnate Son is like this perpetual work of the Father in creation. 'My Father worketh hitherto, and I also work.'

The particle of resemblance used by our Lord may be understood in either of two ways. Both of them place Him on an equality with His Father. It may mean that His work in its continuity and unceasingness is like the work of His Father, and then there is a resemblance which implies equality; or it may mean that His Father works nothing without Him, that what His Father does, He does with Him, on account of the unity of their nature and substance; and then again He claims to be One with His Father. In the first case, there is a distinction implied between the work of the Father and the work of the Son; in the second case, there is the truth implied of the identity of operation of the Father and of the Son. If these two truths are put together, inasmuch as the one does not exclude the other, and as both are necessary for a full understanding—as far as our poor faculties can understand them—of the relations between the Divine Persons and the special work of the Incarnate Son in the new creation, we arrive at the truth, that the new kingdom is to be not less the scene and sphere of incessant activity on the part of God than the old creation, and that in it the work carried on by the instrumentality of the Sacred Humanity of our Lord, is alike the work of the Son and the work of the Father; or, if the unity of operation of the Divine Persons be left to the words of our Lord next following and is not so plainly expressed in these, at least they mean that the work of redemption, of the mission which He had received from His Father, a part of which was the working miracles of power and mercy to authenticate it, was to follow the law of the natural operations of God in the creation and government of the world, and so not to be bound down to certain times and seasons, to be carried on at some and to cease at others. A mission of this kind was above the level of any mission that could be given to prophet or angel, who can but do a definite task and cease at an appointed time. Thus the words imply, as they were understood by the Jews to imply, that when He spoke of God as His Father, He did not speak of an adoptive relationship between His Father and Himself, but of a natural filiation in the strictest sense of the term. Nor, again, was it the language of an angel or a prophet to speak of God in this way as His Father. This single appellation, so constantly used by our Lord, was enough of itself to convey the truth as to His filiation to the minds of any thoughtful hearers. So abundant and overwhelming is the evidence, from our Lord's own mouth, that He claimed to be the only-begotten Son of God.

Those to whom this answer was addressed could hardly take it in any other way. At other times, as has been said, our Lord pleaded the instance of David, which was justified by necessity, of the priests in the Temple, which rested on the requirements of the Divine service, or of the practice of circumcision, in which the spiritual benefit to a soul superseded the positive injunctions of the law, or of the rescue even of animals from danger on the Sabbath, which, again, was justified by necessity. All these reasons might have availed for the merely human instruments of some Divine dispensation, and from our Lord's language in a later passage of this same Gospel of St. John—where, on His next visit to Jerusalem, He refers again to the charge brought against Him on account of the miracle at the pool, justifying it by the precedent of circumcision, as commonly practised by themselves—[1] it is clear that He might have used that answer on this occasion also. But He did not so choose. What He had done needed no human precedent, nor was it to be justified by any human example. It was the very truth that it was a Divine work, a part of the great work which His Father had given Him to accomplish in the world, the work of redemption and enlightenment, and as such, a work which in no way fell under the restrictions of the law of the Sabbath, a work which was regulated by no rule and no pattern short of the operations of the Godhead in which He was One with the Father.

'Hereupon, therefore,' continues St. John, 'the Jews sought the more to kill Him, because He did not only break the Sabbath, but also said God was His Father, making Himself equal with God.' Thus early in the history, then, do we come upon the simple and naked truth as to the claims of our Lord and the manner in which they were instinctively understood by those who were to oppose Him. There was no other course open to them but to acknowledge His Divine authority and even His Divine Person, or to reject Him altogether. They were to acknowledge His Divine mission and authority because of the many evidences by which these were accredited, and of which we shall presently have to speak in commenting on our Lord's discourse, and, after acknowledging His Divine mission, they were to acknowledge the Divinity of His Person, not precisely because the evidences could not have been given to authenticate the mission even of a creature, such as the mission of a prophet or a teacher less than a Divine Person, but because the Person, in witness to Whom these evidences were accumulated, declared that He was God and not only Man. If He had said that He was

---

[1] St. John vii. 23.

a mere man, the force of the evidences would have gone to prove that what He said was true, and, as He said that He was God, they equally implied that that was true. Here, again, as in the case of the miracle wrought in proof of the power of the Son of Man to forgive sins, we see the exact logical force of the miracles of our Lord or of the Church, and, indeed, of the other evidences, as that of prophecy or of the results of the Gospel upon the world. These things prove that what our Lord or His Church say concerning themselves must be true, for they pledge, as it were, the veracity of God in their support, by means of the displays of supernatural power which they embody. The cogency of the proof rests upon the impossibility that God could authenticate a lie. It is more respectful to Him to deny the truth of miracles, than to deny the truthfulness of the messengers who are endowed with the power of working them. But to choose for ourselves what we will believe and what we will reject is exactly the same thing, with respect to the authority of God's messengers, as to refuse to believe altogether. It is more unreasonable than the Jews themselves, to admit the Christian or the Catholic evidences, and then choose what we will assent to and what we will reject out of the message delivered by those to whom these evidences bear witness.

Before we proceed to the discussion which followed on these words of our Lord, we may well pause a moment to endeavour to feed our souls on the contemplation of the truths they convey. If we consider these words to refer, as has been said, especially to that work of redemption which is the object of the kingdom of the Incarnation, we see in them a comparison between that constant activity of God in His creation in the natural order, of which we have spoken, and the incessant working of our Lord in the kingdom which He came to found, the new creation. When we contemplate, as far as we are able, the full truth about the activity of God in the former order, we set before ourselves the manner in which God supports and sustains the whole world which He has made, so that no portion of it has life or existence or operation without that support. We reflect that He concurs actively to every exercise of every faculty with which He has endowed any of His creatures, so that the whole life of the whole world is the work of God, moment after moment. We consider how His creatures, as far as they work and move and energize, as it may be said, for themselves, do this in imitation of Him and following the laws of His ineffable and unfailing activity. Thus we get a picture of the life of all God's creatures, from that of the highest angels down to that of the lowest of the beings that can be said to live or to exist, in which life the order of the universe consists. The higher they rise in the scale of being, the greater and more noble, because more like His, are the activity and energy by which they glorify their Maker; while the perfect harmony and order of the whole gives Him, again, another kind of glory, which may be distinguished from that which results from the life of each in itself, and the effects it has to produce and the influence it has to exert on the being and life of other creatures.

And now our Lord tells us, as we may contemplate, that in His new kingdom and creation He is ever at work as the Father is ever at work in the natural world. He supports, animates, concurs in, all the spiritual energies of the millions of saints in Heaven and souls on earth or in Purgatory. We can thus enter into some of the glowing language of St. Paul, when he speaks of our Lord as 'working in him in power,'[2] or as being the

---

[2] Coloss. i. 29.

'Head from Whom the whole body' of the Church, 'being compacted and fitly joined together, by what every joint supplieth, according to the operation in the measure of every part, maketh increase of the body unto the edifying of itself in charity.'[3] Or, again, when he says, 'There are diversities of graces, but the same Spirit, and there are diversities of ministries, but the same Lord, and there are diversities of operations, but the same God Who worketh all in all,' and, again, goes through the various manifestations of the Holy Ghost, the word of wisdom, the word of knowledge, faith, the grace of healing, the working of miracles, prophecy, the discerning of spirits, divers kinds of tongues, and the interpretation of speeches, and then adds, 'All these things one and the same Spirit worketh, dividing to every one according as He wills.'[4] All this is the work of Christ in His Kingdom. But the Apostle is here speaking of the more visible and extraordinary manifestations of the presence of the Holy Ghost, such as were so common in the early Apostolic Church; as in the parallel passage, to the Ephesians, he speaks of the more directly spiritual offices which are discharged by various members or orders of the ministry, when he says that our Lord has given 'some apostles, and some prophets, and other some evangelists, and other some pastors and doctors, for the perfecting of the saints, for the work of the ministry, for the edifying of the body of Christ.'[5]

These passages taken together may be said to give us a twofold picture. That is, they represent to us our Lord as working in each one of those in whom His spirit dwells, and to whom He communicates His graces, and also as working through them, according to the law of His Kingdom, for the benefit and perfection of the body in general, and of each other. There is a close analogy

[3] Ephes. iv. 16.   [4] 1 Cor. xii. 7—11.   [5] Ephes. iv. 11, 12.

in this between the natural and the supernatural kingdom of God. For in the natural kingdom also, God not only works on His creatures immediately, by the support and assistance which He affords to them in the use of their natural powers, according to the various grades of His creation in which He places them, but He also affects them by and makes their life depend on their ministrations, so to say, on one another. It is the same in the Kingdom of Christ, and the activity of our Lord is exercised in our favour in the one way as well as in the other. This consideration contains under it the immense work which our Lord does in our souls by the means of others, of the Saints in Heaven whose office it is to intercede and plead for us, of the Angels who guard us and present our prayers before the throne of God, of the Holy Souls who are interested in us, and of the friends or superiors or ministers of His grace, alive or dead, present or at a distance, from whom in various ways we derive benefit, as also of the whole sacramental system which He has established, and of the Adorable Sacrifice and the Priesthood. Rising up once more in our contemplation of our Lord to things which it was not to the purpose of St. Paul to mention particularly in these great passages, we may think of our Lord's intimate and secret action upon each individual soul, in all the various and most marvellous stages of His communications of Himself in prayer, and His guidance of the whole body of the Church in her warfare with the world. It takes a moment to write or read the words which convey these ideas, but the range of power and energy and charity which they embrace is like a vast universe, world upon world of beauty and magnificence. The dealings of our Lord with a single chosen soul, such as St. John, or St. Paul, or St. Francis, or St. Teresa, are enough to furnish the angels of Heaven with matter for praise and thanksgiving throughout eternity. And in another place [6] St. Paul has a word or two, which, in like manner, suggest another glorious work of our Lord, the greatness and beauty of which no one but Himself can measure—that continual intercession of His which He is for ever pouring forth for us in Heaven, not in the manner of prayer, which implies need or weakness, but in the way of the continual aspirations and desires of His Sacred Heart, thirsting and longing for the salvation and perfection of men. And, finally, it must be remembered that the work of our Lord, in all these departments, so to speak, into which it may be divided, is yet the accomplishment of a great whole, the creation of a new universe, each part of which is in its due relative subordination to the rest, and to the whole as such, the one great end of all being the glory of the Father, the object of every part and item, of every individual beauty and glory, being combined into a grand harmony and unity, in itself more beautiful and more glorious than all its elements, singly and disconnected. And yet, when we have said all this, we have but set down in the most meagre measure, some drops, as it were, of that fulness of meaning which these words may have represented to His own Sacred Heart, when He said, 'My Father worketh hitherto, and I also work.'

[6] Heb. vii. 25.

CHAPTER XIII.

Unity of the Divine operation.

St. John v. 18—30; *Vita Vitæ Nostræ*, § 42.

BUT we must pass on from the quiet contemplation of the great range of truths suggested to us by the words of our Lord to these Jewish rulers, in order to consider the discussion to which they gave rise and the revelations concerning Himself and His relation to His Father which our Lord therein vouchsafed to make, for the instruction of these poor enemies of His, who were about to hurl themselves in unbelief against the rock of His Divinity, but who might have been saved from their miserable ruin by the explanations as to the distinction of Persons in the Godhead which He here makes. When we are dealing with the words of men like ourselves, we may expect, in some measure at least, to be able to grasp, not only the meaning of their several statements, but the connection of their argument and the object at which it aims. But in commenting on the Divine words of our Lord we must often be content to adore without being able to rise to any certain intelligence of all these points, and, indeed, they would not be His Divine words if we could fully comprehend them. But, as has been said, it seems to have been at least one chief object of our Lord in the first part of the discourse which we are now considering, to explain to the Jews that when, as they perceived, He 'made Himself equal with God,' it was as His only-begotten Son, One with His Father in the full possession of the Divine Nature, but distinct from Him in Person as being His Son, and so receiving from Him, and not independently of Him, that Divine Nature itself and all its power and operation. Thus it was impossible that any exercise of the power and operation of the Godhead on His part could imply any derogation from the single Majesty of His Father, any rivalry between them, any equality in the human sense, in which what is equal is not identical. And our Lord was looking forward, doubtless, to the Church in all succeeding ages, and especially in those in which the doctrine concerning His Divine Person was to be the great subject of the conflicts raised by heretics, and for her He was providing weapons to be furnished by His own words, which might be used in the elucidation of the truth as handed down from His Apostles. Nor need it surprise us that these disclosures concerning His Divinity should have been made rather in answer to the cavils of His enemies, than in private conversation with His friends and disciples. For in this also our Lord seems to have submitted Himself to that rule of His Kingdom, as it was afterwards to be set up in the world, whereby it is to be by the assaults and questionings of adversaries that the great definitions and explanations of the Christian doctrine are to be chiefly drawn forth. The present discourse of our Lord is immediately connected by St. John with those last words of His on which we have commented in the last chapter. 'Hereupon therefore the Jews sought the more to kill Him, because He did not only break the Sabbath, but also said God was His Father, making Himself equal with God.'

The long discourse which follows, and which embodies the solemn teaching of our Lord on this occasion in Jerusalem, is naturally, therefore, divided into two parts.

In the first, our Lord lays down certain doctrines about Himself, and His relation to His Father, which might serve to explain to the Jews, to whom He was speaking, the difficulties occasioned by His former words. In the second part, He insists on the evidences with which the providence of the Father had furnished His hearers, in order to lead them gently and forcibly to that faith in Him that was the condition of salvation and of their reception of all the blessings which were conveyed in the Incarnation. We are not told where this Divine discourse was held. The Evangelist was probably present, with others of the Apostles, although the Apostolic band had not yet been formed. We may suppose that the report which is given by St. John is like that of the Sermon on the Mount as given by St. Matthew, or that of the Sermon on the Plain as given by St. Luke, or those of other discourses of our Lord in this same fourth Gospel. That is, we may suppose that we have here the heads and substance of the disputation in our Lord's own words, although we cannot be certain that no other words were uttered by Him on this occasion besides those which are here recorded. For the report is far shorter than such a conversation is likely to have been. And the same remark holds good with regard to the other instances of similar reports just now mentioned, especially those of the great Sermons. The argument is complete, though many of the passages have not been preserved to us. Such, indeed, is the natural inference at which we might arrive from the internal evidence furnished by the discourse itself. For no argument is expanded or amplified, while yet the truths themselves are so deep and pregnant as to admit of explanation and amplification to almost any extent. And yet, as we shall see, the report cannot be a mere abstract. In such an abstract we should not have the repetitions of the same statements, which are here to be remarked. We should not have the ineffable majesty and pregnancy of the words of Him Who spake as man never spake. We now proceed to consider a little more fully the first part of this great argument.

It has naturally been remarked[1] that this discourse of our Lord has, as it were, two elements which seem to become prominent alternately. In the first place, there are many most sublime truths concerning Himself and His Eternal Father which are here set forth. In the second place, these are intermingled with other statements, which seem to breathe an air of humility, lowliness, and dependence. Truths of the first sort are those statements which assert, for example, that the Son of God does whatever He sees the Father do, that He giveth life to whomsoever He wills, that He has received from the Father to have life in Himself, and the like. Statements of the other kind, speaking in terms of dependence of the Son of God, are those in which our Lord declares that He can do nothing of Himself, that the Father shows Him what He is to do, that He receives His power from the Father, that He judges as He hears, and such as these. That is, our Lord seems to have mixed up a number of such statements, which are true of Him, in one sense, in His Divine Nature, and in another sense, in His Human Nature and mission, with those others which assert His equality with His Father. This He may have done in order to explain His relation as Son to the Father, and also to illustrate the truth concerning His Sacred Humanity, which required continual assertion and explanation, as well as for the purpose of condescension to the weak faith and possible difficulties of His hearers, that so He might lead them on from the humbler class of

[1] See Pererius and Salmeron, *in loc.*

truths, so to call them, to those which relate more directly to His Eternal Godhead and Person. It is very probable that few of these men understood the teaching of the Scriptures, that the Messias was to be the Son of God. We find our Lord, at the very end of His long struggle with their blindness and hardness of heart, putting to them a last question as to whose Son Christ was to be, and when they answered, the Son of David, He put to them the difficulty out of the Psalm, in which David spoke of Christ as his Lord. This was the truth of which they were in need, and to which, some at least, might be led. For in all these discourses with the Jews, whether at Jerusalem or at Capharnaum, as in the instance of the discourse which follows next upon this, in St. John's Gospel, our Lord was careful to treat His hearers with the utmost benignity and gentleness which the case permitted, and so to give them occasion to dwell on things which were less difficult, and from them to rise to the knowledge of other truths which were more sublime.

We shall find our Lord acting in this same manner in His other discourses and dealings with the Jews, especially, it may be said, with these same authorities at Jerusalem. It was a part of His beautiful and tender condescension to do this—to seem almost, if we may so speak, to modify His own words, for the purpose of bringing them to accept the truth from Him. In the present instance it is not to be denied that our Lord says many things of Himself, which may be understood of His Human Nature. But it seems to have been His more direct object to enlighten the hearers of this discourse as to the doctrine of His generation from His Father and the distinction of His Divine Person from the Person of His Father, while, at the same time, He asserts the unity of the Divine Nature and operation.

The language which seems to speak of dependence on the Father, on the part of the Son, is understood in Christian theology as language explanatory of His Eternal generation, in virtue of which He has the whole of the Divine Nature and Power, only by way of communication from the Father. The language of which this is to be understood will be explained presently. But it is well to observe at the outset, that our Lord seems to deal with these Jewish rulers as with persons who had already sufficient reasons furnished to them for faith in His word, whatever that word might propose to them as true. They could perceive well enough, and it was the ground of their hostility to Him that they did perceive, that He claimed to be God. If in God there was but one Person, His language could not be understood by them, otherwise than as implying a seemingly impossible claim to an equality which involved a contradiction of the truth of the unity of the Godhead. But if, as they ought to have known, the Christ Whom they expected was to be God and the Son of God, One in Nature and Essence with His Father, then this doctrine of the distinction of Persons in the Godhead would have saved them from opposing Him as a blasphemer.

It has been already said that the theologians of the Church, when they desire to put into form and draw out in its fulness the doctrine of Sacred Scripture concerning the adorable Godhead and the Three Divine Persons, make use of many of the sayings of our Lord in these discourses with the Jews, as related by St. John. It cannot be surprising if it should help us very greatly to understand particular passages like the present, to cast back upon them, so to say, the light which they, in conjunction with others of the same kind, have shed upon the labours of the Doctors of whom we speak.

We are ever apt to conceive lowly and inadequately of Divine things, and yet Divine things are expressed to us in our own poor language and have to be conceived of by our poor processes of thought. The passage before us is hardly the principal passage in St. John's Gospel on the subject of the generation of the Son, and yet it may be well to remind ourselves, in order to its more full understanding, of some few principles of theology which relate to that great truth. The only true and full instance of Paternity and Sonship is in God, 'of Whom all Paternity is named in Heaven and on earth,'[2] and these relations, as they are seen in created beings, very imperfectly fulfil the idea of which we speak, while yet we have to rise from these, its imperfect expressions, in order to form our notions of the Divine relations. We must use human language, therefore, but correct it and enlarge its meaning as we proceed. Thus when we speak ordinarily of a 'son,' we speak of a person, or hypostasis, who proceeds from another person by that special communication of nature which is called generation. In created things, there is no generation, and, therefore, no 'sonhood,' in pure spirits, but only in beings which are corporeal. Nor, in created things, does generation come about by the communication of the whole substance of the principle which generates, but by the separation of some part of the substance of that principle from the rest. Thus the unity of nature which exists between father and son in created things is not a numerical unity, but a specific unity only, and the father as a person is prior to the son. Thus also the persons, or hypostases, of father and son, are not only distinct, but separate in numerically different natures, with all the diversities which follow upon this distinction between them, and hence, also, the resemblance or

[2] Ephes. iii. 15.

likeness between the two is not absolute or perfect, for this can only be between two persons having one numerically identical nature. These imperfections in unity of nature and substance belong to generation in created things, and they may help us to comprehend better the perfection of the Divine Generation which is altogether free from them.

The other name by which, in Sacred Scripture, the Divine Son of God is called, the Word, is a name which belongs solely to intellectual generation such as can be in pure spirits only. It is a word which can, in a certain sense, be used of a kind of 'generation' even in created intellectual natures, for a created spirit by comprehending or understanding itself produces a 'word' of itself. Thus the Fathers use this analogy to illustrate the Divine Generation of the Word of God. 'Attend to your own heart,' says St. Augustine, 'when you conceive a word which you are to utter, you desire to say a thing, and the conception itself of the thing in your heart is already a word, it has not yet gone forth, but already it is born in your heart, and it has yet to go forth. . . . You have in your heart the word which you speak, and it is with you, and is a spiritual conception—for as your soul is spirit, so also is the word, which you have conceived, spirit, for it has not yet acquired sound, so as to be divided into syllables, but remains in the conception of your heart and in the mirror of your mind. Just so did God utter His Word, that is, beget His Son. Thou indeed, in time, begettest thy word in thy heart, but God, without all time, has begotten *His Son, by Whom He made all ages.*'[3] The use of this comparison is enough to make it easier to exclude from our ideas of the Divine Generation all those imperfections of corporeal generation of which we have just spoken. On this account

[3] St. Aug. *in Joannem*, Tract xiv. n. 7.

the Fathers urge strongly that, in order to attain to some sort of intelligence of this great subject, we should insist on the ideas contained in the name 'Word,' as well as those contained in the name 'Son.'

There are three things involved in this order of generation: (1) the proceeding of one living being from another; (2) that this procession should be out of the substance of the being that generates; and (3) not only this, but that it should be the effect of some internal principle of fecundity, the end of which is the propagation or communication of the nature of the generator. This last condition is wanting, for instance, in the production of Eve from the side of Adam, which was the work of the creative power of God, not of any interior principle of fecundity. If these notes are considered, it becomes evident with how much of truth it is that theologians say that generation in created things is imperfect and inadequate. In created things the principle of communication is not the whole substance of that which generates, and in a compound nature, such as that of man, it belongs to the lower part of the compound, and it works not by communicating the whole substance, but by the external separation of a part. Thus, further, what is communicated is not the same numerical nature which generates, but only what is enough to produce another nature of the same species, but numerically distinct. Again, in created things, generation is a transient act, not necessary for the intrinsic perfection of the principle which produces it. Lastly, it is an act of the sensitive and animal life, natural and corporeal, and so essentially inferior in order and imperfect.

The enumeration of these imperfections enables us in some sort of way to rise to the idea of the opposite perfection, which belongs to the Divine Generation. It is intellectual; it is a pure act, absolutely necessary, of the substantial Intelligence of God, not therefore transitory, as being the result of a change from capacity to action, but an eternal, necessary, and complete act, the communication of the whole Divine Nature, and its term or product, its Word, ever immanent in Itself, is eternal. The principle of fecundity, so to speak, is the act itself by which God comprehends Himself, and this is as necessary as it is that He should comprehend Himself. The Divine Essence is the very substantial Intelligence Itself producing its own Word, and, in so far as it is Intelligence producing the Word, or in relation to the Word, it is that Essence identified with the Person Who produces, and thus the procession or production here is of the whole essence or substance of that Person. The Divine Essence is infinitely simple, and so has no parts. Thus, in the Word produced by the Divine Intelligence whereby the Father perfectly comprehends Himself, the Divine Essence that is produced is not numerically other than His, but it is the same one Essence that is communicated as the light in its ray.[4] This is the only true generation, in which the life that produces and that is produced is most perfect, in which there is the most

---

[4] 'Generatio ibi est intellectualis, actu purissimo absolute necessario intellectionis substantialis, et ideo non est transitus a potentia in actum, sed eternus necessarius actus completus cum termino eternaliter producto sibi immanente. Hic ipse actus ut terminum immanentem productum habens Verbum, est intrinsecum principium fecunditatis; adeoque principium fecunditatis non est in potentia vel habitu, sed est ipse actus necessario ex intrinseca sua perfectione semper completus. Unde generatio, . . . tam necessario est in actu, quam necessario Deus est intelligens seipsum et ipsa vita intellectualis. Porro, essentia divina est ipsamet substantialis intellectio, et quatemus est intellectio producens Verbum, seu relativa ad Verbum immanens, est essentia identificata cum persona producente, adeoque processio ibi est secundum totam essentiam seu substantiam producentis, quod alioquin evidens est, cum substantia divina simplicissima non habeat partes' (Franzelin, *De Deo Trino*, ch. xxx. p. 432).

perfect production out of the substance of Him Who generates, in which there is the most perfect communication and unity of nature in both, in which the principle of fecundity is most intrinsic and essential and perfect in its act. In human generation all these things are very imperfect, in the Divine Nature alone they are perfect. Thus it is true of these Divine processes, as of the attributes of God, His wisdom, power, and the like— our ideas of them are formed from human and created things, but these are in truth only partially, and in a shadowy way, the images of the realities as they are in God.

The point at which this whole doctrine illustrates the passage before us is that which teaches us that the whole Divine Essence is eternally communicated to His Son by the Father, and that this is His Generation from the Father. This implies first, that there is nothing of the Divine Essence which He has not, and, secondly, that there is nothing of the Divine Essence which He has not by way of communication and generation. These two truths explain the language reported to us by St. John here and elsewhere. Thus He says in His prayer to His Father, 'All Mine are Thine, and Thine are Mine," and at the same time, 'All things that Thou hast given Me are from Thee.'[5] Again He says, 'I am the Life,' and still, 'as the Father hath life in Himself, so also hath He given to the Son to have life in Himself.'[6] He is the Light, yet St. Paul calls Him 'the splendour,' or effulgence, (απαυγασμα) of the glory of the Father.[7] He calls Himself the Truth, and yet He elsewhere says, 'What the Father hath taught Me, these things I speak in this world.'[8] So in this passage He says that the Son does whatever the Father does,

---

[5] St. John xvii. 7—10.
[6] St. John v. 26 ; xiv. 6. [7] Heb. i. 3. [8] St. John viii. 28.

and at the same time that the Son can do nothing of Himself but what He sees the Father doing. St. Paul applies to Him[9] the words of the Psalm, 'Thou, O Lord, in the beginning hast laid the foundation of the earth,' and at the same time he says that He it is by Whom God the Father made the world.[10] He says of Himself, 'I and My Father are One,'[11] and yet the Son is said to be the figure of the substance of the Father.'[12]

This, then, is the doctrine which lies behind, so to speak, the whole of our Lord's argument in this place. He is directly occupied, as has been said, in asserting the unity of operation of Himself and His Father, and the language which He uses is to be understood of this, according to the doctrine just now laid down. And this is not a doctrine which is true of and applicable to some operations only of the Godhead which are past and over, according to our mode of conception and intelligence, but to the works of which there was question when our Lord was challenged for working on the Sabbath Day, and to others of which He is presently about to speak as future. To us these things are past, present, and future, and so our Lord speaks of them; but in the operation of His Divine Nature, as in the generation of the Divine Son, there is no time, but one simple eternal act. He asserts this unity of operation in two ways. There is a series of statements which assert it affirmatively. Such are the words in which He declares that His Father worketh hitherto, and He also works; or again, that whatever the Father doeth, that also the Son doeth likewise; or when He says, that as the Father raiseth the dead and maketh alive, so also the Son maketh whom He will to live. Then the same truth is set forth

---

[9] Heb. i. 10.   [10] Heb. i. 2.
[11] St. John x. 30.   [12] Heb. i. 3; 2 Cor. iv. 4; Col. i. 15.

negatively; as when He says that the Son can do nothing but what He seeth the Father doing; or again, that of Himself He cannot do anything, that as He hears He judges, and the like. And the foundation of these statements is also set forth, for it is because the Father generates the Son, in the manner already explained, that the Son can do nothing of Himself, and that whatever the Father worketh that the Son likewise worketh, 'For the Father showeth unto Him everything whatsoever He Himself doeth.' If we call to mind what has already been said as to the Generation of the Son, or Word, by way of intelligence, this language becomes easier to us. The word to 'show' is used because the Son is the Eternal Wisdom and Intelligence of the Father.

Having said thus much by way of preface to this whole passage, we may proceed to examine it more in detail. The first words of the report of this answer of our Lord given in St. John's Gospel connect that answer directly with the previous statement, that the Jews sought to kill Him, 'because He made Himself equal with God.' 'Jesus therefore answered and said to them, Amen, amen, I say to you, the Son cannot do anything of Himself, but what He seeth the Father doing, for what things soever He doth, these the Son also doth in like manner.' The truth directly here declared is that of the unity of operation of the Father and the Son. This unity of operation is exactly the unity of the Divine Nature. The Son has the Divine Nature from the Father, and as the Nature, so also the operation. And He has this from the Father, not as a simple instrument in the hand of a workman, as if the Father only worked through Him. But the Son works with full freedom and inherent power, whatever He seeth His Father doing. For the whole Divine Essence is communicated from the Father to the Son by His Generation in the manner already mentioned. His will is His own, and His operation is His own, and He is said to work what He 'seeth His Father do,' because He proceeds from the Father by the way of intelligence. Thus the inability to do anything of Himself, which our Lord here asserts of Himself, is the inability, not of impotence, but of the highest power, for it is nothing else than that He has one and the same power with the Father, and that nothing can be done by the Father which is not done by the Son. He can do nothing of Himself, because He worketh with the Father as One Who receives from the Father that He does work.

This truth, thus set forth by our Blessed Lord, seems to add a further degree of light to what He had before said, and to give a still more cogent reason for the Jews to desist from their opposition to Him. The first words He had spoken might be understood of imitation of His Father's continual activity, and in that sense might have been taken as defending the action of even an adoptive son, desiring, in the work which He had to do on earth for the glory of His Father, to be as unceasing in His labour of devotion and service as the Father Himself in His continual activity in the preservation and government of His Kingdom. At least, such an interpretation might have been possible, although the activity spoken of would not be inherent, or independent, and would be limited to the narrow capacities of a created nature. But in a certain sense, angels and saints may say with joy, 'Our Father worketh hitherto, and we also work' —making the tranquil activity of God Himself the pattern of their own obedient labours in His universe. It is something more than this for our Lord to assert, not only the faithfulness of His imitation of the Father's activity, but the identity of operation between the Father and the Son. For this last can only be asserted of the Son Who is One in nature and substance with the Father. Thus, if the Jews were in the first instance warned not to blame the work which was after the pattern of the Father, they are now warned not to blame the work which is, in truth, the Father's work as well as the Son's. There is something like this in the discourse of our Lord to His disciples at the Last Supper, where He says, 'The words that I speak unto you, I speak not of Myself, but the Father, Who abideth in Me, He doeth the works.'[13] The Father was their God, Whom they claimed to know, and thus our Lord could assume, in His gentle reasoning with them, that they would be shocked at the thought of questioning a work in which He had been the agent. But so it was with this miracle —it was the work of the Father and of the Son, and of the Son, in the sense in which He speaks, because it was the work of the Father. 'For,' He goes on, 'the Father loveth the Son, and showeth Him all things which He Himself doth, and greater things than these will He show Him, that you may wonder.' What they had seen, then, was a proof of the Father's love as well as a work of His power. The love of the Father for the Son ought to lead all those who honour the Father to be ready to welcome the Son and to love Him for the sake of the Father. It belongs to the nature of the Father to generate the Son and to make known to Him Himself and all things in Himself. The love of the Father for His Son must be a self-evident truth to all who know the Father. But He begets His Son as His Word, by the way of intelligence, as has been said, and so it belongs to His nature to show to His Son all that He doeth. Thus it seems plain that this argument, so to call it, of our Blessed Lord consists in the statement,

[13] St. John xiv. 10.

that the miracle which had caused this attack upon Him on the part of the Jewish rulers was, in truth, one of a series of acts and works of His Sacred Humanity which were the works of the Eternal Father and of Himself, the Son of God, acting and working with His Father. To Christian ears, this is happily a truth beyond doubt, and one which contains nothing which is difficult to faith. It is a truth which fills us with joy, gratitude, reverence, and devotion to all the actions of our Lord as recorded for us in the Gospels. This miracle has no character in itself which is not shared by the others, and thus we are able to adore in each one of them the ineffable condescension as well as the infinite power of God.

And yet it may seem to us strange, or, at least, it may be more than we should have expected, that our Lord should have chosen to meet the difficulties of these priests and scribes by a point of doctrine which requires a certain amount of theological cultivation in those who are to appreciate it. We must remember, in the first place, that the miracles, taken in conjunction with the assertions, explicit or implicit, of our Lord concerning Himself, were distinctly directed, in the providence of God, to the purpose of proving the truth of the Incarnation of the Divine Son. Looked on in this light, they left no alternative to those who witnessed them and heard our Lord's declarations concerning Himself, the truth of which they attested, but either to admit this truth or to deny the miracles themselves as the works of God. This last alternative was, in truth, adopted a little later on by the opponents of our Lord. But it had not yet been adopted by them, and there must have been many among His hearers on this occasion who would never go so far as to adopt it. But the arguments or statements of our Lord, of which we have now been speaking, contain an explanation of the Incarnation, as well as an assertion of its truth—an explanation informing the hearers of the true character and rank of those works of His which were the fruits of the one Divine operation of His Father and Himself. There were certain actions of our Lord, as when He prayed or fasted or walked or talked or ate, which were not the works of the Father in the sense in which He now spoke, for they were the actions of His Sacred Humanity, of His Divine Person in His Human Nature. But the miracles were Divine works, though wrought by the instrumentality of the Sacred Humanity. Now the right understanding of the Incarnation depends upon the right intelligence of the doctrine of the Ever-Blessed Trinity as its foundation, and it requires the intelligence of the relations of the Divine Persons the one to the other, and especially the doctrine of the unity of the Divine operations. Otherwise there was danger, such as seems to have existed in this case before us, of supposing that equality with God meant rivalry with Him, and that if the Son, as well as the Father, was God, they were therefore two Gods. On the other hand, this truth once explained and grasped, the Incarnation became easier of comprehension, and the proofs of our Lord's Divinity, as has already been said, could be accepted without any derogation to the unity of the Godhead.

It must also be continually repeated, that our Lord was speaking to a number of persons of many very various characters, and among whom there were many great varieties of disposition towards Himself, and towards the acceptance of the truth concerning Him. At this great distance from the time, and without any particular knowledge of the persons, we are naturally inclined to class all these priests and Scribes and Pharisees together, as perfectly alike in their spiritual condition, and to assume that because men like Caiaphas and Annas ruled them, and ultimately guided the action of the whole Hierarchy into that miserable aud detestable line of bitter enmity to our Lord which issued in His murder, therefore the whole body was made up of persons like Annas and Caiaphas. It is not so in any large body of men, nor is there any historical ground for thinking that it was so in this particular body. In the Gospel of St. John, which tells us more than the others about these Jewish rulers, we are continually finding glimpses of the true state of things among them. The body followed its natural leaders in its public acts, which, as is so often the case, were more unscrupulous than any that individuals, as such, might have ventured on. But we are continually finding that there were differences of opinion among them about our Lord and about the right manner of treating Him, and it is highly probable that Nicodemus and Joseph of Arimathæa, who came forward at the last to take our Lord's part at the time of His burial, were not alone in their reluctance to join in the measures against Him. We find Nicodemus, timidly indeed, taking His side at the time of the last feast of Tabernacles,[14] and St. John tells us before the Passion that 'many of the chief men also believed in Him, but because of the Pharisees they did not confess Him, that they might not be cast out of the Synagogue, for they loved the glory of men more than the glory of God.'[15] If this was the state of things at that time, much more may it have been the case that, at the outset of our Lord's preaching in Jerusalem, there may have been many who were well disposed towards Him. Our Lord, in His infinite benignity and carefulness for souls, might find it well worth His while to reason with such persons calmly and lovingly, even opening to them great theological truths, of which they ought to have had some

---

[14] St. John vii. 50.   [15] St. John xii. 42, 43.

kind of knowledge before. We gather from His discourse with Nicodemus, that He had a right to expect to find in him more than He actually did find, of intelligence as to the loftier mysteries of religion. This seems to be the true way of understanding this and other of our Lord's discourses to the Jewish authorities. He was scattering seed which might take root in some hearts. And He could know that among those who listened to Him, though there were many whose hearts were already closed against Him, still there were others like Gamaliel, the master of St. Paul, St. Stephen, and St. Barnabas, who were to become His disciples and even His saints, if not before His Passion, at least after the descent of the Holy Ghost on the Day of Pentecost.

CHAPTER XIV.

Resurrection and Judgment.

St. John v. 19—31; *Vita Vitæ Nostræ*, § 42.

THE substance of this part of the discourse of our Lord on which we have been speaking seems to amount to this—that the Jews are warned by Him not to question the work which He has wrought, for it is the work of a Divine Person, one in Nature and Essence with the Eternal Father. In setting this truth before them our Lord condescended to speak to them in language, difficult, indeed, to those altogether unused to Divine things, and especially to the theology concerning the Divine Nature and Persons, but still not too difficult for the apprehension of the 'Masters in Israel,' the doctors of the law, the keepers of the Divine revelation, the heirs of the traditions of the prophets of old, the men who might be expected to be deeply versed in the Sacred Scriptures of the Old Testament. He vouchsafed to explain to them, virtually at least, something concerning the manner of His own eternal Generation, and the communication to Him therein of the Divine Essence, power, and operation. There He might have stopped, for they were already bound to accept His words as true, and these words were sufficient to open their eyes to the danger which they might incur by further cavil and resistance. But our Lord was not pleased to rest here in His communications to this assembly of the most learned men of the nation, in which were included its ecclesiastical rulers and princes. He went on to tell them that He should soon make other and even higher demands on their faith and admiration, as well as to argue with them, with ineffable condescension, as to the proofs of His mission on which their faith ought to rest.

If we compare this discourse of our Lord with the Jews with His conversation with Nicodemus, which bears the greatest resemblance to this, as might naturally be expected, we shall find that in each our Lord sets forth great and sublime truths, which He seems to marvel that His hearers should have any difficulty in receiving, and that He seems to have more to say than the time permits, as One Who had few opportunities indeed of delivering Himself of a great message. This, again, must be considered in examining the subject-matter of each discourse. As a matter of fact, He was but little in Jerusalem, on account of the strange perversity of the rulers, who might have profited more than any others by His teaching, if their hearts had not been full of self-love and pride. Those among His audience, however, who were better disposed to the truth than the rest, on account of their better lives and purer and humbler minds, were not to be cheated by the wickedness and obstinacy of their superiors, of the teaching which was so important for their salvation. And after this time they were not to see or hear our Lord for a long interval, till the Feast of Tabernacles in the autumn of the following year. Our Lord seems to have determined to give them what might help them on—great Divine truths and promises and prophecies, for which His word was to be their warrant, because, as He most carefully explained to them, His Father had furnished them with abundant evidence that His words must be true. There is something like this, also, in the discourse to Nicodemus to which reference has already been made. For in that also our Lord spoke of having higher things to tell him than any which He had as yet taught him, and He hinted even at the doctrine of His Passion, and of redemption to be wrought thereby, as Moses had foreshadowed in the lifting up the brazen serpent in the desert.[1] And, in somewhat the same way, when Nathanael had been won to place faith in Him by His revelation to him, as it seems, of his secret thoughts or actions, He had at once promised higher favours and wonders. "Because I said to thee I saw thee under the fig-tree, believest thou? greater things than these shalt thou see. Amen, I say to you, you shall see the heavens opened, and the angels of God ascending and descending upon the Son of Man."[2]

In the same way it seems that our Lord goes on in the present discourse to raise the hopes of those who might be disposed to believe Him and to treasure up His words, telling them of some far greater works of the Father which He was to show to the Son, and the Son to perform—in accordance with the doctrine as to His Generation, already more than once explained in this commentary—and also to give them a summary

[1] St. John iii. 11—14.   [2] St. John i. 51.

knowledge of the reasons with which God had furnished them for believing in Him. 'The Father loveth the Son,' He says, 'and showeth Him all things which He Himself doeth. And greater things than these will He show Him, that you may marvel.' It has been already said that the Father eternally generates the Son by the way of knowledge, and this is, in truth, the manifesting to Him all things that He doeth. But although this manifestation is eternal, and so above and beyond all time and succession, still, as eternity embraces and encompasses all time, it is allowable to use the language of time concerning the works of God, which are to us successive in our knowledge of them, though not in their manifestation to the Eternal Son, and to speak of things that are past to us as past in it, and of things that are future to us as future in it. Thus there are some things future, or which were future at the time at which our Lord spoke, and these were to be manifested to the marvelling of the Jews. These coming marvels were to surpass altogether what they had lately seen. For this is the law of God's action in the world, according to that saying concerning the bridegroom at the marriage feast at Cana, that he kept the best wine for the last. God's works and manifestations of Himself are ever rising higher and higher, and becoming more and more magnificent. Three of these are spoken of by our Lord in the passage before us. The first of these is the raising of the dead to life by the Incarnate Son. 'For as the Father raiseth up the dead and giveth life, so the Son also giveth life to whom He will.' The Son has the same power with the Father, and will exercise it for your wonder. This power of raising to life is the unquestionable prerogative of the Godhead, and is so spoken of in Sacred Scripture. This will be done by the Son. He will raise 'whom He will,' and for no other reason than because He wills—one therefore and not another, if it so please Him, as the son of the widow at Naim, or the daughter of Jairus, or Lazarus, close to Jerusalem and under the eyes of these same priests and rulers who are so indisposed to admit His Divine authority. The second great work which is here mentioned is the Judgment of all men, which is committed by the Father to the Son in His Sacred Humanity, and which will be executed at the end of the world. The third great work here spoken of, which must not be confounded with the first already mentioned, is the General Resurrection of all for the purpose of the General Judgment. Our Lord, as is often His custom, mentions these things twice over—once in a more summary manner, and then again with somewhat more of detail. Thus, at first, He does not distinguish the two instances of the power of raising the dead of which He speaks—one instance of which was to occur in their immediate neighbourhood during His lifetime, and the far more magnificent exercise of the same Divine prerogative which is still future, the General Resurrection of all mankind. This may be understood as showing us that the raising of Lazarus and of others in our Lord's lifetime, may be considered as belonging to and anticipatory of the General Resurrection, which, together with the Judgment, makes up the greater marvels which are here promised. What He seems to desire especially to put before His hearers, therefore, is the great Day of Account and the previous Resurrection of all men. These things, then, seem to have been chosen by our Lord, for purposes of His own Divine wisdom, as marvels which He foretells to these Jewish priests and scribes, with whom He is now conversing, and whom He is endeavouring to lead to the recognition of the Divinity of His Sacred Person. He adds also the object for which the Father had conferred these powers on the Son—in the sense in which they are conferred—namely, that the Divinity of the Son may be recognized and honoured with equal honour with the Divinity of the Father, that He might be known, in truth, to be One God with the Father. 'For as the Father raiseth up the dead and giveth life, so the Son also giveth life to whom He will. For neither doth the Father judge any man, but hath given all judgment to the Son, that all men may honour the Son, as they honour the Father. He who honoureth not the Son, honoureth not the Father Who hath sent Him.' And then, as this statement of the future works which they were to see, either soon, as the work of the raising of Lazarus and the others, or at the end of time, as the General Resurrection and the Judgment of the world, was to be received by them on the faith of His own word, and without further present proof than those evidences which showed that He was to be believed implicitly, He adds at once a fresh declaration, which He had made to Nicodemus—'Amen, amen I say unto you, that he who heareth My word, and believeth Him that sent Me, hath life everlasting, and cometh not into judgment, but is passed from death to life.'

The verses which follow contain more explicitly, as is so usual in these reports of our Lord's discourses in St. John, the same truths which have been already asserted more generally. First, our Lord explains more circumstantially the power given to the Son to raise the dead, whether in the time of His sojourn on earth or at the end of the world. 'Amen, amen I say unto you, that the hour cometh and now is'—it is not only something in the remote future, but something which is present and of which you will have present proof—'when the dead shall hear the voice of the Son of God, and they that hear shall live. For,' He repeats, 'as the Father hath life in Himself, so hath He given to the Son also to have life in Himself.' Here again we must remember the doctrine of the eternal Generation of the Son of God, which is set forth in all these statements of our Lord. It belongs to the Divine Nature to be the only and essential life, and to be the source to all God's creatures of whatever life, spiritual or material, they may share or be capable of sharing. The whole Divine Nature is eternally communicated to the Son in the act of His Generation, and so the Father gives to the Son this essential infinite life and the power of communicating life to His creatures. The life here spoken of as given by the Son to His creatures, need not be limited, in our interpretation of this passage, to the life of the body alone. The direct and first meaning of our Lord may be to promise them the marvels which they can see and, as it were, touch, and thus the spiritual life of the soul, being invisible and imperceptible to the senses, may not belong to this first and direct meaning. But this life of the body is worth nothing without the life of the soul, and in the words which form the connecting link between the two series of statements of our Lord on which we are dwelling, He speaks plainly enough of the spiritual life. For He says, as we have just seen, that he that heareth His word and believeth His mission, has everlasting life, and does not come to judgment, but is passed from death to life. This statement is true of the spiritual life of the soul, which is the fruit of faith, by which man is justified, according to the doctrine of St. Peter and St. Paul.

But there is another great power inherent in the Divine Nature, and this also our Lord has declared is to be exercised by the Son. Thus He goes on to explain in like manner the conferring of the judicial power. 'And He hath given Him power to do judgment, because He is the Son of Man.' That is, He has made the Son the executor and administrator of His judicial power—a power inherent in the Divine Nature itself as such—because He and not the Father has taken upon Himself the nature of men, who are the persons to be judged. As it belongs to the Divine Nature to judge mankind and all creatures, it cannot be said in every sense that the Father does not judge. And, indeed, as our Lord afterwards said to these Jews, the Father was to seek the glorification of His Son, which had been refused Him by them, and to judge them for their refusal.[3] But He is here speaking of that judgment at the end of time, which is visible and cognizable by all, and this will be executed by the Son of God in His Human Nature—'Because He is the Son of Man.' There are many thoughts connected with this statement scattered up and down the writings of holy men, as to the mercifulness of this arrangement on the part of God, as to the equitableness of the judging mankind by One Who has shared their nature and known its trials; or, again, as to the additional pang which it will give to the wicked to be tried by Him Who has died for them, and to Whose example they have been so unfaithful, while, on the other hand, to the just and good the thought that the Son of Man, Jesus Christ, to Whom they have given their hearts and the service of their lives, is to be their Judge, is one of infinite consolation. But the thought more directly suggested by our Lord's words seems to be that of the honouring of the Eternal Son in His humiliation, by angels and men alike, at the Last Day—angels, so many of whom fell from Heaven because they refused to humble themselves to adore Him in His Human Nature when it was re-

[3] St. John viii. 50.

vealed to them; men, among whom He has lived and dwelt like one of themselves, among whom He has set up His Church to represent Him, and with whom He has even condescended to remain, day after day and night after night, in the holy tabernacle of the altar. For He has said just before this that the Father has given all judgment to the Son, that all men may honour the Son as they honour the Father. 'He that honoureth not the Son, honoureth not the Father Who hath sent Him.'

Our Lord then goes on to speak of the other great truth, which He here proposes to their faith in connection with the Judgment—the truth of the Resurrection. 'Wonder not at this,' He says, do not marvel at what you have been told about the Son raising to life whom He will. This is indeed a great and Divine work, but it is but a part, and a small part, of what is to be in this way hereafter. The raising of certain dead persons to life will be but the anticipation of what is to take place as to the whole race of man by the same power. 'Wonder not at this, for the hour cometh'—He does not say as to this that the hour already is come—'wherein all they that are in the graves shall hear the voice of the Son of God' —it will not be the calling of one single man back out of the grave, but all the graves in the world shall give up their dead—'and they that have done good things shall come forth unto the resurrection of life, but they that have done evil, unto the resurrection of judgment.'

It is certainly remarkable that our Lord should have chosen these words, out of all others of which He might have spoken as future, to impress on the minds of this audience of priests and rulers. But in making this choice it is at all events evident that He acted as He did at other times also to the same people. The mention of judgment seems to rise to His lips very frequently when He is dealing with these persons. We find it even in the discourse to Nicodemus,[4] which has already been mentioned as, in some respects, parallel to this before us. We find it again in the discourse in the eighth chapter of this Gospel, after the incident of the woman taken in adultery,[5] and we find it again in the last-recorded words of our Lord before St. John begins his history of the Last Supper.[6] The last word also that our Lord spoke to His enemies in His Passion, when He gave His answer to Caiaphas, that He was the Christ, was to refer them to His second coming in the Day of Judgment. If it was His purpose now to put this truth before them, and so to warn them of the terrible responsibility which they were taking on themselves in rejecting His mission, and in preventing His acceptance by others, He could not have done this more gently, and at the same time more forcibly, than by this prediction, which spoke of a truth to which the natural conscience bears witness, and which was probably a part of primitive tradition as well as distinct revelation, which is found so constantly implied in the Old Testament, as in the Prophets and the Psalms. All this ought to have made the thought of the future judgment one which it was very easy to arouse within them. And now it was set before them as resting on our Lord's word also, and on the communication of the Divine Nature by the Father to the Son. His manner of speaking of it now implied no direct threat to them. He did not in so many words warn them of what the judgment might be, in the case of those who set themselves against the work of God, which His Father had committed to Him to perform. He left the great truth to make its own way with their consciences, and certainly it was plain enough to make them tremble.

[4] St. John iii. 17, 18. [5] St. John viii. 50. [6] St. John xii. 46, seq.

There is also much of warning in the language with which our Lord closes this part of His discourse to them, for He speaks no longer of the Son of God in the third person, but of Himself; and while He again asserts that all that He does is the work of His Father, on account of His absolute unity with Him, He still speaks with the utmost majesty of the righteousness of His judgment. 'I cannot of Myself do anything'—words which must be understood, as has already been explained, of the unity of operation of the Father and Himself—'as I hear, so I judge'—the judgment which I shall pass will be perfectly impartial and just, for it will be based simply on the state of the souls before Me, which I shall know by My Divine wisdom, in which I am One with My Father, and also by the infused knowledge of My Sacred Humanity which is given to it by God—'and My judgment is just, because I seek not My own will, but the will of Him that sent Me.' The will of God cannot but be that all should be judged according to His own Divine and perfect justice, and this justice is guided to its decisions by His absolute knowledge of the hearts and deeds of men. This is the will of God as to the judgment of mankind, and there can be nothing but this before the mind of our Lord in making that judgment. For the only things that can make a judgment perverse or erroneous are ignorance or bias—a failure to perceive the truth, or a fault in the will which warps its decision from that perfect accuracy which the full perception of the truth ought to engender. But the intelligence of our Lord cannot err in its perceptions, nor can the will of our Lord err in its decisions. Thus His judgment is infallible. As far as it is the work of His Divine nature, His will and judgment are the same identically with the will and judgment of the Father, and this is what He means when He says that as He hears, He judges. As far as the judgment is the work of His human will and soul, these are enlightened by the infused light of the Divine Wisdom communicated to Him as Man, and He can have no intention, or bias, or desire, or thought, or estimate, that is not perfectly in harmony with the dictates of that Divine Wisdom.

Thus does our Lord set before these ecclesiastical rulers of the holy nation the coming Judgment, and the resurrection of all men that is to precede that Judgment. There were among them, we cannot doubt, many men of bad lives and impure hearts, to whom the thought of the great Day of Account was terrible, because of the miserable state of their consciences for the many violations of the moral law with which they had to reproach themselves. In this they were like the ordinary mass of sinners, to whom the mere mention of the coming Judgment is odious, suggesting thoughts which they would fain escape if they could. But our Lord's further language to them in this place seems to press rather on the point as to which many of those present might be in danger, whose lives were free from the pollution of immoral passions. Men are constantly prone to forget that they have to render an account of their intellectual responsibilities, as well as of those which relate to the moral law, or, in other words, that they may break the moral law by intellectual perversity and dishonesty and obstinacy, as well as by the indulgence of the lower passions. This is the great trial of men of intelligence and education, of those who are the teachers of others, the leaders of thought and opinion, men of science and letters and learning, to whom the evidences of religion and the vouchers for the claims of the Church are presented by Providence in generations like our own, as the evidences for our Lord's Divine mission were presented to the Jews when He was upon earth. This is the constant danger of heretics, especially of heretical or schismatical teachers, who strain their intellectual conscience even to what is, in itself, flagrant dishonesty, for the sake of the false position which they have made for themselves, or in which they find themselves, in rebellion against the Church of God. As faith is the condition of salvation, and faith is an intellectual act, it is certain that the probation of man, in his present state, turns very mainly on the manner in which his intelligence deals with the truths of revelation as they are presented to him. It is of little avail, then, to lead a correct life, if the mind is darkened by pride and the will obstinate in its resolution not to submit to teaching. Pride and obstinacy of this kind may be produced in certain cases by the indulgence in lower passions, by covetousness, or ambition, or jealousy. But they may exist without these causes, and wherever they exist they are sins which will have to be accounted for at the day of God's Judgment, as well as sins of the flesh, or injustice, or blasphemy. Thus it is that there are so often men whose greatest danger is in that part of their probation which relates to the management of their intelligence, and the importance of faith in the Christian scheme, the choice made by God of a visible Church as the organ of salvation to mankind, and the extreme sinfulness of heresy and of separation from the centre of unity, make this danger very great and very common in days like our own.

It is very possible that something of this kind may have been the case with the men to whom our Lord was speaking. There may have been among them men lost to morality itself, men of ambition, or men unscrupulous in their pursuit of wealth, but as a body their trial was, for the present, in the manner in which they dealt with the evidences of our Lord's mission. Their treatment of

Him hitherto had not been such as to afford much ground for hope that reasoning would bring them round to the truth. The truth and its evidences required to be looked at, considered, examined, in order to be accepted, and there were as many obstacles to this process in the minds and hearts of a great part of this ecclesiastical body, as have ever been found in heretics or schismatics of later times. But our Lord would not, for this, forsake them, or deprive them of the opportunity which was now afforded, especially as He knew that among them, as in all bodies of the same kind and the same magnitude, there were many whose hearts were more right with God than the hearts of others. Thus we find Him proceeding at once, from His mention of the coming Judgment, to a calm and affectionate attempt to place before them the chain of these evidences, and then to point out to them the moral reasons why they had hitherto found a difficulty in giving its due weight to the overwhelming testimony by which His Father had accredited Him to them.

CHAPTER XV.

Witnesses to our Lord's Mission.

St. John v. 31—39; *Vita Vitæ Nostræ*, § 42.

OUR Lord had now set before these Jewish rulers a number of very high and difficult truths concerning Himself, for which they were to take the warrant of His word. He had done this, moreover, in vindication of His own act of authority, in enjoining on the man who had been healed at the pool an action which was, in itself, and apart from the circumstances which gave it a peculiar character, a violation of the strict law of the Sabbath, and He had also Himself seemed to them, though not truly, to violate the same law by His own work of mercy. Yet for this He had given no reason, such as on other occasions He alleged in defence of such conduct, but had rested His explanation on the fact of His Oneness with His Father, which in itself was a claim which required proof before it could be received. And, as if this were not enough in the way of demand on their faith, He had further added statements about the future wonders which He was to work, statements which implied that He was the Son of God, that He would raise the dead to life, and that, in His Human Nature, as He stood before them, He would judge the world, and assign to the just and to the wicked the eternal retribution which they deserved. These were indeed lofty claims and promises, and, as has been said, they were to be accepted on His word. It is therefore natural that He should next pass on, in His infinite condescension and consideration for those with whom He was dealing, to some kind of recapitulation and summing up of the testimonies which had been vouchsafed to them, in evidence of the truth of any claim that He might make. This is the main purpose of the passage in this discourse on which we are now to occupy ourselves. It is very probable that the actual discourse at this point was much longer than the report which St. John gives us. Our Lord passes rapidly from one point of evidence to another, and though we may be sure that St. John has omitted no head of testimony of those alleged by our Lord, it seems unlikely that He would not dwell to some extent on each. The whole passage sets before us, in great conciseness, the evidences on which our Lord's mission rested.

He begins by a general statement, which seems to imply the necessity of the evidences which He is about to adduce. 'If I bear witness of Myself, My witness is not true.' These words must be understood as spoken in a particular sense. It is not the case that anything that our Lord might say of Himself could be false, for He is the eternal and immutable Truth. Even in His Human Nature, apart from His ineffable Divinity, He could not possibly either deceive or be deceived. Falsehood is impossible to Him. Later on, moreover, in speaking, many months after this time, to these same enemies of His own at Jerusalem, He says Himself, 'Although I give testimony of Myself, My witness is true, for I know whence I come and whither I go, but you know not whence I come or whither I go.'[1] It is therefore clear that our Lord cannot mean to say here that His assertions as to Himself could not be true. The words, therefore, are either a repetition of an objec-

[1] St. John viii. 14.

tion which He saw in the hearts of His hearers, or which they actually uttered on this occasion—a repetition of such an objection, which He makes for the purpose of refuting it—or they are to be understood of technical testimony as such, the true character of which makes it impossible for any one to be his own witness. Witness, in this sense of the word, means the declaration that another person did this or that, or was this or that, and to say that a person's witness to himself was not true witness, was the same as to say that He was not another person, but Himself. In the same way St. Paul seems to say, in the Epistle to the Galatians, that God cannot mediate between Himself and man, because a mediator cannot be one of the persons between whom mediation is made.[2] That this is the sense here, seems proved by the fact that our Lord immediately proceeds to adduce a chain of testimony of various kinds, which confirmed His Divine mission and so accredited His declarations concerning Himself. For it must be remembered that the effect of any testimony, however powerful and multifarious in kind, in the case of our Lord, was not only to prove that He was the Son of God, but also to impose on those who received it as true testimony, the obligation of believing all that He said, whether about Himself, or on other points. And thus the other statement of our Lord just now quoted, which seems to contradict this, is confirmed, that although He bears witness of Himself, yet that witness is true. The witness of others first proves Him to be ineffable Truth, and then His own statements are to be received as the utterances of that Truth. Thus the Samaritan woman was the witness by means of whom her fellow-townsmen were brought to the knowledge of our Lord, telling them that He had told her all things

[2] Galat. iii, 20.

'whatsoever she had done'—and afterwards, as St. John says, 'Many more believed on Him because of His own word, and said to the woman, We now believe, not for thy saying, for we ourselves have heard Him, and know that this is indeed the Saviour of the world.'[3]

The witnesses to whose evidence our Lord now appeals may be considered as five, three of which were special to the times of His mission, the other two having existed before it. First He says, 'There is another that beareth witness of Me, and I know that the witness which he witnesseth of Me is true. You sent unto John, and he gave testimony to the truth . . . he was a burning and a shining light, and you were willing for a time to rejoice in his light.' Here, then, is the first appointed witness, the testimony of St. John Baptist. Then our Lord proceeds: 'But I have a greater witness than that of John. For the works which My Father hath given Me to perfect, the works themselves which I do, give testimony of Me, that the Father hath sent Me.' This, then, is the second witness—the miracles which our Lord wrought, as given Him by His Father. Then follows a third head of testimony—'And the Father Himself Who hath sent Me hath given testimony of Me. Neither have you heard His voice at any time, nor seen His shape. And you have not His word abiding in you, for Whom He hath sent, you believe not.' Fourthly, our Lord mentions the testimony of the Sacred Scriptures in a way which implies that this at least was acknowledged by them. 'Search the Scriptures, for you think in them to have life everlasting; and the same are they that give testimony of Me.' Thus the Sacred Scriptures are alleged by our Lord, as a distinct head of the testimony to Him, though in this case He is speaking of a kind of testimony which was

[3] St. John iv. 39, 41, 42.

not new, for it embodied the predictions of the prophets who had been, as St. Zachary says in the *Benedictus*, 'from the beginning.' In this respect the testimony of the sacred writings was not like the other heads of witness of which He had already spoken. And the same is to be said of that other, which is mentioned towards the end of the whole passage before us—the testimony of Moses. In that latter part of this passage, our Lord leaves the enumeration of the heads of testimony to Himself, so as to make something else the main subject of His discourse. That other subject embraces the causes, moral and spiritual, which had brought about, in the Jews, the blindness or the obstinacy, which prevented them from accepting the witness which was furnished to them concerning Him. But He does not fail to adduce this other kind of witness, the testimony of Moses, which He mentions last of all. This may be considered as a witness to some extent independent of the general witness of Sacred Scripture, for Moses was a Lawgiver as well as a writer of Scripture and a Prophet, and the witness which he rendered to our Lord, even by his writings, was contained not simply in predictions, but in the whole body of his legislation, and especially in the system of typical sacrifices and rites which it had been his office to establish in the name of God. These, then, are the five kinds of testimony to which our Lord appeals here, though to the last two in a different way from the others; the witness of St. John Baptist, the witness of His own miracles, the witness of the Father, the witness of Scripture in general, and the witness of their own Lawgiver Moses.

With regard to the first of these heads of testimony to which our Lord now appeals, a good deal has been said in a former volume of this work. We know that the ministry of St. John Baptist was of short duration, that he never appeared in the Holy City itself as a teacher, that he worked no miracles, and that he confined himself mainly to the preaching of repentance and the administration of his baptism. His witness to our Lord was, to the great majority of those who heard of it, prospective only, though those who may have been present when our Lord was baptized may have understood that he pointed Him out personally, and he certainly did so to those of his own disciples who joined our Lord in His last visit to the Jordan. The disciples who remained with St John after that time could speak of our Lord to him as 'Him to Whom he had given testimony.'[4] In many respects, therefore, the witness of the Baptist to our Lord, though it had been clear and intelligible, was not so conspicuous and direct as to force itself on the attention of those who were unwilling to receive it. Still our Lord makes the Chief Priests, who sent a solemn embassy to St. John to ask him who he was and why he baptized, responsible for their treatment of him. And this method of treating them on the part of our Lord is continued to the very end, for in His last teaching in the Temple, at the end of His Ministry, He refused to answer them as to His own authority, unless they would first tell Him whether the baptism of John was of God or of man.[5] For St. John was the appointed forerunner and herald of our Lord in the providence of His Father, and not to receive him was the same thing as to reject the message of God. The Evangelist of the same name speaks of the Baptist, in the great passage about the Incarnation with which his Gospel opens, in language which shows us how very far the intentions of God in the mission of St. John surpassed the results which were actually produced by that mission. 'He was sent to bear witness of the light,

[4] St. John iii. 26.   [5] St. Matt. xxi. 24, seq.

that all men might believe through him.'[6] And in the same way the language of St. Zachary, the father of the Baptist, in his canticle, the *Benedictus*, is very strong and large in its description of the mission of his child, echoing, in this respect the words of the angel who was sent to announce his birth, who said that he was 'to go before the face of our Lord in the spirit and power of Elias, to turn the hearts of the fathers unto the children, and the incredulous to the wisdom of the just, to prepare unto the Lord a perfect people.'[7] So it is with the great spiritual designs and instruments of God—their mission is very glorious and their work very magnificent in the Divine counsels and in the eyes of Heaven, but they pass swiftly before the eyes of a drowsy and inattentive world, their message falls on dull ears and hard hearts, it causes but a transient sensation, except in the case of the few. No doubt the preaching of the Baptist had produced a stir over the whole land, and its influence had touched even these priests and rulers themselves. But they had turned away from the teaching of penitence, the one thing of which, more than all other things, they were in need, and the intrigues of the day, the ambitions and jealousies of their own body, the vicissitudes of the Roman politics, their own chances of advancement in the consideration of men, the interests and desires of whatever kind with which their hearts were engrossed, occupied them entirely, so that the appearance of our Lord among them, to claim their allegiance and faith, was a thing unwelcome and startling, which found them altogether unprepared, which disturbed them and revolted them, like the message of death itself coming upon a company of the revellers of the world, the frivolous children of pleasure, or the slaves of greed.

John had appeared suddenly, and for a few months

[6] St. John i. 7.   [7] St. Luke i. 17.

the whole country was ringing with his name. These priests at Jerusalem had allowed the movement which he had occasioned to go on—they could not have stopped it if they would, but they seem to have taken an interest in it, and even to have rejoiced in the improvement among the people which followed from it. Then he became so influential and prominent, that they sent him an official deputation to ask him about his person and his authority. They received an answer which they did not take the pains to understand, a reference to some One greater than he, and then, after his influence had already begun to wane, he was imprisoned by Herod, and his voice could be lifted up no more. Among none of the people was the impression which he had produced more transient than among them. All passed away from them, and yet now, a year or so after, our Lord calmly and sternly reminds them—'You sent to John, and he gave testimony to the truth. But I receive not testimony from man, but I say these things that you may be saved. He was a burning and a shining light, and you were willing for a season to rejoice in his light.' This then was the first witness which the providence of God had furnished to these rulers of His own people. A whole chain of prophets had prepared the Jews for the coming of our Lord, and they could tell, as we see from the history of the Wise Kings,[8] even the particular village in which He was to be born. They knew the times and seasons of His coming, and they could have answered many other questions concerning Him as truly as they answered the question of Herod. But God had, lastly, sent one single messenger, whom our Lord declares to have been more than a prophet in his office, to make the immediate preparation for Him, by the preaching of repentance, and even to point out

[8] St. Matt. ii. 5.

His Sacred Person. John had come, and gone. He was now in the prison to which the impure passion of a wicked King had consigned him. The voice of John was no more to be heard, and the priests could breathe more freely at the thought of their own rejection of his importunate call to repentance. As to his witness to Him Who was to come after him, the latchet of Whose shoes he was not worthy to loose, it had made no impression at all on them.

But the providence of the Father in witnessing to His Son was not exhausted by the mission of St. John. That chosen messenger of His had worked no miracles, in this respect being unlike many of the prophets who had preceded him. This witness to His Incarnate Son had been kept, as it seems, by the Father for that Son Himself, and when He had begun to preach, His path through the country had been marked by a profuse display of miraculous power, in which all the old prophecies concerning the times of the Messias had been fulfilled, and by which the hearts of the people had been drawn to Him in a way and to a degree in which nothing else can draw the hearts of men. In truth, whatever may be the cavils of would-be philosophers, nothing brings home to the ordinary mass of mankind the truth that God is visiting them in the same way as a great display of miraculous power. This, then, was another head of evidence, presented to the Jews by the providence of God, in favour of the mission of our Blessed Lord. 'I have a greater testimony than that of John for the works which the Father hath given Me to perfect, the works themselves which I do, give testimony of Me that the Father hath sent Me.' It has been said more than once, that this is the true logical inference to be drawn from miracles—that God, Who works them through one who is, or seems to be, a man like ourselves, has sent him, whose authority is thus proved to be from Him, with a special message and for some special purpose, and that the messenger thus accredited is to be received as speaking in the name of God. But what our Lord said in the name of God was, that He was Himself God, and the Son of God. This therefore was a witness which they could not rightly set aside, and it brought home to them the truth which our Lord was now setting before them—that He was indeed the Son of God.

It may be said that, even if this had not been so, the miracles of our Lord were such, and attended by such circumstances as to the manner in which they were wrought, as to imply of themselves that He was God. For instance, it is certainly true that He worked miracles in His own name, and by His own power, whereas prophets and saints worked them in the name of God, and very often by means of prayer. Again, our Lord's miracles were not confined to this or that class of wonders, or worked at certain times and places only, as is the case with the miracles of the saints. And, if we are to include in the number of the works of which He here speaks such marvels as those which He had just predicted, as the raising of the dead, the giving spiritual life to souls, nay, the resurrection of the whole human race at the end of time, these works certainly transcend the sphere of the miracles of mere created agents altogether. It may be said that these miracles, at all events, had not as yet been worked, and some of them are not to be worked till the end of the world; others again, of the same stupendous power, such as the reading of the hearts, or the resurrection of Lazarus, or His own Resurrection and Ascension, and the giving of the Holy Ghost, were to come sooner, but had not yet been seen. Our Lord may speak in general of all the works of various kinds which He was to work by the power of the Father, in the course of His Ministry on earth, or even after His Resurrection and Ascension—for He is here summing up the different kinds of evidences which were the vouchers of His mission. Or again, as has been said, we may be satisfied with the formal and logical power of even the miracles of the lesser order, such as that which had just been worked, in the knowledge of these rulers, in the cure of the man who had lain so long under the infirmity from which our Lord had delivered him at the pool. For the formal force of such miracles was to prove the truth of the message on the part of God which was so accredited. And in this sense, as in the others, there can be no comparison made between the witness even of so great a saint as St. John, which, after all, was the word of a man, and the series of these miracles, which was, in truth, the word of God. Even in the case of a saint, there might still be a human element in what he said. But in works above and beyond the power of nature there could be no human element.

Here, again, we may remark upon the direct manner in which our Lord seems to force upon them the responsibility which His miracles brought home to men in their position. The miracles had been wrought, almost exclusively, at a distance from Jerusalem, and they knew of them only by the popular voice, which hailed them as the fulfilment of the promised signs of the Messias Who was to come. They might have said, perhaps, that they were not bound to attend to them, though that would have been strange language in the spiritual rulers of the holy nation, who were especially obliged to be on the look-out for the fulfilment of the promises of God. But, even putting aside the miracles of which they had heard only by the universal witness of the people of those parts of the land in which our Lord's ministry had hitherto been chiefly exercised, at least a year before this time He had been among them in Jerusalem itself, and had then worked the miracles which satisfied Nicodemus and others that God was with Him. And now, instead of welcoming Him as God's messenger, they were actually, as it were, in arms against Him, on account of one of those very miracles which He had worked, almost before their eyes, on this Sabbath day.

Could there be anything more direct than the witness of God to His Son by the way of miracles? It seems as if there could be. That is, if God would vouchsafe, or if He had vouchsafed, to make Himself heard from Heaven in confirmation of the same truth. But this had actually taken place at the Baptism of our Lord by St. John. 'And the Father Himself, Who hath sent Me, hath given testimony of Me.' For it must not be supposed that so solemn and wonderful a mystery as that of the Voice which was heard from Heaven at our Lord's Baptism, 'This is My beloved Son, in Whom I am well pleased,' could be meant to pass as of no importance, or, rather, as of any importance short of the very highest. It is of course true that the voice which was heard was formed in the air by the angels, who are the ordinary ministers of God in all apparitions and other manifestations of the kind—but the words could belong to no one but to the Eternal Father, and could be true, in their Divine fulness, of no one but the Eternal only-begotten Son. This being the case, they became another head of the evidence on which these Jews were bound to receive our Lord, and to accept His teaching concerning Himself.

This would be true, even if there were no more to be said as to the mystery of the voice which was heard at the time of the Baptism of our Lord. But the words of the passage before us, in which our Lord seems distinctly to refer to the promise made by God to the Israelites at the time of the promulgation of the Law, seem to involve a further meaning or interpretation as to the manner of this witness of the Father of which our Lord speaks. This is dwelt upon by some of the best commentators on this passage.[9] We must remember that, at the time of the giving of the Law on Mount Sinai, we are told of the great terror of the people which made them implore Moses that he might be an intermediate between them and God. 'And all the people saw the voices and the flames and the sound of the trumpets and the Mount smoking, and being terrified and struck with fear they stood afar off saying to Moses, Speak thou to us and we will hear, and let not the Lord speak to us lest we die.'[10] And in the similar passage in Deuteronomy, in which this history is recapitulated, we have the great promise of the Prophet, which was always understood of the Messias: 'The Lord thy God will raise up to thee a Prophet of thy nation and of thy brethren, like unto me, him thou shalt hear; as thou desirest of the Lord thy God in Horeb, when the assembly was gathered together, and saidst, Let me not hear any more the voice of the Lord my God, neither let me see any more this exceeding fire, lest I die. And the Lord said to me, They have spoken all things well. I will raise up to them a Prophet out of the midst of their brethren, like to thee, and I will put My words in his mouth, and he shall speak to them all that I shall command him. And he that will not hear his words which he shall speak in My name, I will be the avenger.[11] This passage is quoted by St. Peter in his

---

[9] See Toletus, in loc.   [10] Exodus xx. 18, 19.
[11] Deut. xviii. 15—18.

discourse to the people in the Temple, after the first Apostolic miracle, as it may be called, that on the man who lay at the Beautiful Gate.[12] St. Peter applies it, of course, to our Blessed Lord. It is very natural to consider that our Lord's official designation, if we may so speak, as the Prophet, whom the chosen people were to listen to, as they had listened to Moses, who was to plead for them, and make intercession for them to God, and to be, as Moses is called, a Mediator for them, was indicated on the occasion of His Baptism, and that the Voice of the Father conveyed this designation. Considering the passage thus, the Voice of the Father is not only a simple attestation of the authority of our Lord's mission, like the witness of St. John or the witness of miracles, but it is an attestation on the part of the Father declaring His own faithfulness in the fulfilment of the promise which He had made to the people at the most solemn moment of the history of His dealings with them, and also declaring the punishment which He would inflict on them if they were disobedient to the teaching of the Prophet whom He had both promised and sent. Thus St. Peter quotes the final words of the text in Deuteronomy in a different manner, explaining the sense in which God would be the avenger in case of such disobedience. 'And it shall be, that every soul which will not hear that Prophet, shall be destroyed from among the people.'

Thus, when our Lord says to the priests to whom He is now speaking, 'Neither have you heard His voice at any time, nor seen His shape,' it is very probable that those commentators are right who consider that He was alluding to this passage in the Jewish history. The allusion enables Him, also, to meet by anticipation the objection that might rise to their minds against His last

[12] Acts iii. 22.

declaration that His Father had given testimony of Him. His Father had given this solemn witness at His Baptism. True it was, indeed, that they had not heard His Voice, nor seen anything with their eyes which revealed to them the presence of God. But, after all, this was what they had desired in old times—they had asked for some one to stand between them and God, and this had been promised to them and was now fulfilled. But even this was no excuse, for the word of His Father had come to them, as St. Paul says in the opening words of the Epistle to the Christians of their nation, 'at sundry times and in divers manners,'[13] and it had not sunk into their hearts nor remained there like a seed of good and truth. And the proof of this was before their eyes; for now that God had sent Him Whom He had promised to send, Who was the end and the burthen of the whole revelation of God from the beginning, Him they did not receive.

Another interpretation of these words of our Lord may be mentioned, as suggested by His own manner of speaking of the silent drawing of men to Him by the Father, which is necessary in order that any may truly and efficaciously come to Him. Thus, he says, in those famous words in which He gives thanks to His Father for the revelation of the truths of His Kingdom to little ones—'I confess to Thee, O Father, Lord of Heaven and earth, because thou hast hid these things from the wise and prudent, and hast revealed them to little ones.'[14] That is, He speaks of the knowledge or discernment of Himself by those who do discern Him as the work of the Father. Again, when St. Peter made his great confession of faith in this very truth of our Lord's Divinity, which is the subject of the discourse on which we are now occupied, he says to him, 'Blessed art thou,

[13] Heb. i. 1.   [14] St. Matt. xi. 25.

Simon Bar-Jona, because flesh and blood hath not revealed it to thee, but My Father Who is in Heaven.'[15] And a little before that time, in His disputation in the synagogue in Capharnaum, after the miracle of the multiplication of the loaves for the five thousand, our Lord said, 'No man can come unto Me, except the Father, Who hath sent Me, draw him, and I will raise him up at the last day. It is written in the Prophets, "And they shall all be taught of God."[16] Every one that hath heard of the Father, and hath learned, cometh to Me.'[17] And then He adds words which remind us of the present passage, saying, 'Not that any man hath seen the Father, but he who is of God, he hath seen the Father.' These words may be explained more fully hereafter, but for the present it is enough to point out that they suggest a witness of the Father, which had been going on in many hearts which had been drawn to the Incarnate Son since His mission began, and in this sense the adhesion of so many faithful souls to the teaching and person of our Lord was a witness of the Father to the truth of His mission. In a certain true sense, all that believed in our Lord had seen the Father, for He says to St. Philip, in the conversation before the institution of the Blessed Sacrament, when the Apostle had said to Him, "Lord, show us the Father, and it sufficeth,' 'So long a time have I been with you, and have you not known Me, Philip? He that seeth Me, seeth the Father. How sayest thou, show us the Father?'[18] According to this manner of understanding the passage before us, the whole success of our Lord's preaching, the conversions which He had wrought, the disciples who had gathered round Him, the effect which He had produced in souls —all this was the witness of the Father to the truth that

---

[15] St. Matt. xvi, 17.   [16] Isaias liv. 13.   [17] St. John vi. 44—46.
[18] St. John xiv. 9, 10.

He had sent Him. All this had been going on under the eyes of these Jewish priests, at least within their knowledge, and yet they themselves had remained outside, spectators of the movement of grace, and themselves taking no part in it, but even opposing it. 'You have not His word abiding in you, for Whom He hath sent, Him you receive not.'

These words are the first of direct reproach which our Lord here addresses to these Jewish rulers. They very naturally suggest the idea of the Sacred Scriptures, which were the monuments and archives of the revelations of God, and by means of which, therefore, those to whom they were confided might have prepared themselves for the fulfilment of those revelations. And here, at least, there could be no question between our Lord and those to whom He was speaking. They might doubt of the Divine mission of St. John Baptist, they might even cavil at the miracles of our Lord, they might question the fact of the Voice of the Father heard from Heaven when He was baptized. The authority, at least of the Sacred Scriptures they could not question, and yet, if they could but grasp the true and plain teaching of the Scriptures, all would be well with them. Our Lord's words may be understood, either in Greek or in the Vulgate translation, as either declaring a fact or enjoining a practice. It may be either, 'Search the Scriptures,' or, 'You search the Scriptures.' Perhaps the common English translation, according to which our Lord bids them search the Scriptures, has the greatest probability in its favour. For it is ever the way of our Lord, as of the Apostles and the Church speaking in His name, to take those who are addressed on their own ground, and to begin the process of their conversion or enlightenment from the truths which they clearly perceive and the authorities which they already acknowledge. Thus it may be understood that, after having enumerated the various kinds of evidence which the Providence of God had brought home to them, but which they had not accepted, our Lord bids them turn to evidence which they cannot question. Their knowledge of the mere text of Scripture was marvellous and exact, and they could insist on such a point as that as to which they afterwards bade Nicodemus 'search the Scriptures'—'that out of Galilee a prophet riseth not.'[19] But the whole teaching of Scripture concerning our Lord was lost upon them, just as the whole teaching of the New Testament concerning the authority of the Catholic Church is lost upon so many Protestants and Anglicans in the present day, who may know the sacred text, as far as they acknowledge it, from beginning to end, and with a far more humanly critical knowledge than hundreds of uneducated Catholics, and yet are blind to the noon-day truths of the articles of the Creed which they profess with their lips and yet obstinately deny in practice.

'Search the Scriptures, for you think in them to have life everlasting, and the same are they that give testimony of Me.' The Scriptures contained what St. Paul calls the 'words' or oracles 'of God,'[20] the possession of which he declares to have been the chief privilege of the chosen people. Life was promised to the keepers of the law, and the knowledge of the law—of the path, therefore, of life—was conveyed by means of the Scriptures. They also contained, as has been said, the whole revelation of God's counsels for the redemption of man, and thus for the attainment of eternal life. In a thousand ways and with a thousand voices they witnessed to our Lord, and to show how this was, was the greater part of the argumentative task of the Apostles and teachers of the Church, as He Himself had begun the explanation in so

[19] 1 St. John vii. 52.   [20] Romans iii. 2.

many points. The whole witness of the Scriptures to our Lord need not be drawn out here, but it is well to remark that this head of evidence, to which our Lord appeals in the last place, is fitly placed where it is, because the other kinds of testimony, already spoken of, may be said to be in some sense included under that of Scripture. That is, the mission of St. John and his designation of the Messias was a part of prophecy, and was so spoken of by St. John himself and by our Lord. Again, the testimony of miracles was undoubtedly foretold in Scripture, and indeed, as has already been shown in this work, the witness of miraculous signs, as an evidence of religion, may not indeed rest on prophecy, but it is secured by it. Again, if we take the view that the Voice from Heaven of the Eternal Father, as heard at the Baptism of our Lord, was in some measure a fulfilment, or the announcement of the fulfilment, of the promise made to the Jews of the sending of a prophet like to Moses, then this also is connected with the witness of Scripture, and may be said to rest upon it. Thus, apart from the testimony to our Lord of which the Scriptures are full, and for which they may be said to have been given, they also confirm and illustrate the other heads of divinely appointed testimony to which our Lord appeals.

CHAPTER XVI.

Causes of our Lord's rejection.

St. John v. 39—47 ; *Vita Vitæ Nostræ*, § 43.

THE last part of our Lord's discourse to the Jewish rulers, as reported to us by St. John, passes from the heads of evidence on which they ought to have believed in Him, to the internal causes on account of which they failed so to do. Here we have the Judge of all men putting His finger, so to say, on the moral sores and the seeds of evil in the hearts of those to whom He was speaking. Or, if we must not yet speak of Him as the Judge, He is rather the wise and tender Physician, Who, after finding His treatment of the sick under His care fail, points out to them gravely and lovingly the reason why it has been so—a reason not inherent in the treatment itself, which had ample power to cure them, but in the evil dispositions or habits of the patients, which deprive the wholesome medicine of its efficacy, either by directly counteracting its influence, or by making the patients unfit to take it. We must here again remember that our Lord was addressing a body of men, the individuals among whom were by no means all in the same moral state. There were many on whom He might hope that His words would have effect, many who were to profit by them, though not at once, others on whom they would be wasted, except to harden them to greater obstinacy. So it is always with the Word of God. Its fortunes in the world are described by our Lord in the parable of the sower and the seed, and yet we see that the Divine Sower of the Word does not let the small return that He may get for the greater part of the seed which He scatters so profusely and so widely, paralyze His exertions or chill the fire of His charity, but rather, that He is content, for the sake of the fruitfulness of the few souls who are as the good ground, to scatter much that must fall by the wayside, or among the thorns, or where there is no depth of soil. The words of our Lord in the few verses which remain of this Divine discourse, seem abrupt and severe, but they may have been even sweet and gentle as they fell on the ears of some who heard them—grave, indeed, and full of truths of awful solemnity, yet still expressed with loving gentleness, as far as so piercing a reproof admitted of such expression. We have now to examine in detail the words in which our Lord opens to them the wounds of their own souls, and by so doing points out the remedy which may still save them.

In the first place, the reason why they did not surrender themselves to all this accumulated evidence in favour of His mission is said to lie in the will. 'You will not come unto Me that you may have life.' He seems to refer to their belief that the Scriptures could show them where life was to be found, and to explain how it was that with all that belief to urge them on they could not understand the witness of the Scriptures concerning Him. The reason lay in their unwillingness to come to Him for life. Why did He point this out? Not certainly for His own sake, but for theirs, as He had said about the testimony of St. John, that He did not receive testimony of men, but said what He did that they might be saved. 'I receive not glory of men. But I know you, that you have not the love of God in you.' The love of God, again, is in the will, and this would have led them to our Lord, if they had had it. The proof that they had not the love of God was that they did not receive our Lord, Who came, in a special way, in the name of God. 'I am come in the name of My Father, and you receive Me not; if another shall come in his own name, him you will receive.' So it will always be—the men who do not receive the messenger and the message which God sends them, will receive other messengers and other messages which do not come from Him. This runs through the whole history of mankind, and there is no difficulty, therefore, in believing that it will be as our Lord says to the end of time, and in the days of Antichrist.

Our Lord then proceeds to point out to them the obstacle to faith which was the fruit of their want of the love of God, and which raised the barrier which shut them out from all capacity of a true and simple faith. This obstacle was their love of human respect, their desire for praise and esteem on the part of men, which supplanted in their hearts the single desire of pleasing God and standing well with God. 'How can you believe, who receive glory one from another, and the glory which is from God alone you do not seek?' It was this that prevented their will from doing its office in the genesis of faith, in directing the intellect to the consideration of the grounds of evidence for the truth proposed to them, and in enjoining its assent thereto. Their will was turned in another direction, in the direction of disbelief, for the slavery to human opinion under which they lay imposed on them the necessity of adhering to the fashionable creed, with which it was a kind of heresy to accept the providential witnesses of which our Lord had been speaking. He goes on to tell them of the accusation against them on the part of Moses, in whom they trusted. If it were true that the

Father had sent Him in His own name, and had provided those to whom He sent Him with so many proofs of the Divine authority of His mission, it might certainly be expected, according to ordinary rules of judgment, that the Messenger of God, thus despised by them, would raise against them a complaint before the Majesty Whose message He had borne in vain. All these things would be witness against them before the throne of God, and would, as our Lord said afterwards of the Queen of the South and the men of Ninive, rise up against them in the Day of Judgment. Our Lord now says that He will not be so much their accuser as that messenger and message of God which they did not question, and yet to which they had not attended. For the refusal to receive our Lord was, in truth, a rejection of the teaching of Moses himself, whom they professed to revere and to trust in. Their case was that of men who were condemned for not believing what they professed to receive—as St. Paul says of heretics, that they are condemned by their own judgment, for they profess the Creed of the Church, and yet refuse to obey the Church, of which the Creed speaks. This is the general meaning of the last words of this discourse of our Divine Lord, 'Think not that I will accuse you to the Father. There is one that accuseth you, even Moses, in whom you trust. For if you did believe Moses, you would perhaps believe Me also, for he wrote of Me. But if you do not believe his writings, how will you believe My words?' This will suffice for a general account of the contents of the passage now before us.

The first great truth on which our Lord here dwells, is that after all difficulties that could be alleged as to the reception of the message which He came to deliver which might be raised on the score of its evidences, the true reason why men did not believe lies in the will and in the heart. He is speaking, of course, to men who had had set before them all the array of evidence of which we have lately been speaking, and it is not meant that all the unbelief in the world, either then or now, is to be laid to the charge of a perverse will. For there were, we know, even among these very priests at Jerusalem, many souls whose hesitation as to faith in Him was afterwards overcome, and who had some real intellectual blindness,—such as so often comes from the existence in the mind of false conceptions as to our Lord or the Church, which have been imbibed in youth or derived from the teaching of some heretical school— and until this blindness was removed, their will could not be free to embrace the faith proposed to them. Much more may such blindness exist in times like our own, when there is so much confusion of religious teaching, and when the enemies of the Church have been so long in possession, as the chief teachers of mankind, in matters of history, of the explanation of the Sacred Scriptures, and of the natural sciences. The immense prejudices which have thus been raised against the Church and the Faith are often under-estimated, and some persons are thus in danger of judging too hardly those who are outside the Church, as if the mere fact of their remaining so were a proof of their bad faith and dishonesty. Our Lord is speaking of persons who had no right to plead such excuses as this. Taking them as a body, they had had a full and over-abundant amount of evidence presented to them, and they had no true reason for passing by its consideration as unnecessary. To them, more than to any others in the world, the whole mass of the evidences for His mission had been addressed. They were in some respects like the teachers and clergy of an heretical or schismatical body in times of some great Catholic movement, providentially aroused by God for the conversion of the people among whom they minister—they, more than all others, were bound to make themselves acquainted with the cardinal points of the controversy, and to consider dispassionately the grounds of the position which was called in question. Alas, they were to be the first instances in the history of the Christian preaching and faith, of a class which has had its representatives in every succeeding age of the Church—the class of men on whose assent to or rejection of the Christian and Catholic evidences, the spiritual welfare or ruin of thousands has depended, men who have first turned away from the surrender which the truth claimed of them, and then become its most bitter opponents and most successful persecutors. The truth was brought home to these Jewish rulers far too clearly for their rejection of it, as a body, to be attributable to circumstances of individual dulness or to a distorted view of the truths which they already might be supposed to know. Our Lord presently puts His finger on the particular evil which paralyzed their wills in the process of faith, but He begins by declaring, as has been said, that it was in the want of will that their paralysis lay.

To say that the action of the will is all important in the genesis of faith, is only to say, in different words, that faith is a meritorious act of the intellect, and therefore not a necessary act. It has pleased God from the beginning, as St. Paul is so fond of arguing, when he has to vindicate the rights and prerogatives of faith, to make the free assent of the mind to the truths which He reveals the condition of acceptance with Him, a condition so necessary, that no one can be saved without faith who is capable of it, and so efficacious, that faith and repentance have always and will always avail for the pardon of sins through our Lord. But the assent, which has this wonderful power and privilege in the Kingdom of God, cannot be the simple intellectual grasping of truths which are self-evident, and which cannot be questioned without rebellion against the laws of thought, such as are the truths which lie at the foundation of the exact sciences, or such truths as, if not known as such the moment they are proposed to the mind, can at least be proved to be infallibly true by reasoning from other truths which have been established beyond all question. If this were the case no one could help believing, and the most perfect faith would be that of the man who has the keenest natural intelligence. Nothing that is necessary can be meritorious, and all merit lies in the choice of the will. On the other hand, it is certain that the Christian grounds of faith are not wanting in true cogency and convincing power. How then can they be questioned? How can it be a matter of choice, and so of merit, to accept them and yield to them? The answer is, that their cogency is that of moral evidence, not of mathematical. Moreover, the will has a perpetual office in the guidance of the intelligence, as to what it will consider and attend to and what it will neglect and turn away from. It may force the mind to entertain the evidences of religion, or not to entertain them. It may occupy the mind with other things, it may tie it down to grovelling studies and frivolous and sensual thoughts; it may debauch it and stunt it and blunt its edge, by the use which it imposes on it as habitual, the tastes or the pursuits on which it employs the energies of the immortal soul.

Thus, practically, and for the great mass of mankind, it may and does depend on the will, whether the mind of any one is capable practically of grasping Divine truths and their evidences, because the will may make the mind absolutely averse to all such speculations as require vigour, and exertion, and purity, and elevation above the things of sense. And when the time comes for the consideration of a particular question or line of argument, the will may impart to the mind its own aversions and repugnances, and so prevent the process of conviction, by hindering that of examination and reflection, which must precede the other in the order of nature. And then, again, when the arguments of the faith have been considered and weighed and even allowed their natural influence on the intelligence, it still remains in the power of the will to command or to forbid its adhesion to the conclusion. But the decision of the will must depend on its own direction and bias. It cannot make true false, or false true, or turn probabilities into certainties, or raise conjectures into realities. But, as it could in the earlier part of the process compel attention and consideration, so here also it can order the intelligence to reason firmly and courageously, to set aside difficulties and place itself with docility on the ground irradiated by the light of the word of its Maker.

Thoughts such as these explain to us the power of the will in the formation of faith, or in the rejection of the evidences of Divine truth. It must be remembered that this is the human side only in the formation of faith, and that the other part, the part of God, must be taken into consideration if we are to have a full view of this great grace. And it must be remembered in particular that the assent of faith is to the word of God, and that thus, by God's bounty, the security and certainty of faith partakes of the stability which belongs to everything that is Divine and eternal. The grace of God works with the human agents in the formation of the act of faith all through, from the beginning to the end, and especially it works beyond and above human power in the certainty and peace of the soul which believes. But nothing more is required than this simple statement of Catholic theology to let us see the immense difference, as to the result of which we are speaking, between the soul in which the love of God dwells and rules, and the soul in which the ruling power is the spirit of the world, or self-love, or ambition, or sensuality, or any other evil principle. The one all-sufficient principle for the due formation of faith, as it has been explained, is the love of God. Where that exists there can be no hesitation, except in the case of persons who are under the influence of some mistaken teaching, which makes them for a time accept as true and as from God what is false and not from Him. But as all truth comes from Him, and is a reflection of His ineffable light, no truth can be really discordant from another, and, more than that, each truth that is duly recognized by the mind of a sincere lover of God, under any dispensation or in any circumstances, must lead on naturally to others and so to the whole chain. And on the other hand, if there be no love of God in the soul, the spring of all spiritual energy and progress is wanting. And it may be said that it is never the case that there is no love of God, without the substitution for that love of some other principle, which acts as powerfully in the turning away of the mind from the recognition of the truth, as that love might have acted in bringing the mind to recognize it. Thus, to say that there is no love of God in the soul, practically includes the further assertion that the love of the soul is given to other and lower objects, which have influence enough to engross it, although they cannot satisfy it.

The next words of our Lord, 'I receive not glory from men,' seem, like others in this and other discourses of His in this Gospel, to be either an anticipation of, or an answer to, some objection that might rise to their minds or their lips upon what He had just said. Men are ever prone to think that others are actuated by the motives which rule themselves, and so these Chief Priests may have thought of retorting upon our Lord that He was saying all this about faith in Himself for the purposes of His own glory. And so, in His ineffable condescension, He turns away this cavil. What, indeed, had He to gain from the homage of the whole universe of created beings that could add to His own intrinsic and eternal glory? They could add nothing to Him, but on their acceptance or rejection of Him, their own salvation and that of many others depended. It was nothing to Him, except so far as their salvation was the dearest interest of His Sacred Heart. 'I say these things, that you may be saved.' And then He returns to the subject of which He was before speaking. 'I know you,' He says, 'that you have not the love of God in you.' He knew them by His Divine knowledge, as God, whereby He reads all the hearts and thoughts of all His intelligent creatures. He knew them also by the infused knowledge which was given to His Sacred Humanity at the moment of the Hypostatic Union. And He knew them also by the experience which His dealings with them had added to His other kinds of knowledge. He had tried them, and found them out, as it were, for He had put them to the true test, and the thoughts and characters of their hearts had been brought out into daylight. The proof of what was in them was the result of the presentation to them of the Divine evidences of His mission. They had rejected Him, and that was the all-sufficient proof that the love of God was not in them. And so He pronounces the sentence on them, and on all like them, of which we have already spoken—'I am come in the name of My Father, and ye receive Me not; if another shall come in his own name, him you will receive.'

The whole character of our Lord's mission was that

of the work of One Who was sent by another. He might have come in His own name, that is, by virtue of His own authority, and, as the works of the Ever-Blessed Trinity are the works of each of the three Divine Persons, it was true that He did come, in this sense, in His own Name.. And, from time to time, we find Him asserting His own inherent authority and majesty, and this was so apparent to His hearers, that it became a matter of remark, that He did not teach as the scribes. And there are passages in this very discourse of which we are now speaking, which wear this character of dignity and royal independence. But there are also many others in which the language which He uses is best to be understood by remembering how faithfully, if we may so speak, He maintained throughout the character of the envoy of His Father. And perhaps it was a part of the Divine counsel that it should be so, for the very purpose of distinguishing His bearing in this respect from that of those who might come after Him, 'in their own name,' as He says, and who might, perhaps, pretend in words to be sent by God, but who would have neither any true mission from Him, nor any humility or lowliness and meekness, such as become the messengers of the Eternal Father. Thus our Lord came in the name of His Father, both because He was sent, according to the theological meaning of mission in the Divine Persons, for this special work, and also because He uniformly spoke and acted as dependent and as a messenger, not come in His own name or by His own authority.

On the other hand, it is the characteristic of all false teachers to differ from our Lord, in the first instance, in that they have no true mission, neither directly from God, nor from him who holds on earth the place of God, as to all spiritual and ecclesiastical mission whatsoever. Even when the teachers of falsehood and separation profess to come in the name of God, as Mahomet and other founders of false religions, that profession of theirs is false, as well as everything else which they impose on the world of their own. And ordinarily, also, they differ from our Lord in the absolute independence of all other authority which they claim for themselves, especially of the authority of the Church, against which their first efforts are directed—always either claiming to have a special and personal mission from God, or professing to rest on some authority which cannot speak to repudiate them, such as Scripture interpreted by themselves, or the ancient Church, not as it exists in the Church of their own day, which has a voice, but in any literary monuments which may happen to exist of the early centuries, which they can interpret for themselves as well as the Sacred Scriptures. This is in fact to come in their own name, because they do not acknowledge any living authority to which they are responsible. And, besides this mark of their independence, they have also usually an immense pride and arrogance which make them, practically, their own gods, and which may be hidden for a time, on account of the necessity incumbent on any teacher who professes Christian doctrine, to ape the manners and virtues of our Lord and His Apostles, but which are sure sooner or later to become manifest when they are contradicted or called to account, even if they do not provoke God to let them fall into some open and flagrant sin in the eyes of the world, in order to unmask them, and give them by disgrace the one last chance of repentance open to them.

Our Lord had before Him as He spoke all the series and generations of mankind, and He saw the fortunes of the Church to the end of time, and how the nation which had once been His own, and on which He had lavished so many precious favours, would be ready, at the close of the world's history, to welcome the great opponent of God, the Man of Sin, who was to come in his own name, according to the meaning of these words already explained. But all through this discourse our Lord is speaking with gentleness and meekness, and His words are rather those of remonstrance and pity, than of anger and reproach. And so He does not put His prophecy of this miserable error of the Jews at the end of the world .in the form of a direct prediction, but hypothetically—'if another shall come in his own name, him you will receive'—for, as has been said, it is ever the lot of those who turn away from the message and the revelation of God, to become the dupes of imposture and the slaves of disgraceful and degrading superstition. The mind of man requires food from without for its cravings after truth, as the heart of man requires something to love as a satisfaction for its powers of affection. If the mind is fed on the truth, and the heart on the true goodness and beauty, then the soul is happy and at peace; but if they do not find their proper food and object, they will wander in search of something on which to fasten, let it be the husks of swine or the mire beneath their feet. And so, if men do not believe the truth which God sets before them, they will be the prey of falsehoods, one more monstrous than the other. The whole system of Paganism was an imposture palmed off on the hungry souls of men who had fallen from that knowledge of God, which was given to the race on its outset in life. Superstition imposes on its subjects a yoke far harder to bear than the yoke of God's truth and law. The insolent dogmatism of heresiarchs has always been more stringent in its claims on obedience than the teaching of the Catholic Church. The sham priesthoods of modern times have bound men in personal bonds of the most exacting kind, by the necessity of their position outside the true Church. The lay power, when it has usurped the place of the rightful government of the Church of God, has been far more severe in its rigours against the disobedient than the Church could ever be, and the superstitions and follies, into which philosophers, who have aimed at the emancipation of mankind from the yoke of faith, have fallen, have sometimes been as degrading as anything that is to be found among the savage heathen themselves. So it always must be—men who will not submit to the government which God has appointed, will have to serve a harder bondage in the house of error. And even in the Apostolic age, as we learn from St. Paul, the arrogance of the false teachers had risen to such a pitch as to constitute an easily cognizable test of distinction between them and himself. 'You suffer,' he says, 'if a man bring you into bondage, if a man devour you, if a man take from you, if a man be lifted up, if a man strike you in the face.'[1] Thus does the exemplification of our Lord's words meet us in every age—'If another shall come in his own name, him you will receive.' And most of all, we may be sure, will they be true in that particular time of which He now speaks, for Antichrist will be the worst and most cruel of all the persecutors of the Church, the most exacting and tyrannical of the masters who impose themselves on the credulity of the unbelievers outside her pale.

Our Lord then goes on to point out, as has been said, the one particular evil to which, more than to any other in their case, it was owing that they did not believe His preaching. Not only did they not believe, but it was not possible that they should believe. They had in their hearts a principle which was enough to shut out the possibility of that ready faith which His words demanded. We have already seen how it is that the

[1] 2 Cor. xi. 20.

will has to act in the formation of faith, and how a fault of the will will stop that formation, whatever be the evil motive which forbids the will from acting as it ought. This is the general account of all unbelief when the evidence of the truth has been set before the mind. But the special motive is not the same in all cases, nor, we may suppose, was it the same in the case of every single individual alike in all the crowd of priests to whom these words were addressed. But there are in such bodies general and prevailing temptations, which serve to account for their unbelief as far as it is common to all in its grounds. There may have been among them some very bad cases of the lower sins, and one more than another of them may have been the slave of ambition, or of priestly jealousy, or of avarice and the like. But there was one dominant fault among all, which accounted in the eyes of our Divine Lord for their general obstinacy in resisting the force of all the accumulated witnesses of which He had been speaking, and He mentions this as the cause of the blindness of which He is complaining. He selects the common fault, as if for the sake of sparing the more flagrant sinners before Him, who might have been reproached with individual sins of greater shamefulness than this, and, in the same spirit of mercifulness, He mentions a sin lighter in itself than many others of which He could have spoken. Indeed there is a kind of mercifulness in the form itself of His reproach, for He seems to put their fault upon inability rather than on wilful error.

'How can you believe, who receive glory one from another, and the glory which is from God alone you do not seek?' This then was the ruling fault, the common danger, of these priests at Jerusalem. It is the fault of persons in positions such as theirs. It is the fault which may be fatal to persons who are outwardly serving God, and keeping His commandments. It consists in nothing more than a desire to stand well with and to gain the approval of men, as the first and great object of life to which all things else are subordinate. It is not wrong to seek the approval of men, in a certain sense, for that may be a means to the service of God, and we are told by our Lord Himself to let our light shine before men, that they may see our good works and glorify our Father in Heaven for them. But when we look no further than the esteem of men, and make that our ultimate end, to which everything else gives place, we may be led, as these priests were to be led, to any length in opposition to the truth of God or the designs of God. The light that is in us may become darkness indeed, for we may guide ourselves and form our intentions according to it, and, when there arises a conflict between conscience or duty or the truth, on the one hand, and this human estimation on the other, the right principle may give way—indeed, must give way, and the wrong prevail. These men were the slaves of human respect and opinion, and thus they had no principle to raise them above the influence of the world. The glory that is of God alone they did not seek. The one approval which is of any value at all to a right conscience, is the approval of God, and this would have led them, if it were necessary, to despise the human interests and esteems which were all-powerful with them, for the sake of accepting the messenger of God and yielding their assent to truths witnessed to by so many proofs which God alone could furnish.

The way in which the paralysis of the will in consequence of the influence of an imperfect or bad motive can make the formation of faith impossible, could not be more clearly illustrated or explained than by the case of these men, nor could the mischief that results from this miserable self-induced blindness have a more complete exemplification than in their instance. The argument is complete here. There is no more needed to unveil the wiles of Satan and the evil which he may work, even in those who are by profession the servants of God, when he induces them gradually to make another principle than that of the service of God the rule of their lives. And it must be remembered, that as faith has many measures and degrees, so its growth as well as its birth may be hindered by the usurpations of human respect. Thus the evil which our Lord deplored in these Scribes and Pharisees, may not be unknown even in those who belong to Him in the Church. The esteem of men keeps thousands from embracing the creed and submitting themselves to the gentle yoke of the Church, and we see the effects of this evil constantly in the difficulty which stands in the way of many a conversion, especially in countries where a false Church is established, or again, in the case of persons who have been brought up in the free-thinking tenets, which have been so fashionable in France and other continental countries since the age of Voltaire. The power of human respect is shown in the occasional defeats which it suffers in the case of persons who become Catholics and disavow their infidelity on their death beds, when the delusions of earth are already beginning to vanish and the worthlessness of human applause is proved by the near presence of the Judgment from which every evil conscience shrinks instinctively. For one poor infidel who has the courage or the opportunity to reconcile himself with his God at that last moment, who shall say how many there are who miss such a grace? The influence of the love of human praise may be measured by the answer to that question.

In such cases as these the miserable power of human

respect is written, so to say, in large letters, but its influence in dwarfing the growth and chaining down the efforts of the soul, especially of those who might perhaps do great things for God, is not the less true and real because it is less perceptible. The love of human applause has often tempted men to compromise in a great cause, or it has been the fertile spring of jealousies and animosities in the servants of the sanctuary itself, at which the children of the world have laughed. It has stopped many a high vocation, it has stifled many a generous enterprize for God, it has made men in authority niggardly in their encouragement of the efforts of others, and so guilty of that sin peculiar to their position, the standing in the way of good which God has prompted, and on which the salvation of many souls may depend. Nay, more, it has before this been the real origin of schisms and of heresies, as it is the constant reason why schismatical and heretical teachers do not submit themselves to the Church. In all these, and in a thousand similar cases, the words of our Lord hold good, that the love of human honour hinders the growth of faith, and by hindering the growth of faith; prevents the generous and noble acts of which a strong and clear faith is the essential foundation and condition. For it is by faith that all that is great in the Kingdom of God is wrought, and a Christian writer might make a catalogue of the achievements of the great saints and servants of God in the history of the Church, and celebrate them, as St. Paul has celebrated the deeds of the heroes of the Old Covenant, in the Epistle to the Hebrews, saying that by faith all these things were done.[2] The love of human credit is essentially a want of faith—it is the fruit of a false view and a purblind perception of the great truths of our religion, of the

[2] Hebrews xi.

dignity of man and the majesty of God, of the value of the soul and of grace, and of the worthlessness of all earthly things. Thus it is an evil as mischievous in the Christian ages as in the Jewish Synagogue, and it is not without reason that when our Lord put His finger on the bad principles which turned against Him these Jewish rulers who were at last to be guilty of His murder, He points to their love of human esteem as the root of all their perversity.

Our Lord does not only say that these priests sought the honour which they might gain from the approval of men and of one another, but that they were wrong negatively also, in not seeking the glory or approval which is from God alone. His words seem to suggest, not only the reproach which He brings against them, but also the remedy which would have saved them from the spiritual ruin which they were bringing on themselves and on so many others. It is as if He had said, 'I do not forbid you to seek approval and credit, but there is approval and there is credit which are worth having, and which, as the servants of God in His sanctuary, you in particular are bound to seek above everything else, and singly, and with your whole heart—the approval and praise which God can give you, and which He desires to give you for your faithfulness to Him, if you will but be at the pains to deserve it. And the way to deserve it is simple and easy, for you have but to seek it. God is not like other masters, who may be displeased at the efforts which their servants make in their ignorance and good faith, intending to advance the interests of their lords, but failing to do so. Human masters discard such servants, and blame them as useless, but God rewards those who fail as well as those who succeed, provided only they seek His approval in simplicity. This is the aim which will elevate you and strengthen you, and make you courageous and fearless in the service for which you are where you are in His synagogue. The petty ambitions and jealousies, the fears and timidities, the clinging to attachments and personal interests, the anxieties as to the future, the apprehensions of failure and of possible risks, from a thousand different quarters, which now keep you back, will all seem small and unworthy of your thoughts when you have set your hearts truly to seek the Kingdom of God and nothing else.' He had spoken in the same kind of way, at least implying the same great principle, to His own disciples in the Sermon on the Mount, in the passages on which we have had to comment, concerning the absolute confidence in God which He desires to see in those who are to do anything for His service. The best of the men to whom He was now speaking, men like Nicodemus and Joseph and Gamaliel, may have been kept back by this want of the habitual earnest single pursuit of the approbation of God alone which is here suggested to them, as much as the more energetic and ambitious and pushing men, like Caiaphas, were forced onwards in their enterprizes of iniquity by their devotion to human success. The saints tell us that the very beginning of the spiritual course is the realization of the truth that we are to live as if there were nothing in the world to be attended to except God and our own souls, and that this is the essential foundation of all true liberty and of all true virtue.

The remainder of the passage before us may be considered as exemplifying the immense compassionateness and love of our Lord for these poor souls, who were to be so miserable in their opposition to His work and person. He seems to try to win them by His protest of pity and mercy for the miseries of their spiritual state, and of the consequences which it involved. He seems to speak of things which were before His own mind rather than before theirs—deep realities of the unseen world, the effect which their conduct must produce in their position before the eyes of God, and as to the judgment which He must form of them. Their consciences may have been uneasy with feelings of dissatisfaction at their state, while still they may not have cared much to probe their own wounds, or have had any great anxiety as to their position before God. They were blind and careless, and their hostility to our Lord was becoming a sort of passion, intensified by its want of success. Such a passion would give them little encouragement to enter into their own hearts silently and seriously, and calmly to consider how they stood, and what might be the issue of their attitude towards this new messenger of God, with whose claims they were inclined to deal so summarily. And all the time their responsibilities were mounting up before God, and their worship of human respect was writing itself in His books, as the cause of a most heinous unfaithfulness to their duties as the spiritual chiefs of His own people. Well indeed might He accuse them to His Father. He was the bearer to them of the most merciful and loving message that ever God, in His infinite goodness, had sent or could send to His creatures. His message was carefully authenticated and accredited by proofs and witnesses which they could not gainsay, and yet they had turned away from it in passion, on account of their love of human position and credit. In such cases an earthly messenger would return to him who had sent him, and complain of the treatment which he had received, and the king, whose envoy he was, would proceed at once to avenge his own honour by punishing the offenders. Such had been the prophecy of Moses. God had said that if they did not hear the words of the prophet who was to be sent, He would Himself be the avenger. Perhaps our Lord may allude to that passage of Moses. No, He seems to tell them now, no act of His should have the aim of hastening on the judgment which God might be preparing for them, He would make no charge against them, He was all on their side, His only desire was their salvation. This would be the one object in all His future dealings with them, in all His dealings with His Father regarding them. He was to pray for them and to plead for them to the very end, and when He was being crucified, He was to allege the excuse for them to His Father that they did not know what they did. This was a very different thing from accusing them to the Father. 'Think not,' He says, 'that I will accuse you to the Father.' The whole of His conduct to them was the conduct of One Who most tenderly loved them, and Who waived all His own rights of complaint against them out of love. He was not come now to judge, but to save. He was about to retire from their immediate neighbourhood, and even in Galilee, whither He was bound, when they sent their emissaries to watch and persecute Him, He was about to keep out of the way and in the background in the discharge of His great mission, in order not to provoke them too soon, and force them, by any act of His, to heap up greater guilt before God by their resistance to Him.

Afterwards, at the end of His Ministry, and just before His Passion, He said, what seems to illustrate this passage, as if the thought in our Lord's mind had then been of the same tenour, 'If any man hear My words and keep them not, I do not judge him, for I came not to judge the world but to save the world. He that despiseth Me, and receiveth not My words, hath one that judgeth him, the word that I have spoken, the same shall judge him in the Last Day.'[3] It cannot be denied that the words of

[3] St. John xii. 47, 48.

our Lord will rise up in judgment against these Jews and against all who at any time and under any circumstances have despised them, but He seems to promise that He will so conduct Himself as to let them have as little as may be to account for, and that He will now plead for them rather than accuse them. Or it may be understood, according to the idiom which our Lord so frequently uses, that His will not be the only or the chief accusation against them. As if He had said, it is not necessary that I should accuse you to the Father, the Judge of all mankind, for your accusation is already urged by Moses in whom you trust. 'There is one that accuseth you, even Moses, in whom you trust.' Not that Moses is to be supposed as pleading against the Jews before the throne of God's justice in the way in which, perhaps, the angels of little ones who are scandalized plead before the throne on high against those who have caused their ruin; but the accusation is already formed, because the words and writings of Moses were given them by God to lead them to our Lord, and their misuse and neglect of this means of grace was in itself an accusation. And He goes on to give the reason why the words of Moses will constitute their accusation and condemnation rather than His own, because they had turned away from Him through nothing else than neglect of the teaching of Moses. They could not have been faithful in their use of what Moses had left behind him without being led on to faithful submission to our Lord. And their unfaithfulness in regard of Moses and his writings involved, as by a necessary consequence, unfaithfulness in their treatment of our Lord, of Whom Moses wrote. But our Lord puts this also in a kind of hypothesis, speaking, as all through this discourse, with the utmost gentleness and modesty, 'For if you did believe Moses, you would perhaps believe Me also, for he wrote of Me. But, if you do not believe his writings, how will you believe My words?'

The solemn words of our Lord on this subject of the witness to Him of the great Jewish lawgiver and prophet, are full of significance to all time, for they show that the appointed means of grace, of whatever sort, of which men fail to avail themselves, are reckoned in the eyes of God as so many witnesses against them, or rather, as so many heads of accusation against them. We may, as has been said, even understand our Lord to mean, when He says that He will not 'accuse' them to the Father, that He will withdraw Himself from them for a time, in order not to increase their responsibility while they were so indisposed to listen to the voice by which God was addressing them. This is a principle, then, in the Kingdom of God, as regards the moral probation of men, and it suggests many thoughts of caution and warning, especially to those who have the greatest opportunities, either of listening to the invitations which God makes to them to enter the fold of salvation in the Catholic Church, or, if they are inside that fold, to make themselves perfect by all the rich supplies of grace which He furnishes therein. We have already seen how a little self-love, or a little cowardice in resisting human respect, may often be the cause of a declension from the upward path to which a strong clear faith invites the soul. And the concluding words of our Lord imply a different but not a less important lesson. They seem to teach us the principle that the manifestations of God are vouchsafed, as we may say, in a continuous chain, and that the links of this chain are meant to lead men on, the one to the other which comes next in succession. Thus it may be said, that natural religion is meant to lead men on to revelation, and that the earlier grades of revelation are the steps by which access is obtained to the higher. To turn away at the first step is to turn away from all that follow. On the other hand, the faithful use of the teachings of natural religion and conscience, in whatever state of society, and under whatever dispensation of God, will certainly prepare the soul for the acceptance of revelation, whenever the evidences of revelation are set before it, and the habit of faith which has begun by exercising itself on the few truths which had come down by primitive tradition, remains the same habit when its sphere is enlarged by the further declarations of God proposed to its acceptance, as the great counsel of redemption is matured. To believe Moses was implicitly to believe Christ, of Whom Moses spoke, and those who did not really believe Moses could not believe Christ. Our Lord says elsewhere, in His parable about the rich glutton and Lazarus, that if men did not believe Moses and the prophets, they would not be convinced if one went to them from the dead.[4] The words were exactly fulfilled in these Jewish rulers, and in the mass of the nation which followed them in their unbelief. They were already certain to reject all the further evidence of the Church. The Resurrection of our Lord from the dead, and His Ascension into Heaven, and all the wonders that followed on the giving of the Holy Ghost, fell on their ears and eyes as on the senses of the deaf and the blind. It is the same with the resistance to the Catholic Church in all ages. Men are found who profess the Catholic Creed, and declare that they stand or fall by the early Fathers. But they do not believe the Creed or the Fathers, any more than these rulers at Jerusalem believed Moses. For the Creed speaks of the indefectible existence of the Church as a matter of faith, and gives the notes by which she is to be known from

[4] St. Luke xvi. 31.

all other bodies falsely calling themselves churches. In the same way, the early Fathers witness to the obedience due to the Church; nor is there any single fact more clear in all history, than the fact that the Church, according to the Catholic doctrine, cannot fail, and that it is a mark of heresy to appeal from the living Church of our own day to a supposed 'holy undivided Church' of past centuries. Thus it is always true that the spirit of faith is incompatible with resistance to the Church. Those who are outside her pale have a certain number of fragmentary truths which they profess to believe, as the Jews professed to believe Moses, but if they really believe them they will be led on by them to the full faith of the Church, and if they do not accept the evidences of the Church, when they are set before them, it is a proof that they have never really believed the fragments which their systems of opinion have retained. They have thought them true, and accepted them as in harmony with their own researches, or their own conceptions of what ought to be, but they do not hold them on faith.

CHAPTER XVII.

The Disciples in the Cornfields.

St. Matt. xii. 1—8 ; St. Mark ii. 23—28 ; St. Luke vi. 1—5 ;
Vita Vitæ Nostræ, § 43.

THE incident of the miracle on the man at the Probatic Pool, and the long discussion between our Lord and the Jewish rulers which followed upon that miracle, must be regarded as marking a very important point in the onward progress of His Public Life. It was now plain that the authorities at Jerusalem would henceforth be our Lord's opponents, unless some marvellous change were wrought in them by the power of Divine grace. The disciples who had accompanied Him to Jerusalem must have found out that they, as well as their Master Himself, were the objects of hatred and suspicion from those to whom they had been accustomed to look up as the appointed teachers of the law of God, the guardians of the sacred deposit of prophecy and doctrine, and of the traditions of the elders, which were scarcely less venerable than the law itself. On the one hand, they had listened to His discourse with these rulers of Israel, and had heard Him assert things concerning Himself which may have enlarged very much indeed their own ideas concerning Him and His mission. They must have understood, as well as the Jewish rulers themselves, that He claimed to be the Son of God, and they may thus have risen to higher conceptions of His unity of nature with His Father, and the consequent dignity of His Person and of His works, than they had before formed. On the other hand, the Jewish rulers themselves had been brought into close personal collision with this marvellous Teacher, of Whom such fair reports had reached them from the distant parts of the country to which His Ministry had hitherto been mainly confined. They had been eye-witnesses of the effect of one of His great miracles, and, far more than that, they had found out that He claimed powers which seemed to override the law of God in so important a matter as the observance of the Sabbath Day. And, when He had been questioned by them and had argued with them, He had met them with language which in no way receded from the very highest pretensions and claims which could be imputed to Him. He had confronted them with singular majesty, though also with wonderful gentleness, and with the tenderest consideration for their spiritual maladies. But He had abated in nothing from the claims which implied Divine power and authority, and He had left them with solemn warnings and even with implied threats of judgment. It was evident that He was independent of their authority, and would take no heed of their injunctions. They might yield to Him, but He could never yield to them. In this position of things the seeds of all that was to follow were already germinating. The movement which had been begun might die away—if it continued, if it made advance, and gathered volume and strength, it must inevitably break on them in force, and either sweep them away or be itself shattered in the collision.

This visit of our Lord to Jerusalem, which seems to be mentioned by St. John chiefly for the sake of the discourse which was then delivered by Him in answer to the questionings of the priests and authorities of the Synagogue, after the miracle on the man at the pool, is not recorded by any other of the Evangelists, for reasons stated already more than once in the course of this work. St. John's account ends abruptly, with the last words of the discourse itself, and we are therefore left without any information as to what ensued after that discourse. It is probable that if our Lord had at that visit taught in the Temple for any number of days, something would have been said about that teaching by St. John, and it seems most reasonable to conjecture that He very soon indeed turned His back on the Holy City, the rulers of which were so ill-disposed either to receive His teaching themselves or to encourage others to receive it. Humanly speaking, as we may judge from St. John's language, it was unsafe for our Lord to remain in that neighbourhood, as the priests had already determined to seek to put Him to death. It may be that at this time He formed or cemented His loving friendship with Lazarus and his sisters, at least with Martha, for the blessed Magdalene had not yet been won to make herself His disciple, though even at this time she may have heard His conversation. He may have seen something of Nicodemus, and a few others who were inclined to the faith, if they had not already embraced it, and this may have been the extent of His success at this, His first visit to Jerusalem after His public preaching had begun. It must have been a strange disappointment to the ardent hearts of His disciples, who had seen Him work so many wonders in Galilee, and had been accustomed to see thousands hanging on His words wherever He went. It was one of the trials to which their faith in Him was necessarily to be exposed, in the providence of God, a trial of a kind which was now to begin to be more frequent with them. They may have gone up to Jerusalem with their hearts bounding with joyous expectation, looking forward to triumphs of their Master in the Temple which might eclipse the glories of His teaching in the synagogues throughout the country, and hoping to see Him recognized as the promised King of Israel and Son of David even by the multitude of Jews who would assemble for the feast from all parts of the Empire, and who might go back to their own countries with His name on their lips and His words and deeds in their hearts. What a prospect for the burning zeal of Peter, for the 'Sons of Thunder,' James and John, for simple Andrew and generous Philip and meditative Nathanael, for Thomas, slow of mind but as deep as any in his personal devotion, for Matthew, lately called, and already full of the accomplishment of the prophecies of his nation in every action and characteristic of our Lord! They had expected a crisis, a deciding point in the rise of the new Kingdom, and the crisis had come, in the form of what looked like a crushing defeat,— a single miracle had been wrought, a single great discourse delivered, and then their Master's life was in danger from the authorities, and He seemed obliged to withdraw and give up all His prospects at Jerusalem to save His life.

No contrast could possibly be greater than this between the reception of our Lord in the capital of the holy nation, and the immense and triumphant success, as it seemed, which He had met with in the province in which His home had always been all through the history of His Life. We can trace the contempt with which the learned men at the centre of ecclesiastical authority regarded 'the Galilæan.' But they could not but fear our Lord, though it was very true that they attempted to despise Him. It was, no doubt, a relief to these rulers at Jerusalem that our Lord did not remain long in the city after the feast was over. He never seems to have made any stay of more than a few days there, and the human reason for this must have been the attitude of these priests and doctors of the law towards Him. His field of predilection, the sphere of labour which He chose out, as had been prophesied of Him, and where He had as yet met with but little of hostility from rulers, either secular or ecclesiastical, was the despised land of Galilee, the country, as they afterwards said, out of which no prophet came. Thither then our Lord seems to have turned His steps almost as soon as the feast was over, and the second-first Sabbath, as it was called, in the first week after the Pasch, found Him and His little band of seven or eight disciples, either already in Galilee or not far from it. They were, as it seems, pushing on in their journey as far as the Sabbath Day's regulations would permit, and their way lay through the ripe cornfields, for it was now the same season of the year as when He had passed through Samaria, had sat by the well-side on the close of His day's walk, and when speaking to His disciples of the harvest of souls, He bade them lift up their eyes and see the countries, that the fields were white unto harvest. The merciful provisions of the Jewish law gave the wayfarers a right to pluck the ears as they passed through the fields, or even the grapes as they passed through the vineyards, and on this occasion the disciples were so hungry that they availed themselves of their privilege without scruple, and without hindrance from their Master. More than once we come upon little hints in the history, which speak to us of the poverty and hardness of life to which our Lord trained His disciples, after His own example, and it would seem also that they habitually thought but little of any provision for the morrow which they might need, as our Lord had taught them in the Sermon on the Mount. And perhaps His Divine words and the sweetness of His companionship made them even more forgetful of material things than

His teaching of itself might have made them. They had their Lord with them and that was enough. Their minds may have been full of the solemn teaching which they had just before listened to at Jerusalem, not primarily addressed to themselves, but more fruitful in their hearts than in the hearts of those to whom and for whose sake it had been delivered. The truths set forth had indeed been high, and the range of doctrine immense, embracing the whole of the evidences which the Providence of the Father had arranged for the conviction of all men of goodwill as to the mission and Person of His Son. Hearts like those of St. John and St. Peter would be full enough of these great truths to forget the necessities of the body, and besides, the journey which they could take on such a day could not be long, and they might well have set out before the time for their usual meal.

'And it came to pass, on the second-first Sabbath, that as He went through the cornfields, His disciples plucked the ears and did eat, rubbing them in their hands. And some of the Pharisees said to them, Why do you that which is not lawful on the Sabbath Days?' It seems from the other Evangelists that, as was often the case, the reproach, which was aimed in the first instance at the Master through the disciples, was immediately addressed by the same persons to our Lord Himself. 'The Pharisees said to Him, Behold, Thy servants do that which is not lawful to do on the Sabbath Days.' It is not certain from the text of the Gospels whether the supposed illegality consisted in the eating the ears of corn on the Sabbath, or in the slight manual labour involved in rubbing them in their hands, in order to extract the grain. It can hardly be supposed that the first was regarded as unlawful. We seem to find here, as in the remainder of the history of this immediate period, the traces of the very great impression which had been made by the miracle on the impotent man at the pool. It is not likely that the miracle remained unknown to the people at large throughout the day on which it had been worked, and the long argument between our Lord and His questioners must have produced a very deep effect on their minds. It is not likely that the rulers would have given to others a favourable version of the position assumed by our Lord in that disputation, and it might easily have got about that the Prophet of Nazareth had incurred the suspicion of violating the Sabbath, and even of advancing claims to a Divine authority which had seemed to the appointed guardians of orthodoxy and of ecclesiastical discipline inadmissible. When a piece of formalism takes possession of the minds of persons of an exterior profession of sanctity and regularity which is far from corresponding to the interior of their hearts, it is well known by experience how bigoted they can be in their rigour against what appears to contradict their own hard rules. It is well known also how quickly the bigotry of a few can communicate itself to a multitude in such a case, and how the news of some formal violation of an external rule will fly over a whole community, and set people everywhere on the watch against the supposed offender. It is certainly surprising, according to ordinary rules of experience, that what had passed at Jerusalem should be so soon communicated to other parts of the country, so that it should not be possible for our Lord and His disciples to pass through a field of corn in their passage from one part to another, without exposing themselves to criticism by what they did. But everything at this time seems to combine to show us that the attitude assumed by the priests at the capital, had an almost immediate effect in other parts of the country.

The answer which our Lord made to His critics on

this occasion has been carefully summarised for us by the Evangelists. It differs very importantly from the answer which, as we have seen from St. John, was made by Him to the priests at Jerusalem. There He had at once gone to the root of the objection, and had cut it off, as it were, at once, by telling them that He was the Son of God, and the Lord of all. He had not only not excused Himself, but He had implied that they were in great danger from their ignorance or their determined blindness as to His authority. He, as it were, called them before the tribunal of His own majesty, and made them the accused instead of Himself. In the present instance, and in all the other instances of which we have any subsequent record as to this kind of objection, He began by placing Himself on their own ground, and arguing as they might have argued, in defence of men like themselves. It is remarkable, however, that here also He tells them, as we shall see, that He had authority over the Sabbath, but He first of all defends the action of His disciples on the grounds of which we speak. And in this perhaps He was considering the future action of His Church with regard to this law of the Sabbath, which was not to limit itself to a change of the day on which this great solemnity was in future to be observed, in honour of His own Resurrection, but was to extend itself also to the manner of the observance itself, making it far more spiritual and less carnal than before. Nor does He in His Church alter any positive Divine laws without such considerations of mercifulness and care for man, as are here suggested in the answers which He now makes.

The grounds, then, of our Lord's answer on this occasion are altogether five. First, He alleges the example of David, who in case of necessity had seen that the positive law of God as to the incapacity of mere laymen to eat the 'loaves of proposition' which had been set before the ark of the Lord in the tabernacle, might be made to yield to the natural law which enjoins the preservation of human life by every lawful means. 'Have you not read what David did, when he was hungry, and those that were with him? How he went to the house of God, and did eat the loaves of the proposition, which it was not lawful for him to eat, nor for them that were with him, but for the priests only?' In the next place our Lord alleges the example of what was done every week in the Temple, where, in order that the sacrifices might be duly offered, the law of the Sabbath, according to the strict letter, was violated by the priests, who killed and prepared the victims, offering them on the altar as holocausts or otherwise, a service which involved a very considerable amount of labour. 'Or have you not read, in the Law, that on the Sabbath Day the priests in the Temple break the Sabbath, and are without blame?' To this answer He adds a few words which imply His own great dignity. It might be said that what was done in the Temple was for the service of the Temple, and the worship of God, and that there could be no argument to ordinary practice from such an example. This objection our Lord meets by a direct negative: 'But I tell you, that there is here a greater than the Temple.' The next part of His answer is an appeal to the principle of 'mercy and not sacrifice,' of which He had already spoken in His reply to the first criticism of this kind which He had had to meet—the criticism on His conduct in not insisting on the observance of fasts and other public works of mortification on the part of His disciples. 'And if you had known what this meant, I will have mercy and not sacrifice, you would not have condemned the innocent.' The fourth head of His reply is related to us by St. Mark: 'And He said to them, the Sabbath was made for man, and not man for the Sabbath.' And this leads up to the last head, which is given by St. Matthew and St. Luke, as well as by St. Mark, though those two Evangelists omit the declaration about the Sabbath being made for man— 'For the Son of Man is Lord, even of the Sabbath.' These are the heads of doctrine on which our Lord here rests His justification of the conduct of His disciples, and of His own permission thereof. In the next chapter, when we have to speak of the miracle on the man whose hand was withered, we shall find Him arguing on another ground again. For the present we must consider a little more in detail each of these arguments, which combine with those which are used elsewhere, in similar matter, to make up a complete account of the reasons on which a positive law like that of the Sabbath may be dispensed with.

The example of David which is here cited by our Lord is to be found in the First Book of Kings.[1] David was flying very suddenly from the injustice and murderous designs of Saul against him, and had no provision of food for himself and the small band of followers who accompanied him. He went to Nob, where the Tabernacle and Ark then were, and prevailed on Achimelech, the high priest, who was assisted and afterwards succeeded by Abiathar, his son, to give him the twelve 'loaves of proposition,' which had been set before the Ark, and which had lately been removed, as was the custom each week, to be succeeded by other loaves. It was not lawful for any but the priests themselves to eat of this consecrated bread, which was placed before the Ark, week after week, to testify that God was the feeder and guardian of the twelve tribes. But on this

---

[1] 1 Kings xxi. 6.

occasion David had had no scruple in taking these loaves for the necessities of his little company and himself, and the priest had willingly given them, though he was afterwards put to death at the command of Saul for so doing. This, then, was an instance of the suspension of a positive law by the natural law of necessity. If it be applied to the case of the disciples, we must understand from the fact that our Lord thus reasoned, that the necessities of the little band of future Apostles were great and urgent, and we thus see that they were indeed leading hard lives in their following of their Divine Master. If the soldiers of David were thought worthy of the 'loaves of proposition' in their extreme need, the Apostles were in the like case, and, even if it had been a violation of the strict law to eat as they had done, they were justified on the same grounds as the soldiers of David. Our Lord takes for granted that the example of David, one of the great saints of God, will suffice for His critics. For, at all events, such an action would not have been recorded in Sacred Scripture, unless it had been an action worthy of admiration and praise.

His next argument is taken from the weekly violation, or apparent violation, of the Sabbath, in the Temple itself. And here, as has been remarked by some commentators, every word is emphatic and seems to add to the force of the argument. The priests themselves, in the Temple itself, and on the Sabbath itself, and for the purposes of the Divine worship itself, violated or seemed to violate the Sabbath, week after week. The law, therefore, of the Sabbath might yield to something else besides the necessities of preserving life. It might yield to the exigencies of the service of God, even the simple liturgical service, which after all, is a matter of positive law only. All that was required to justify the violation of the Sabbath by the priests themselves, was the rule as to the daily sacrifices which might be or might not be. It is here, however, necessary, in order to apply the argument to the case before Him, that our Lord should allege some such reason for the act of the disciples as existed in the case from which the argument was drawn. He does this without hesitation, and at the same time, as always, with the utmost modesty and meekness. The reason which made the example of the priests in the Temple applicable as an answer to the cavils of His critics, was His own personal dignity. The priests were dispensed from the law of the Sabbath, because they were the ministers of the Temple and of the worship, which was there carried on. It is clear that our Lord's argument implied that the Apostles were His ministers, and as such, equally entitled, or much more so, to the privilege of the priests. So He says plainly, though without speaking of Himself in the first person: 'But I tell you, that there is here a greater than the Temple.' That is, the disciples were engaged in His service. They were labouring in the instruction of the crowds who flocked to His teaching, their whole time was spent in the work which He set them to do, and, even if they were at rest on the Sabbath, still they were to be considered as men who were prevented from making the ordinary provision for themselves and their sustenance, and so were allowed to seek it in extraordinary ways and at unusual times. All that they did for their own sustenance, for the preservation of their bodily health and vigour, was to be considered as a part of the service of One greater than the Temple, and so as exempt from the ordinary laws against work of that kind on the Sabbath Day.

Our Blessed Lord's third argument is a repetition of the quotation from the Prophet,[2] which He had used in

[2] Osee vi. 6.

answer to the critics who had found fault with Him for eating and drinking with publicans and sinners. 'If you knew what this meaneth, I will have mercy and not sacrifice, you would never have condemned the innocent.' In the former case the words of the Prophet had been alleged to justify an apparent departure from the strictness of social intercourse which was a kind of service to God, inasmuch as it enjoined on those who professed religiousness of life, to abstain from the company of persons of laxer ways and looser habits, such a departure being allowed for the sake of charity, and of the opportunities which it might afford of doing good to those who could be approached in no other way, or in no other way so well. It was an act of mercy to go among the publicans and sinners, to condescend to their rude ways and conversation, for the sake of winning their affection and confidence, and so gradually leading them on to better things. To abstain from such intercourse was not wrong in itself. It was in a certain way an act of religion, inasmuch as it honoured God by the assertion of a high principle and a strict standard of virtue. But God preferred mercy to sacrifice, as the Prophet had taught, and so the other conduct was the higher of the two, at all events in cases like that which was censured by the Pharisees. How does this principle apply here to the case of the disciples? It seems to apply in two ways. In the first place, the observance of the strict law of the Sabbath, if it applied to the case of the disciples in their great hunger, would have been an act of religion—a sacrifice of their sufferings in order not to break that strict law. But to indulge them in their need, and to encourage them to supply their wants in the way that was open to them, was an act of mercy, and that was more pleasing to God as such, than the act of religion at so great a cost to them. In the second place, the words of our Lord may be understood as applying to the judgment which the Pharisees had formed of the act of the disciples. No doubt there might be cases in which such a judgment might seem to be prompted by a zeal for the honour of God, by the observance of the strict law. But it was an act of mercy to interpret favourably all that they saw, and therefore they might easily have concluded that there was some strong reason of necessity for an act like that which they censured so severely, in persons who were certainly not likely to be acting in that manner without some good motive. The disciples could hardly be accused of being gluttons or self-indulgent persons, and the act which they had done, after all, did not amount to a very great self-indulgence. Thus our Lord might mean to say that a little more mercifulness in judging would have saved the Pharisees from a censorious judgment, which was contrary to the spirit of the prophetic saying which He quoted. As the word 'innocent' is in the plural number in the original, it seems most natural to adopt this interpretation.

Two more heads of argument remain as alleged on this occasion by our Blessed Lord. 'He said to them,' says St. Mark, 'The Sabbath was made for man, and not man for the Sabbath.' The meaning of this seems to be that the institution of the Sabbath was made with the direct intention and end that it should serve man, both in his physical and spiritual interests, by providing him with wholesome rest and recreation for the body, and by securing him a special time set apart for the worship of God and the care of the affairs of his soul, which would be neglected and forgotten if there had been no such fixed time for them. Therefore, it would follow, if at any time the observation of this institution was found, from particular circumstances, to be injurious instead of beneficial, to these interests of man, then the end of the institution would be lost by its observance rather than served. Thus we find in the history of the Machabees, that the Jews found that they must not observe the law so strictly as not to fight in self-defence on the Sabbath Day,[3] although it would have been easy for God to defend them by some miraculous interposition if they had endangered themselves by the observance of the precept under such circumstances. This would hold good in case of any sudden danger or emergency. It would be wrong not to put out a fire or not to stop an inundation, not to secure a harvest when there was danger of bad weather coming on, and the like, on the Sabbath, or to force persons, to whose health it would be injurious, to attend the service of Mass, or the like, on a day on which they could not leave their homes. On this ground then, also, that is, on the general principle that the end is of greater importance than the means, our Lord defends the apparent violation of the Sabbath of which His critics complained.

It need hardly be said, how important the principle which our Lord here lays down has proved in the formation and administration of the Church after Him. We can trace its working in a hundred different ways, notably in all that concerns the sacraments themselves. For it seems to be on this principle that they have been made so simple and common in their form and matter, and also that the Church is so extremely indulgent in dispensing with the safeguards which might naturally be insisted on to protect them against disrespect. She shows her reverence for these blessed means of grace, and especially, of course, for the Sacrament of the Eucharist in which our Lord makes Himself present in a new way, by the regulations on which she insists as to those who minister them and those who partake of

[3] 1 Mach. ii. 41.

them. But, at the same time, the precautions of her reverent love are almost over-ridden in many cases by her extreme condescension to the wants of her children, for whose sake these precious treasures are entrusted to her care. And when we consider the immense humiliations to which our Lord is sometimes exposed by His love for men, in that last-named Adorable Sacrament, no further commentary on this sense of the maxim now before us can be needed. It is remarkable that the same spirit of rigorism, which made the Pharisees and Scribes so severe in their interpretation of the law of the Sabbath, should always have been rife in men of the same character in Christian times. Rigorism is the natural companion of hypocrisy, but it is not always confined to the hypocritical. There will always be found men who have an instinctive tendency to severity—and it is one of the prime devices of the Evil One to make such men his instruments in his war against souls. These are the men whose maxim it really is, in contradiction to our Lord's teaching, that men are for the sacraments and not the sacraments for men. They teach practically that men are never good enough to approach the sacraments, whereas our Lord and His Church have arranged certain clear and not exacting conditions on which men are to receive the sacraments, not being saints before they are worthy to receive them, but receiving them in the hope of becoming holy by their use. The saints of God have often had to fight a hard battle against this deadly rigorism, in order to persuade men not to be afraid of the fountains of life and spiritual strength, which our Lord has provided for them. Thus we may see that our Lord was legislating for all time in the Church, when He insisted on this simple proverbial maxim, which embodies so much of His Divine wisdom and love for man.

The last reason here alleged, which is mentioned by all the three Evangelists who speak of the incident before us, is contained in the words, 'The Son of Man is Lord also of the Sabbath. In St. Mark's account, in which, alone of the three, the words just now commented on about the end of the Sabbath, occur, this last reason is connected with the former by the particle 'therefore.' 'Therefore the Son of Man is Lord of the Sabbath also.' This connection is wanting in the other Evangelists. If we are to insist on it, as it is put by St. Mark, it would signify that, as the institution of the Sabbath was for the benefit and not for the injury of mankind, our Lord, as the Son of Man, the Head of the human race, the new Adam, might be understood as having power and authority from God to alter or interpret the law of the Sabbath, or to dispense with it or take it away, as it might seem good to Him for the advantage of the race of which He was the Lord and King. This would imply, as to the case of the disciples who had given scandal to the Pharisees by eating the ears of corn, that our Lord, if it had been necessary, might have granted them a dispensation for that particular liberty which they had taken with the law, on account of the circumstances in which they were at the time. It could hardly be expected that this claim would be acknowledged as valid by His enemies. But it belonged to the completeness of the treatment of the whole subject which might be convenient on such an occasion as this, that the claim should be asserted, especially as the time was to come in His Church when this power of the Son of Man was to be actually used, for the purpose of transferring the observance in question to the Christian Sunday. And, if we are not to see in the words before us that particular connection with the preceding words of which we are speaking, then the words before us are a simple assertion of the power and authority of the Son of Man. This then was another of the royal prerogatives of our Lord in His Human Nature, that He might alter and rearrange, if it so pleased Him, even the positive institutions of the Divine law, and thus we have another link added to the chain of revelations concerning His own dignity, of which the disciples might take heedful note, although the words might convey nothing more than a fresh appearance of arrogant assumption to the ears of the Pharisees to whom they were more immediately addressed.

It may seem at first sight somewhat strange, that our Lord should have insisted so very strongly as we see that He did insist, on laying down, in the clearest possible manner, and in face of great risk and great opposition, the true doctrine concerning the Sabbath and the rights of the Son of Man concerning it. At the very time that He was retiring from before His enemies, and condescending in so many ways to humour their prejudices, He was nevertheless peremptory and unflinching on this single point. Without entering more fully on this particular point of controversy, we may be able to see that His care to provide, beyond all mistake, for the prerogatives of the Church, which were to be founded on those which He claimed for Himself as the Son of Man, had a large share in determining this part of His conduct. We have seen how peremptorily He refused to bind His disciples to any Jewish customs as to public and general fasting, and that He gave as His reason for this that the time had not yet come for the regulations of the new Kingdom in these respects, and also that He hinted that, when the time did come, those regulations would be altogether in accordance with the new spirit of the Gospel dispensation. All this was reserved for the Church after Him. That was a matter of positive legislation, and on the other hand, there were to be many points of legislation committed to the Church, which were to be actual innovations and changes from what had before prevailed in the synagogue. The principle on which all these changes were to be made, was that which He enunciated in the words of which we are speaking—that the Son of Man is Lord also of the Sabbath. If He was Lord also of the Sabbath, He was Lord of the whole sacrificial and ceremonial system of worship and the like, He was Lord of circumcision, He was Lord of such matters as the difference between meats, clean or unclean, He was Lord even of the law of marriage and divorce, He was Lord of the whole system of the law of Moses and of the positive institutions of God which were even older than that law. Thus, when He said what He did about the children of the bridals, and the new wine and new bottles, He implied that He had a whole system of His own, rites and laws and priesthood and sacrifice and sacraments, which He was to introduce when and as He thought fit, and with absolute independence and royal authority. And when He said that He was Lord also of the Sabbath Day, He claimed authority over all that was old in this way, as well as over what He chose to establish as new.

It was most important that this claim should be put forth by our Lord Himself, and in such a way as to leave no possible opportunity for mistake as to His meaning. It is therefore fair to suppose that He chose the question of the Sabbath for this purpose, not only for the sake of leaving on record His teaching as to the right manner of observing the Sabbath itself, but also that it might be established beyond all question that His authority extended to all such matters as the

Sabbath, that is, to all the positive institutions of the Divine Law as the Jews had received them. No better instance could possibly have been taken, both on account of the importance of the Sabbath in the Jewish system, and on account of the prominent and conspicuous character of any departure that He might practise, or enjoin on others, from the established usages on this point. To tell people not to circumcise, or not to offer the sacrifices of the Old Law, was to tell them something that might have passed without notice. But to tell them, or encourage them, to seem to break the Sabbath, was a thing as to which no mistake was possible. The Church has gained immensely by His doctrine and example as to the observance of the Sabbath, for if He had not done as He did, a thousand good works of mercy and charity would have remained unsanctioned or proscribed, on the very day of all others on which they are the most pleasing to God, and most open to the generality of mankind. And if our Lord had not laid down the law, that the Son of Man is Lord of the Sabbath, a very large part of the field on which the Church has exercised her power over the positive institutions of religion for the benefit of her children, would have been closed against her. Such is the momentous importance of these incidents in our Lord's Ministry. It is quite possible that the more acute of His enemies understood the extent of His claims, and that their resistance to Him was not caused so much by the difference of opinion between Him and them, as it might seem, as to the lawfulness of this or that act on the Sabbath, as by the instinctive feeling that made them perceive in Him the Lawgiver of a New Dispensation, claiming powers that went even higher and further than the powers of Moses himself.

CHAPTER XVIII.

The man with the withered hand.

St. Matt. xii. 9—14; St. Mark iii. 1—6; St. Luke vi. 6—11;
Vita Vitæ Nostræ, § 44.

It seems to have been immediately after this incident of the ears of corn, and the complaint made by the Pharisees on account of the conduct of the disciples, that the question as to the Sabbath was again raised, and the dissidence between our Lord and the Jewish authorities brought to a head, in a manner which made all hope of their toleration of Him impossible. Our Lord acted in this instance with deliberate determination, as if to show that He would in no manner compromise the truth which He had asserted, or allow anything to stop Him from giving the most unmistakeable example as to the right observance of the Sabbath. This incident is related by all the three historical Evangelists, and had, no doubt, a very high importance in their minds. The details of the scene, as in other similar cases, are to be gathered in their entire fulness by considering the Evangelical records as supplementary one to the other. The Evangelists do not all tell the story in the same way, but here, as in other instances, we gain a great deal by their diversity, for every particular addition made by each serves to make the picture more forcible and vivid.

The scene of this incident was different, as St. Matthew tells us, from the spot at which the discussion about the eating the ears of corn on the Sabbath Day had occurred. 'When He had passed from thence,' on another Sabbath, as St. Luke says, 'He entered into the synagogue and taught. There was a man there who had a withered hand, and the Scribes and Pharisees watched if He would heal on the Sabbath Day, that they might find an accusation against Him.' They came to the synagogue, not for any holy purpose of prayer or worship, to listen to the word of God, or gain instruction from His teaching, but to watch Him; and when they saw there the man with his right hand withered, their first thought seems to have been, not for his good, not whether the merciful Wonder-worker Who was there present to teach would vouchsafe to illustrate His words of truth and clemency by removing the disability under which the poor man was labouring, but whether this occasion of the exercise of His healing power might not be turned by themselves against Him, by furnishing the opportunity which they were seeking of bringing Him before one of the ecclesiastical tribunals, under a charge of the violation of the Sabbath. St. Matthew tells us that they asked our Lord, thus raising the question themselves, 'Is it lawful to heal on the Sabbath Day?' and that they did this with a view to accusing Him. Thus our Lord was directly challenged by them, and, as it were, threatened with a serious charge, if He did not give way as to the point which He had lately asserted with so much majesty at Jerusalem.

But 'He knew their thoughts,' says St. Luke, and He determined to give them their answer in the most pointed and authoritative manner. 'And He said to the man who had the withered hand, Arise and stand forth in the midst, and rising he stood forth.' He, then, had faith enough to obey our Lord, Who had no apparent right to command him, and then our Lord turned to His questioners, and, as if to prevent all mistake as to His own meaning, He said to them, 'I ask you'—you have asked Me, and shall presently be answered, but first I ask you to declare your own doctrine plainly—'I ask you if it be lawful on the Sabbath Day to do good or to do evil, to save life or to destroy?' The alternative question seems almost to suggest a reflection on their own malice. He knew their thoughts, and in His sight certainly they were bent on evil, they were contriving a snare for Himself with a view to destroy His life. For no one would have said that it was lawful on the Sabbath, or on any day, to do evil or to destroy life. Yet this, in truth, was the purpose of these men, who all the while were persuading themselves of the purity of their intentions, and taking credit for the zeal with which they were preserving the Sabbath from violation. They had no answer to make to this question, 'and they held their peace.' That is, they would not avow their own unreasonable and self-contradictory rigorism. They were ready enough to find fault with Him if He did what they expected, and apparently wished, but not ready to say in plain terms what they held on the point in question. 'And He said to them, What man shall there be among you that hath one sheep, and if the same fall into a pit on the Sabbath Day, will he not take hold of it and lift it up? How much better is a man than a sheep! Therefore it is lawful to do a good deed on the Sabbath Day.'

This argument, then, must be added to the others already adduced as to the right observance of the Sabbath. It is very like the argument drawn in the last preceding chapter from the example of David, whose conduct in eating the loaves of proposition was to be defended by the necessities of the case. But here the argument is stronger, for it is from life, from ordinary actions, and from the common example of persons like themselves, and from the care of the inferior animals, which were of much less value than man. It does not, however, seem that this simple and gentle argument produced any response from the adversaries of our Lord. They would neither say that they were convinced, nor make any objection to the reasoning—very much as so many adversaries of our Lord in His Church will take no note whatever of her arguments, or of the proofs of their own state of heresy or schism, but remain silent till the moment comes when they may seize an opportunity of bringing against her some accusation which has already been refuted a score of times. 'And looking round upon them all,' and 'with anger,' as St. Mark tells us, from the faithful memory of St. Peter, who was there watching every movement and look of his beloved Master, 'being grieved with the blindness of their hearts, He saith to the man, Stretch forth thy hand,' and he stretched it forth and it was restored to health, even as the other.' It is hardly possible to imagine a more complete discomfiture than that of these enemies of our Lord on this occasion. They were very probably emissaries sent down from Jerusalem, with the express purpose and commission to watch Him, and to accuse Him, if He again violated, as they thought, the law of the Sabbath by working a miracle upon that day. They were therefore the representatives of the central and supreme authority, and so, perhaps, of greater credit and estimation than the Scribes and Pharisees of the province into which they had been sent. They had put the question to our Lord in public, and so practically taken up, in the eyes of the people present, the position of His judges or at least His critics. It was not now a miracle wrought in the midst of a crowd which did not notice at the time what had occurred, but in the synagogue itself, and in the presence of a multitude who were more likely to sympathize with the sufferer who had been relieved, than with the strict formalists who objected to the nominal breach of the law. The miracle was worked after distinct opportunity given to them to express their opinion on the legality of the act, and after they had at all events indirectly but unmistakeably protested against it in the name of the law. And notwithstanding their opposition, our Lord had brushed aside the technical reasons which might be alleged on the side of strictness, and had gladdened the hearts of His disciples and of the multitude, as well as that of the poor sufferer himself, by a display of His miraculous power—a display which implied that He was right and that they were wrong in their view of the legal question, as it involved the sanction of God to the doctrine which He laid down, and the disapproval of God of the doctrine which was opposed thereto.

They had not yet come to their final and most abominable device, of asserting that His miracles were worked by means of a collusion between Himself and the powers of evil; and thus they were driven to absolute silence and confusion. Henceforth it was clear, as our Lord said, that it was lawful to do good on the Sabbath Day. The miracle proved this, as much as the miracle on the paralytic man had proved that the Son of Man had power on earth to forgive sins. God had spoken by the miracle which had been wrought, as He had spoken on that former occasion by the healing of the paralytic. In each case there had been cavillings before the miracle was worked, and these had been put to the test of an appeal to God, when our Lord enjoined the action which showed that the Divine power was at hand to second His words. This being the case, the enemies of our Lord were forced either to acknowledge His doctrine true and their own interpretation of the Law false, or to question the truth of the miracle which had been wrought. This course we find them afterwards adopting in regard to the man who had been born blind,[1] as they would gladly have done in the case of the first Apostolical miracle mentioned in the Acts, the cure of the man at the beautiful gate of the Temple.[2] But there was no possibility in the case before us of any such subterfuge. It is clear that the man was well known, he was among his friends and neighbours, and the fact of his disablement must have been notorious. But instead of giving in their adhesion in consequence of the miracle, they were 'filled with madness,' as St. Luke tells us. 'The Pharisees going out immediately, made a consultation with the Herodians, against Him, how they might destroy Him.' They had come to the synagogue in the execution of their commission to watch our Lord, and probably in hopes that something might happen which they might be able to report. They intended to accuse Him, it is said, by which we may suppose that the local tribunal might have had authority enough to deal with Him as a breaker of the Sabbath. But this was probably made impossible by the conspicuous character of the miracle, and by the feeling of the people in His favour.

There was one other resource open to them, though it was a resource which they might well have been ashamed to use. This part of the country was under the jurisdiction of the Tetrarch Herod, and if he could be persuaded to take any measures against our Lord by their representations, His preaching might at least be stopped, if He were not thrown into prison like His Precursor. The power of the princes of the Herodian family came entirely from their dependence on the Roman Cæsars, and it might have been expected that

[1] St. John ix.   [2] Acts iv. 14.

the stricter Jews would have been unwilling to avail themselves of it for religious purposes. But, just as they afterwards used the Roman power itself as their instrument of bringing about the crucifixion of our Lord, so now men of this class were willing to endanger His life, by making Him an object of suspicion to the Tetrarch and his officials. First they talked with one another, as St. Luke tells us, 'what they might do to Jesus,' and then they 'immediately made a consultation,' or conspiracy, 'with the Herodians against Him, how they might destroy Him.' The Herodians were the courtiers of the Tetrarch and the subordinate magistrates of his government. As a body of men they were of low loose character, in the eyes of the Jews, for the Herods always aped the Roman Emperors and affected the modern civilization of that day, which consisted very much in a certain varnish of Greek 'culture,' as it may have been called, and was practically offensive to the better Jews on account of its low standard of morality and its sceptical consequences. That a princess like Salome, the daughter of Herodias, should have danced a lascivious dance at a public banquet, as we shall presently see when we come to speak of the murder of St. John Baptist, shows well enough the tone of these petty licentious courts, the manners of which were probably about as pure and manly as those of some of the Indian Rajahs of our time. Yet these were the men with whom the envoys of the chief priests, or at least these Pharisees of Galilee, were content to ally themselves against our Lord. It would not be difficult to persuade such men that the immense popularity which He has acquired would be a political danger, either directly to the Government of the Tetrarch, or indirectly to the peace of the province for which he was responsible to his Roman master. Or perhaps the Herodians, as Pilate afterwards, saw through the pretended zeal of these men for the peace and tranquillity of the country, understanding the true motives which made them so eager in their hostility to our Lord. Perhaps it was a jest at the Court of the Tetrarch, that the sanctimonious emissaries of the high priests had suddenly become loyal to the Herodian dynasty, and been taken with an access of zeal for the security of public tranquillity. Perhaps 'it made the laughter of an afternoon,' for the sensual revellers in Herod's magnificent palace on the lake, that these jealous priests should imagine that their envy could successfully hide itself under so poor a device.

We do not hear much of the danger to our Lord which may have resulted from this, the first of a thousand such unholy leagues between the professors of religion and strictness and the rude and profligate world. But there may still have been some danger. As it is, the league is chiefly memorable as having produced a change in our Lord's usual habits of preaching in the cities and towns, and as having set the example which has been only too faithfully followed in every age of the Christian Church down to our own time. Sectarian envy and jealousy have never been scrupulous as to the allies with whom they unite against our Lord and against His Church or His servants. Whether it is Arianism leaguing with the corrupt court of the sons of Constantine, or the enemies of St. Chrysostom with the flatterers of Eudoxia, or the Greeks welcoming the yoke of the Turk as a protection against the Pope, or Anglicanism truckling at the feet of the royal power, or Jansenism making common cause with Madame de Pompadour and the French philosophers against the Society of Jesus, or 'Old Catholicism' fawning on the

German Chancellor—in a thousand different instances in history we have repeated, over and over again, this typical incident of the Pharisees banding with the Herodians against our Lord Jesus Christ.

CHAPTER XIX.

The servant of God.

St. Matt. xii. 15—21 ; St. Mark iii. 7—12 ; *Vita Vitæ Nostræ*, § 45.

SOMETHING has already been said of the effect of the league between the Pharisees and Herodians upon our Lord's movements. It is probable that at this time of His great popularity—for His popularity had hardly as yet begun to wane, even if it ever truly waned until the last—He might have braved His persecutors and aroused the people, if it had so pleased Him, against them. The people are usually fickle and easily misled, but in this case all their natural feelings would be on the side of our Lord. Nothing but fear for themselves could have kept them back. But our Lord was to set an example to all who were afterwards to bear His name and commission, an example of the utmost meekness combined with the greatest firmness, and of extreme gentleness united to courage. His great and only object was the salvation of souls—of the souls of His enemies as well as of those who were ready to listen to Him. It is obvious that the work committed to Him by His Father required the utmost delicacy and forbearance in dealing with those whom He thus came to save, among whom many were at present in a state of mind altogether averse to His teaching, while others were but slightly advanced in the teaching of His school. Our Lord seems to teach us that under such circumstances it is better to be silent or to yield, as far as may be, to the hostility of men, who can never be converted while they are resisted, and that it is to this principle that the Evangelist attributed the line of conduct of which he now speaks.

'But Jesus knowing it,' that is, knowing the designs of His persecutors, and their league with the officials of Herod to destroy Him, retired from thence; 'retired,' says St. Mark, 'with His disciples to the sea'—that is, as appears, to the shores of the Lake of Galilee—'and a great multitude followed Him from Galilee and Judæa, and from Jerusalem, and from Idumæa, and from beyond Jordan, and they about Tyre and Sidon, a great multitude, hearing the things which He did, came to Him; and He spoke to His disciples that a small ship should wait on Him, because of the multitude, lest they should throng Him, for He healed many, so that they pressed upon Him for to touch Him, as many as had evils; and the unclean spirits, when they saw Him, fell down before Him, and they cried, saying, Thou art the Son of God. And He strictly charged them that they should not make Him known.' The picture here given is of one of the busy times of our Lord's ordinary missionary preaching. The only difference between the circumstances here described and those which were ordinary in such periods, is that our Lord was now in the country part of the lake side, not in any town or village, not teaching in the synagogues, but in the open air and from the boat which attended on His movements, and took Him, as it appears, from one spot on the lake to another. This change of place, by means of the lake, gave Him perfect security against the attempts of His enemies, if they had been inclined to make any effort to arrest Him on any charge, either of a political or an ecclesiastical crime;

and His attraction was so powerful that He had no lack of audience for His teaching. St. Mark seems to take a pleasure in recording the many distant parts from which the crowd which flocked after Him was gathered. The whole country from Tyre and Sidon to Idumæa, and from the sea-coast to the parts of the Holy Land beyond the Jordan, was in commotion because of Him, and was sending its pilgrims to Him to be healed or taught. Wherever He went the people crowded after Him, so that the pressure became inconvenient. The great object of the crowd was to obtain miraculous cures for themselves, or for those they carried with them. And the power of our Lord was shown also in the casting out of devils. In their case, as usual, He would not allow the devils to proclaim Who He was, though they were ready enough with their mocking or terrified cries, 'Thou art the Son of God.'

It is here that St. Matthew takes the occasion to draw attention to the fact, which no doubt impressed him, and others like him, so much—the fact of the fulfilment of the prophecies in this conduct of our Lord. This may have been almost the first time that he had himself accompanied our Lord on these missionary excursions. But not even the multitudes which thronged after Him and the numberless cures of all kinds which He wrought, not even the witness of the fearful enemies of God and man in their crouching terror before His feet, were so striking to the mind of the Apostles as the gentleness and forbearance of our Lord. At the very time that He was thus the leader of large masses of people from all parts of the country, at the very time that He was displaying so magnificently the powers of healing diseases and of dispossessing demoniacs which belonged to Him as the Incarnate Son of God, He was still keeping aloof from the towns and villages where He would have been so gladly welcomed, in order not to drive His enemies to desperation and bring on any sudden collision with the upstart power of Herod or the authority of the priests at Jerusalem. This seemed to be more Divine than the exercise of His preternatural powers, or even the teaching with which it was accompanied. And St. Matthew, ever on the look out for the fulfilments of ancient predictions and expectations in our Lord, here quotes a beautiful passage of Isaias on this special point of the gentleness and forbearance of the promised Messias, and by so doing he connects with our Lord a whole chain of predictions which are contained in the same part of the evangelical prophecy. The burthen of these passages is to describe our Lord under the title of the 'servant of God,' and a consideration of the whole series together would furnish us with a very instructive commentary on His character in that capacity. The series begins at the forty-second chapter, which is here quoted, and leads up to the famous description of the Passion and humiliation of the 'servant of God' in the fifty-third chapter of the Prophet. Although there are several places in this and other parts of the Prophet in which the people of Israel is personified as the servant of God, still there can be no doubt that there are many others, in which the words cannot be made to fit the nation as such, especially this passage, and that in the fifty-third chapter just mentioned, in which the Prophet speaks of the servant of God justifying man by his sufferings.

In the passage with which we are now concerned, St. Matthew does not follow quite uniformly either the Hebrew or the Alexandrine version, but the words, as we have them from him, are a free translation from the original. It is remarkable, in the first place, that the words with which he begins are almost identical, except that they do not contain the expression, 'Son,' with the words heard from Heaven on the occasion of the Baptism of our Lord, the voice to which, as we have lately seen, our Lord appealed in His disputation with the priests at Jerusalem, as one of the great heads of evidence in His favour. 'That it might be fulfilled which was spoken by Isaias the Prophet, saying: Behold My servant Whom I have chosen, My Beloved in Whom My soul hath been well pleased. I will put My Spirit upon Him, and He shall show judgment to the Gentiles.' The word judgment in such passages as this seems to mean very much what similar words mean in the Psalms, especially in the long 118th Psalm, that is, instruction in all that relates to justice and virtue, doctrine both practical and dogmatic. The spirit of the Lord is upon His servant, as it is said in the passage which our Lord read in the synagogue at Nazareth,[1] and He is anointed to preach the Gospel to the poor, among whom, under the various forms mentioned in that other place, the contrite of heart, the captives, the blind, and the bruised, the Gentiles, so long deprived of light and true moral liberty, so long afflicted in all ways that concern salvation, hold the first place. This mention of or allusion to the Gentiles is not unfrequent in the Gospel of St. Matthew, written in the first instance for the believers of the Circumcision, and it seems to testify to the readiness of this Evangelist to point to all that indicates the high favours reserved for the Gentiles in the providence of God. We now come to the point in the prophecy which occasions more directly its quotation here by St. Matthew: 'He shall not contend nor cry out, neither shall any man hear His voice in the streets.' The Hebrew word translated 'cry out,' seems to mean 'lift up,' and the omitted word describing what is lifted up has been supplied in this place by the word 'voice,'

[1] St. Luke iv.

according to the sense of the passage on which St. Matthew was intent, while in other versions that has been otherwise supplied, as in the Vulgate in the place in Isaias, where we read, 'accept persons,' that is, 'lift up the face.'

The whole tenour of this great prophetical passage is to describe the immense meekness and gentleness which are to characterize the promised 'servant of God' in His dealings with others: 'The bruised reed He shall not break, and smoking flax He shall not extinguish, till He send forth judgment unto victory.' The meaning of this is, that the servant of God is not to let Himself be provoked into any step with regard to those who are hostile to Him and deaf to His preaching, which might result in the loss of that slender hope which may yet remain of their conversion and salvation. A bruised reed is not yet quite broken, and the servant of God will do nothing to break it altogether. The smoking wick of a lamp almost entirely extinguished has still some fire in it, and the servant of God will do nothing to change that flickering struggling flame into total darkness. This is to be the rule of the kingdom of the servant of God, until the very end. The time will come when there will no longer be room for forbearance, when truth shall finally triumph and the judgment and justice of the evangelical teaching be crowned with entire victory, all men acknowledging the truth and the power of the Kingdom of our Lord at the end of the world. They will acknowledge it either willingly, as its obedient and joyful subjects, or as its conquered and silenced enemies. Then the time for repentance and conversion will be no more, and if the bruised reed has not lifted itself up to the light, and if the smoking flax has not burst forth into true flame, then they must be broken altogether, and extinguished altogether, for the time of grace will be past. But till that moment comes, the servant of God will not hasten on the destruction of any one of His enemies: 'And in Him,' St. Matthew goes on, finishing his quotation with a reference to the hopes of the Gentiles as he had almost begun it in the same way, 'in His Name the Gentiles shall hope.'

We may gather from the use here made by the Evangelist of this famous passage of the Prophet, that the disciples saw in this retirement of our Lord before His enemies the exemplification of a great principle of His Kingdom, which, like so many other of its principles, had been foretold with particularity by the Prophets. It was not simply that our Lord acted in this case with that extreme meekness which always characterized Him. That was perfectly true, and it might have been worth the while of St. Matthew specially to record it of Him on this occasion. But it was not only that He acted now, as, for instance, He acted in the course of His Passion, according to the words of this same Prophet later on—as a sheep before his shearers—dumb and not opening His mouth. It was to be a distinguishing feature of the Catholic Church in all ages, that she was to yield to persecution and not to resist ill-treatment and injury, and for the same reason as that which is expressed in this description of the servant of God here quoted by St. Matthew, that is, for the sake of the enemies them- selves to whom she yields by retirement. This was to be as much a principle of the Kingdom of our Lord as it was to be a principle of the same Kingdom to exercise royal authority over matters like the observance of the Sabbath, or in the forgiveness of sins on earth by the power of the Son of Man. It was a part of the training of the Apostles to learn this principle as well as the other. Our Lord was acting exactly according to the rules which were to last on to the end of time. As the

Church was to be guided in her acts of authority by the example which He set her in the one case, so was she to follow His example also in the other case.

The significance of such conduct cannot be understood without the knowledge of Who He is that acts thus. It has been the characteristic of God from the beginning of His dealings with men. Of all the beautiful attributes the play of which makes up the history of His government of the world, none is more beautiful or more conspicuous in its influence on the course of that government than His infinite and ineffable patience. When we consider Who He is, and how He hates iniquity, how absolute is the dependence of all His creatures upon Him, how pure and holy is His law, and how outrageous men have been in its violation, and in their use of themselves and of His creatures to insult and provoke Him, it is certainly no exaggeration to speak of His adorable patience as the most marvellous of all His attributes, and of the evidence which it bears to His love for men as the most wonderful of the instances of that love. And this, again, deepens our thoughts as to the severity of the future judgments of God on His enemies when at last the time will come for judgment and not for mercy. This patience of God in His providence is the subject of some well-known passages in the Book of Wisdom, in which the holy writer dwells particularly on His mercy on those nations which He had yet visited, after all, with conspicuous severity in the end. Thus, speaking of the chastisements of the Egyptians, he says that God might have destroyed them in a more summary manner than He did—'They might have been slain by one blast, persecuted by their own deeds, and scattered by the breath of Thy power, but Thou hast ordered all things in measure and number and weight. For great power always belongs to Thee alone, and who shall resist the might of Thy arm? For the whole world before Thee is as the least grain of the balance, or as a drop of the morning dew that falleth down upon the earth. But Thou hast mercy on all, because Thou canst do all things, and overlookest the sins of men for the sake of repentance. For Thou lovest all things that are, and hatest none of the things that Thou hast made, for Thou didst not appoint nor make anything, hating it. For how could anything endure, if Thou wouldest not? or be preserved, if not called by Thee? For Thou sparest all because they are Thine, O Lord, Who lovest souls.' And he speaks in the same way of the punishments inflicted on the abominably wicked nations of Canaan, whose sins called for vengeance from Heaven. 'Yet even those,' he says, 'Thou sparedst as men, and didst send wasps, forerunners of Thy host, to destroy them little by little. Not that Thou wast unable to bring the wicked under the just by war, or by cruel beasts, or by one rough word to destroy them at once; but executing Thy judgments by degrees, Thou gavest them place for repentance, not being ignorant that they were a wicked generation. . . . For who shall say to Thee, What hast Thou done? Or who shall come before Thee to be a revenger for wicked men? Or who shall accuse Thee if the nations perish which Thou hast made? For there is none other God but Thou, Who hast care of all, that Thou shouldest show that Thou dost not give judgment unjustly. . . . For so much then as Thou art just, Thou orderest all things justly, thinking it not agreeable to Thy power to condemn him who deserveth not to be punished, for Thy power is the beginning of justice, and because Thou art Lord of all Thou makest Thyself gracious to all. . . . Thou being master of power, judgest with tranquillity, and with great favour disposest of us; for Thy power is at hand, when Thou wilt.'[2] On the basis of these thoughts of the Wise Man, a whole history of the world might be written, or rather we may say, that these thoughts may be considered as a revelation of the manner in which the blessed saints and angels of God in Heaven read the history of the world, as it is unrolled before their eyes, age after age.

The character of our Lord in His dealings with His friends and with His enemies, in His magnificent bounties and gifts to those who love Him, and in His almighty forbearance with those who do not love Him, is necessarily a reflection of the character by which God reveals Himself in His dealings with mankind. Our Lord, too, the humble and despised Carpenter of Nazareth, was armed with the Divine power of annihilating His enemies with 'one rough word,' as the Wise Man expresses it, and perhaps there were among His immediate followers hearts which marvelled why that one rough word was not spoken, and who would have been glad, as we gather from another anecdote in the Gospels,[3] to see fire from Heaven descend and burn up His adversaries. This instance, of which St. Matthew takes so much notice, may have been almost the first in the Gospel history when our Lord had occasion to show this Divine forbearance, at least to so great an extent, for we are not told ever before that they actually made a definite plot to take away His life. But, if it was the first instance of this kind, it was not to be the last. From this time forward they were to observe in our Lord this principle guiding His movements and ruling His actions, often shutting Him out from occasions of marvellous and most fruitful activity, and, in truth, becoming the constant cause of failure and disappointment, ending in His entire defeat, as it seemed to men—in His Passion

---

[2] Wisdom xi. 21—27 ; xii. 10—18.
[3] St. Luke ix. 53, seq.

and crucifixion. In proportion as their own faith in His divinity became more clear and strong, just so must this patience and gentleness of our Lord have appeared to the Apostles more and more marvellous. The Incarnate Son of God, sent into the world to redeem the human race, allowed His mission to be frustrated, out of His incomprehensible patience with His opponents. This is the great lesson of the life of our Lord. Never in all these scenes of opposition and yielding, of persecution and flight, of blasphemy and calumny and of silence, of outrage and submission, are we to forget that He Who suffered all this was the Eternal God, of Whom the author of the Book of Wisdom speaks in the language just now quoted. And as our Lord was then, so He is now in His forbearance and indulgence with sinners, in the patience with which He will wait for them, in the gentleness with which He rebukes them, in the love with which He still draws them to Himself.

But if the character of our Lord is a reflection of the Divine character as revealed by God's dealings with His creatures, it has in turn generated a twofold reflection of itself—in the manner in which the Church had been guided by the Holy Ghost to bear herself in the world, and in the lives and actions of the saints. The path of the Church through the world has been signalized by many wonderful displays of wisdom and power and courage; it has been an onward march to empire, and works of mercy and beneficence have sprung up along that path like flowers in the spring. But of all the Divine things that the Church has shown in the world, none has been more Divine than her marvellous forbearance and gentleness. She has never half used her powers, or asserted her prerogatives, and she submits to slights and injuries unprovoked for the sake of peace. She can bear herself royally, but she hides her royalty out of mercifulness. Principle she never sacrifices, but she can and does forbear, over and over again, to force principle by might on an unwilling world. As the history of our Lord's patience is the history in great part of His life, so there is not one of the lessons He has taught her which has been more constantly and conspicuously illustrated by her than this lesson. And it has always been the same with the saints of God, who have studied most deeply in the school of our Lord, and who have been most thoroughly imbued with the true spirit of His religion and of His Church. They have sometimes done very bold and very strong things, as the Church herself has done, but if they have had to act thus, the manner in which it has been done has always been gentle and loving, always a reflection of the manner of Him Who taught His disciples to yield to persecution and to be silent under calumny, when He drew away from the cities and towns of Galilee that He might leave His enemies time to come, perhaps, to a better mind, after He had taught them so boldly and plainly that the Son of Man was Lord also of the Sabbath.

APPENDIX I.

The Sequence of the Miracles.

To the cursory reader of the Gospel history, especially if he have no well-formed or adequate idea of the characteristic differences in design and method of the several books in which that history is contained, the miracles of our Lord may seem to be scattered over the whole field of the narrative, very much as the stars on a frosty night are seen to be scattered over the unclouded sky. There are some of greater brilliancy than others, there are spaces in which they seem to occur but sparsely, and there are groups which seem to form connected clusters, while, on other parts of the field of vision, the stars are crowded in luminous masses, the several particles of which are not discernible one from the other. The multitude of our Lord's miracles must not be estimated by our knowledge of them. Here again, the image which we have been using holds good, for science informs us that, for a score of stars that are seen by our eyes on the darkest and clearest night, there are hundreds more that our faculties cannot reach without aid, and that the discoveries which the telescope reveals to us can by no means exhaust the myriads of these glorious bodies as they shine in the universe itself. We know that the time of our Lord's preaching was limited, and that during considerable portions, even of the three years, His great activity in the working of miracle was to some measure checked. It would be idle to suppose that we have not an account of His greatest and most conspicuous miracles, or that, taking all the statements of the Evangelists as they lie on the pages of the New

Testament, we have not altogether some sort of account of the whole. In this respect we know them better than we know the heavenly bodies to which we have been comparing them. But it may be possible to deepen and even to enlarge our knowledge concerning them by a careful examination of the statements of the Evangelists themselves, and to discover more than is obvious at first sight as to our Lord's method, so to speak, in the working of these wonders, on which He rested, in so large a measure, the obligation imposed in the Providence of His Father on those who witnessed them of believing that He had sent Him.

The chronological order of the miracles is in most important points tolerably clear from a comparison of the Evangelical narratives themselves. It is not intended, in the present paper, to enter on any discussion on this point. Taking them as they are arranged in the harmony which has been adopted elsewhere by the present writer, it will be the object of this paper to show what we can learn in illustration of the divinely-appointed purpose and order of our Lord's mission from the sequence of His miracles. It is not easy for thoughtful students of the Gospels to persuade themselves that this sequence is simply accidental. The first and the last links of the glorious chain of the miracles are almost enough in themselves to prove that this cannot be. The miracles or 'signs,' as St. John calls them, begin with one of the most splendid of the whole series, full of sacramental significance, and wrought, as it appears from our Lord's words, in some sense, at least, before the time, at the intercession of His Blessed Mother. It is a miracle for which, on merely human and ordinary grounds, there was but little ostensible reason, and in this respect very unlike to many of the rest, such as the raising of the widow's son or the healing of the leper. It is therefore fair to consider it as important chiefly on account of its circumstances and doctrinal signification. It was not worked in the presence of a large multitude, and it seems, from St. John's remarks about the faith of the disciples in our Lord which was founded upon it, to have been most directly addressed to them. This is undoubtedly a solemn and providential opening of so magnificent a series of manifestations, and it is natural to think that the following members of the series have the same deeply significant character. The same conclusion is forced upon us by the last of our Lord's recorded miracles, the fishing in the Lake of Galilee by the seven disciples after our Lord's Resurrection, which was the prelude to the scene in which He so solemnly confided to St. Peter the charge of His sheep and of His lambs. This miracle seems to turn our eyes backward to the other fishing in the same lake at an earlier period of the history, when the net was broken and the multitude of fishes countless, and when St. Peter fell down at his Lord's feet with the prayer that He would depart from him, for he was a sinful man. Here again, as indeed in the case of that other fishing, the parabolical and prophetical import of the miracle seems to lie on the surface, and to court our consideration. If this be true of the first and last of the miracles, it can hardly be thought that it is not true of many of the intermediate links of the chain to which these belong. And it is obvious that the relative order of these two miracles could not have been inverted, without evident incongruity.

If, in order to consider them more closely, we classify the miracles, one most obvious division, for the purposes of this essay, will be that which separates off the miracles which are related individually and in detail, from those which we are told of only, as it were, in masses. Of the former, again, some are grouped together in the history, and others stand by themselves. If we may recur to our former image, we may treat the miracles as if we were to divide the stars in the heavens into those which are single and apparently lonely orbs, those which are clustered together in constellations, and those which form shining masses, like the milky way. The miracles which can be considered as belonging to the two first of these classes can easily be numbered, though the number may be variously given by different writers. The differences arise from the various ways of estimating, for instance, such an act as the cleansing of the Temple, which St. Jerome counts among the greatest miracles. Again, harmonists are in the habit of grouping more than one cure together as one miracle, as in the case of the blind men at Jericho, and, besides this, there are incidents which ordinarily count as one miracle as to which we are told that the cures wrought were very numerous indeed, as in the case of the cures worked on the evening of the Sabbath at Capharnaum, or in the presence of the envoys of St. John Baptist, or before the miracles of the multiplication of the loaves. We may speak of these cases presently, remarking, for the present, that the number of the passages in which we are told nothing but that our Lord worked an almost countless number of miracles in general is larger than might be supposed at first. Let us see, in the first place, what the Evangelists tell us as to this.

The first passage of this kind relates to our Lord's first visit to Jerusalem, after He had, as it may be said, openly assumed His public office, that is, after His Baptism by St. John Baptist. The single prominent incident of this visit is the cleansing of the Temple, as it is recorded by St. John in his second chapter. After relating this incident, and the memorable answer given by our Lord to the question addressed to Him as to His authority, the Evangelist speaks quite incidentally of the other miracles of this time. He says that a great many believed on our Lord, seeing the signs which He did. This is language which implies that these signs were not few. In the same way, Nicodemus, who is said to have come to our Lord by night at this visit, witnesses to the effect produced in simple and well-instructed minds like his own by these signs. He says to our Lord that they knew He was a teacher come from God, for no one could do these signs unless God were with him. These words, as has often been remarked, give the exact logical or theological force of the miracles as evidences. They prove the Divine mission of the person who works them. But it is not easy to think that this effect could have been produced by a few isolated miracles. And yet we have no account of these signs in the earlier Evangelists, nor does St. John mention any particulars. In truth, the particulars of a miracle are only valuable 'evidentially,' as adding to its preternatural character, and as having a kind of beautiful correspondence with the dispensation in witness to which the miracle is wrought, which makes it more clear that the whole proceeds from God. Thus, it may be perhaps argued that our Lord's Divine mission might have been proved by portents and signs of power of some terrible kind, such as those which accompanied the promulgation of the Law on Mount Sinai, or the plagues of Egypt, as well as by the series of miracles of mercy and condescension which formed the actual proofs of that mission as chosen by God. And yet it can hardly be questioned that there is a fitness about the healing and remedial character of the Gospel miracles, so perfectly in harmony as they are with the economy of redemption to which they testify, which constitutes a fresh element of proof which would be wanting in simple displays of power.

We pass on to the next stage in our Lord's Ministry, His preaching in Galilee, which began soon after this feast of the Pasch of which St. John has spoken. Here we have language of the very strongest kind, as to the multitude of the miracles of which no particulars are recorded. 'The fame of Him went out,' says St. Luke, 'through the whole country.'[1] St. Matthew's words are much stronger—'And His fame went throughout all Syria, and they brought to Him all sick people that were taken with divers diseases and torments, and such as were possessed by devils, and lunatics, those that had the palsy, and He healed them.'[2] These

---

[1] St. Luke iv. 37.   [2] St. Matt. iv. 24.

words certainly describe a very large and habitual mercifulness in the working of miracles. And it cannot be doubted that, when the Evangelist adds that 'great multitudes followed our Lord from Galilee, and from Decapolis, and from Jerusalem, and from Judæa, and from beyond the Jordan,' he means to imply that the whole country was in motion after our Lord, on account, mainly, of His very numerous miracles. So that it would be fair to say that, in the course of a day of His ordinary preaching at this time, our Lord probably worked quite as many miracles as all that are specially recorded in the Gospels, or a far greater number.

But this statement of St. Matthew is but one of several of the same kind which are to be found in the history. Thus, after the miracle of the leper, which is related by all three historical Evangelists, St. Luke tells us that people flocked to our Lord from all sides—He being at that time unable to enter into the cities—'to hear, and be healed by Him of their infirmities.'[3] This was at a time when He was in comparative retirement. In the same way at another similar time, when our Lord withdrew Himself from the persecution which was occasioned by the miracle on the man whose hand had been withered—a miracle performed, in the face of His enemies, on the Sabbath Day—we are told in the same very wide language, that 'A great multitude followed Him from Galilee and Judea, and from Jerusalem, and from Idumæa, and from the Jordan, and they about Tyre and Sidon, a very great multitude, hearing the things which He did, came unto Him. . . . For He healed many, so that they pressed upon Him as many as had evils, and the unclean spirits, when they saw Him, fell down before Him and they cried out, Thou art the Son of God.'[4] This description of St. Mark may well seem to refer to the same great multitude of which St. Luke speaks a little later, before his account of the Sermon on the Plain: 'A very

[3] St. Luke v. 16.   [4] St. Mark iii. 11, 12.

great multitude of people from all Judea and Jerusalem and the sea-coast, both of Tyre and Sidon, who were come to hear Him, and be healed of their diseases, and they that had unclean spirits were cured. And all the multitude sought to touch Him, for virtue went out from Him, and healed them all.'[5] Some months later we find mention of another of our Lord's circuits in Galilee, after He had paid His last visit, as it seems, to Nazareth, and been able to do very few miracles to them on account of the unbelief of His fellow-townsmen. 'And Jesus went about all the cities and towns, teaching in their synagogues, and preaching the Gospel of the kingdom, and healing every disease and every infirmity.'[6] Again, before the miracle of the feeding of the five thousand, our Lord is said to have seen a great multitude, and to have healed all that had need of healing.[7] And again after that miracle, when our Lord crossed the lake and came suddenly on the 'land of Genesar,' we are told that 'running throughout the whole country, they began to carry about in beds those that were sick, where they heard that He was. And whithersoever He entered, into towns or into villages or into cities, they laid the sick in the streets, and besought Him that they might but touch the hem of His garment, and as many as touched Him were made whole.'[8] The same description is repeated as to the multitudes who were assembled before the second miracle of the multiplication of the loaves— 'And there came to Him great multitudes, having with them the blind, the lame, the maimed, and many others, and they cast them down at His feet, and He healed them. So that the multitudes marvelled, seeing the dumb speak, the lame walk, the blind see, and they glorified the God of Israel.'[9] It is remarkable, that these large general descriptions cease at the time when our Lord passes, in the

[5] St. Luke vi. 18.
[6] St. Matt. ix. 35; St. Mark vi. 6. [7] St. Luke ix. 11.
[8] St. Mark vi. 56. [9] St. Matt. xv. 30.

last year of His teaching, from Galilee to Judæa. St. Luke is the chief chronicler of what passed after this, and before the Passion, in Judæa strictly so called, as St. John gives us the record of the incidents in Jerusalem itself. We can hardly doubt that the miracles of this period of preaching in Judæa were as numerous as those of the similar period in Galilee, but St. Luke's purpose is mainly didactic, and it may be on this account that he omits such general statements as to miracles as those already quoted. Considering his usual silence as to these matters, his mention of miracles, when he does mention them, is significant, as we shall see.

These passages suggest to us some idea of what must have been the ordinary frequency of miracles in the preaching of our Lord. There is no reason for supposing that the Evangelists can speak at random on such matters, nor, on the other hand, is there any reason for thinking that the occasions on which this great frequency of miracles of mercy is mentioned by them, were occasions of a kind in any way singular, and as such did not recur many times over, when no especial mention of them occurs in the Gospel narrative. It is clear that they are introduced, as it were, by the way, in most at least of the instances among those which have been adduced. The great miracles of the multiplication of the loaves are, in the two latter cases, the direct subject of the narrative, and the same may be said of the Sermon on the Plain, which is accompanied by an account of the miracles which took place just before it was delivered. The conclusion to which these considerations lead, is that we have rather the general mention than the particular account of all but a few out of a great multitude of our Lord's miracles, of the purposes of which, in the providence of God, He speaks also in general terms, in such passages as that in which His works bear witness to Him that He was sent of the Father.[10] Nor need it be questioned that many of these miracles, of which we have no direct narra-

[10] St. John v. 36.

tive, may have been as splendid in themselves as those of which the Evangelists speak in detail, nor need it be thought that there was less of individual care and condescension on the part of our Lord in the one case than in the other.

A similar conclusion, as to the frequency of the miracles of our Lord, may be drawn from the consideration of those cases in which it has happened that the Evangelists have been guided to relate the occurrences of a day, or of a day or two, in the active life of our Lord. This has happened on very few occasions, but we may fairly take them as specimens, by no means selected on account of any unusual frequency of the miracles which were then witnessed. The first of these is the Sabbath at Capharnaum, which may be considered as the very beginning of our Lord's formal teaching. It is related, in fact, by the first three Evangelists, though St. Matthew, for a particular reason, gives its incidents separately, and not together. In this account we have, first, the miracle of the deliverance of the man possessed by a devil in the synagogue, brought on by the clamour of the devil himself, then the healing of St. Peter's wife's mother, and then the account of the healing of a multitude of sick and afflicted of all kinds, including demoniacs, which took place after sunset, because the people were prevented by the rules as to the rest of the Sabbath from bringing their sick to our Lord until that rest was, strictly speaking, over. In their accounts of the numbers of persons thus delivered and healed, the Evangelists use the very strongest language—'All they that had any sick with divers diseases,' says St. Luke, 'brought them to Him. But He, laying His hands on every one of them, healed them. And devils went out of many, crying out and saying, Thou art the Son of God.'[11] Another day, as we may reckon it, of which we have a detailed account is that on which, after having delivered many of His parables, our

---

[11] St. Luke viii. 31—40. Cf. St. Matt. viii. 14—17; iv. 23—25; St. Mark i. 21—30.

Lord sailed across the Lake of Galilee late in the evening to the 'country of the Gerasenes.' Here we have first the miracle of the stilling the tempest which arose while our Lord was asleep, wearied out, as it seems, by the exertions of His preaching. Then there is the incident of the dispossession of the legion of devils, who were allowed by our Lord to enter into the herd of swine. Then the whole multitude of 'the country of the Gerasenes' come and beseech our Lord to depart from them, 'for they were taken with great fear.' Our Lord immediately sails back over the lake to Capharnaum, and there a great crowd is waiting to meet Him. Among this crowd is Jairus, the ruler of the synagogue, and he asks our Lord to come and heal his daughter, who is at the point of death. On His way to the house of Jairus, our Lord is secretly touched by the woman with an issue of blood, and this miracle, which He insists on making public, prepares Jairus for the stupendous act of mercy in the raising of his own daughter to life. As our Lord goes out from the house of Jairus, He is followed by two blind men, who cry after Him, 'Have mercy on us, O Son of David.' Our Lord, Who was at this time about to take His leave of Capharnaum, will not heal them in public, but when He has come to the house in which He usually dwelt, they come unto Him, and He heals them. He charges them to let no man know of it, but they publish it all over the country. After their departure, a dumb man possessed by a devil is brought to Him, also, as it seems, in the house, and the devil is cast out and the dumb man speaks. This gives occasion for a renewal of that calumnious blasphemy of which our Lord spoke in such severe terms, that He cast out devils by the prince of the devils. This appears to have been our Lord's last day of wonders at Capharnaum, as the Sabbath already spoken of may have been the first.[12]

If we put all these bits of evidence together, the inference

[12] St. Matt. ix. 18—26; St. Mark v. 22—43; St. Luke viii. 41—56.

is certainly clear that the miracles of our Lord were very numerous indeed, and that we have but a very small proportion of them related to us in detail. It is also clear that the evidence of our Lord's mission, as it rested on His miracles, was very different indeed, on the one hand, to the people who were living in the countries which were the scenes of His labours, and to ourselves on the other hand. If we were asked to prove our Lord's Divine mission from His miracles, we should probably speak of some few of those which were most stupendous and most clearly supernatural, such as those of the raising of Lazarus and of the widow's son, the feeding of the five thousand and the four thousand, or of the giving sight to the man who had been blind from his birth. But a considerable number of our Lord's most wonderful miracles, as we know them from the Gospel history, were worked in the presence of a comparatively small company, and in many cases they were followed by the strictest injunctions not to speak of them. The miracle at Cana, the miracle on Lazarus, the miracle on the daughter of Jairus, those on the impotent man at the pool, and on the man born blind, and on the leper, come under this class. The miracles of which we are told belong in few cases to that great portion of our Lord's ministry when He was most prominently before the eyes of the public collected in great multitudes, that is, to the time which He spent in His great missionary circuits, first through Galilee, and afterwards throughout Judæa. Of these periods the Evangelists speak only in the most general terms. Yet these were the periods during which His Divine mission wrote itself, so to say, on the hearts and minds of the people by this kind of evidence. He would be remembered by them as the wonder-working Preacher, as St. Peter spoke of Him to Cornelius and his companions, the Man 'Whom God anointed with the Holy Ghost and with power, Who went about doing good, and healing all that were oppressed by the devil, for God was with Him.'[13] The miracles which are specially related, therefore, must be considered as specimens out of an immense multitude, and we must find the reason for their selection either in the fact that they are such specimens simply and nothing more, or in the other fact that they stand out in some manner of their own from among the multitude of such works, and that they belong thus to the history, as steps in the gradual development of the designs of God in the economy of the Incarnation, in a way in which other miracles—the intention of which may have been simply mercy or the authentication of our Lord's mission—do not belong to that history.

It is hardly necessary to point out, that there is great antecedent probability in favour of this last hypothesis. It is quite certain that our Lord's earthly course, short as it was, was to be the foundation of the whole life of the Church after Him, and that nothing but the Divine Wisdom itself could have arranged its incidents so as to suffice for this purpose within the narrow space of time to which it was contracted. It is certain that there is an onward march in His manifestations of Himself, the steps of which are guided by the measures of His own eternal counsels. It is certain that a large number of His actions were prophetical and sacramental, looking forward to mysteries of His religion or doctrines of His faith, and no one who has studied the writings of the great Christian doctors and commentators can doubt that they have been right in so understanding a considerable number, at least, of His miracles in particular. Again, we require some reason for the selection of the miracles which have come down to us in detail. The first Evangelist began with some principle of selection. St. Mark follows St. Matthew, not always in the same order, but in the actual miracles which he arranges more in the order of time. St. Luke, whose principle it is, if possible, not to repeat exactly what St. Matthew has

[13] Acts x. 38.

related, still follows the rule of that Evangelist's selection by relating miracles and discourses like those which his predecessor has chosen. Even St. John works, as may be said, on the same lines, though he repeats only once, in the case of the feeding of the five thousand, a miracle which has been related by any one before him. Now, the relation of many miracles which thus stand out in the narrative to the unfolding of the Gospel history is very striking, and not difficult to discover. We are thus led to the conclusion that the chain of these miracles of which we have separate accounts, has a close connection with the development of the providential plan in the arrangement of the life of our Lord, and that, if this can be established, these wonderful works are set before us in a new light and with a new importance, differing in this respect from the immense mass and multitude of wonderful works of which no special account is given.

This brings us to a point in our inquiry at which it becomes natural to give to ourselves some account of the order of these great manifestations. The mere enumeration of the miracles of which we speak is suggestive of much that may help us to the answer to the question thus raised. The miracles of our Lord begin, as has been said, with the great and most significant marvel of the change of the water into wine at the marriage feast of Cana. Apart from the splendour of this miracle, and the effect which it produced on the small band of disciples whom our Lord had brought with Him from the school of St. John Baptist on the banks of the Jordan, it is plainly fraught with a mysterious significance as to two great truths—the power of our Blessed Lady in the Kingdom of her Son, and the use to be made of the simple elements of bread and wine in the great Sacrament of the Eucharist. These are truths which our Lord might have taught in other ways, but which He chose to teach by their connection with this great miracle. The miracle, therefore, may be considered not simply as an evidence 'that God was with Him,' as Nicodemus said, but also as having a doctrinal import, conveying to us the truths of which mention has been made, quite as clearly as if our Lord had taught them in so many words, without working at the same time any miracle at all. The miracle which next follows is of a very different order indeed, so much so that it might be omitted from the list by some commentators. We speak of the cleansing of the Temple of the buyers and sellers and the money changers. This was a moral miracle, for it can hardly be accounted for without the supposition of some preternatural influence on the part of our Lord on the minds of those whom He chased so summarily from the house of His Father. It is clear, also, that this action was entirely our Lord's own choice, not suggested by any one but Himself. But it belongs in a most important manner to the history of the Gospels, because without the knowledge of the answer which our Lord then gave to His questioners, as to His authority—'Destroy this temple, and in three days I will raise it up'—we should not be able to explain the charge brought against our Lord when He stood before the tribunal of Caiaphas. It is clear that the simply 'evidential' force of this miracle is comparatively unimportant, but it belongs very importantly to the history.

The next two miracles in the order of the narrative are remarkable in themselves, on account of their relation to the onward progress of the revelation of our Lord by means of His works of power. The first of these is the healing of the ruler's son at Capharnaum, when our Lord was Himself at Cana, and when He plainly designed to raise the faith of the father of the lad to a higher level before He would grant the cure. For it was a higher level of faith to believe that our Lord's word at a distance could drive away the disease, than to believe that our Lord could work the miracle by coming down to Capharnaum and standing over the sick bed.[14] Here, then, at least we have a distinct

[14] St. John iv. 47, seq.

reason for the working the miracle in the manner in which it was worked, and for its record on the part of the Evangelists, apart from all considerations of what may be called the simply 'evidential' character of the miracle. There is also a special reason for the mention of the miracle by St. John, inasmuch as he is silently engaged, in the course of his work, in filling up what was wanting for the perfect intelligence of the history, as it stood before he wrote. For without some such addition there was as yet no mention on the part of any Evangelist of any wonders at Capharnaum which might explain the language of our Lord in the synagogue at Nazareth, as mentioned by St. Luke.[15] This scene in the synagogue of the town of His childhood and youth is the next event in the Gospel history, and here also we have a miracle contrasting very beautifully with the last, in the escape of our Lord from the hands of His intending murderers at the mount of Precipitation. This is one of those occasions on which our Lord, instead of displaying His powers in a new and more wonderful way, as had been the case in the miracle on the ruler's son, chose to appear weak and helpless in the hands of His enemies, and to use His power only just enough to protect Himself from absolute death. Nor can we be wrong in seeing in this incident an act of humiliation, sought at the hands of others, by which our Lord prepared Himself, as it were, for the great and conspicuous glories which were to signalize His course of public preaching, then about to begin. And, again, this incident may be considered as the first of a chain which all bear witness to the truth that the blessings which our Lord brought with Him were not to be distributed according to any law of natural relationship or even national connection with Him, although He was sent directly to the lost sheep of the House of Israel. In this aspect, the events of this Sabbath at Nazareth are a prelude to the miracles on the Centurion's servant, and on the daughter of the Syrophœni-

[15] St. Luke iv. 17, seq.

cian woman. The next miracles of which we have a detailed account are those of which we have already spoken as having been wrought at Capharnaum on the first Sabbath of our Lord's public ministry there, the deliverance of the demoniac in the synagogue, the healing of St. Peter's wife's mother, and the numerous cures wrought after the sunset of that day. After this for a time the narrative is silent as to any special miracles, and we are left to the general and very large words in which the Evangelists speak of the evidences of our Lord's ordinary public preaching from city to city and from town to town throughout Galilee. We then come to a series of miracles, every one of which may, without any fancifulness, be well considered as having a purpose of its own, independent of its value as a witness to the mission of our Lord.

The series of which we speak begins with the miraculous draught of fishes in the Lake of Galilee.[16] Here we take up again the list of a class of our Lord's miracles which in many respects must be considered by itself—the class of miracles which our Lord wrought without any solicitation on the part of those who were to be benefited by them. It is obvious that such a class must have sprung from some purpose of our Lord's own, and may therefore be considered as very probably having a special bearing on the development of His designs in the foundation of His Kingdom. It is certain that this miracle has always been considered as singularly significant and prophetic, and that its meaning may well be gathered from the words of our Lord which conclude the narrative of it in St. Luke, 'Fear not, from henceforth thou shalt be catching men;' that is, it is a miracle which embodies a prophecy and a promise of the fertility and fruitfulness of the labours of the Apostles in toilsome quest for souls, undertaken at our Lord's bidding; and in this light the unprofitableness of their labours the night before seems to be a part of the same providential

[16] St. Luke v. 1—11.

lesson. This may furnish some answer to the cavils of Protestant critics, who not only dislike, but even ridicule, the common Catholic contemplation of this miracle, according to which there is a special significance in the selection of St. Peter's boat as that from which our Lord preached to the crowd on the shore, and which was afterwards steered into the middle of the lake at His request. Of course there is nothing which forces us to consider every single mention of St. Peter in the Gospels as having a designed reference to the position which was to be occupied by the Prince of the Apostles in the Church. But when the prophetic significance of this miracle is once established, and when it is remembered that the whole series of incidents was directly chosen by our Lord, the application of this mode of interpretation to any single detail becomes very natural indeed. Moreover, it was at this time that our Lord seems to have begun more definitely the preparation of the Apostolic band, of which St. Peter was to be the chief, and this miracle is certainly a very fitting beginning of that preparation. Those which follow immediately, though they are few in number, and are scattered over the space of at least a few weeks, have all, more or less, the same character. They are miracles which prepare the attentive student of our Lord's acts and ways for various truths connected with the powers or doctrines of His Kingdom, of which the Apostles were to be the princes. We can see this character even in the first of the series, which is the miracle on the leper.[17] This was the first occasion on which our Lord took the precaution of enjoining silence on the subject of the great work which He had wrought. This silence was not observed, and in consequence our Lord was compelled to remain for a time outside cities and towns in which He usually preached. The leprosy was no ordinary disease, at least in the estimation of the Jews, and in the view taken of it by the Mosaic legislation. It was far more to heal a

[17] St. Matt. viii. 2—4; St. Mark i. 40—45; St. Luke v. 10—16.

leper than to heal a sufferer of another class, and the regulations of the law, on the observance of which our Lord strictly insisted in this and the other case in which He is recorded to have healed this disease, required a very special amount of examination by the priests and some very peculiar rites of purification. All this must have been in our Lord's mind, at the time when He enjoined on the man whom He had healed to keep silence on the miracle, but to go to the High Priest and show himself, that the cure might be certified as such by the highest authority. This miracle, so considered, is a preparation for the series of the Sabbatical miracles, of which we shall speak presently, and which, as it appears, were to begin at Jerusalem within a short time after this healing of the leper.

But the significance of the other miracles which now follow is more marked still. The next is the healing of the paralytic who was let down in his bed before our Lord.[18] This miracle was not unsolicited, but it was not worked by our Lord until He had asserted His claim, as the Son of Man, to forgive sins on earth, and so made the working of the miracle a distinct proof of the truth of that claim. The next two miracles are equally remarkable in this point of view. They are the two first Sabbatical miracles, if we may use such an expression. That is, they were wrought on the Sabbath Day under circumstances which challenged the attention of the authorities of the synagogue to a new claim of our Lord, that to be considered the 'Lord of the Sabbath.' They were both unsolicited, and due to our Lord's own deliberate choice. The one is that on the impotent man at the Pool of Bethsaida,[19] the other that on the man in the synagogue whose hand was withered.[20] In each case we see that our Lord had a definite object in view, apart, as has already been said, from the general object of all His

---

[18] St. Matt. ix. 2—8; St. Mark ii. 1—8; St. Luke v. 17—25.
[19] St. John v. 1—15.
[20] St. Matt. xii. 9—14; St. Mark iii. 1—16; St. Luke vi. 6—11.

miracles, considered as the appointed evidences of His Divine mission. Nor is it less clear that the Evangelists had a special purpose in recording these miracles, apart from the general value of all miracles in works like theirs. That is, they had it in view to explain the first great cause of the enmity to our Lord which now began to be manifested on the part of the Jewish authorities, who, whatever may have been their real motives, took hold of His conduct with regard to the Sabbath as the ground of their determined opposition to Him which dates from this period. This fact gives these miracles an importance of their own in the Evangelical narrative. It may, indeed, be said, that these miracles have a direct doctrinal importance which can hardly be exaggerated. It was on account of these miracles that the first great conspiracy was formed against Him, and that the rulers at Jerusalem finally threw themselves into opposition to Him and determined to kill Him. The immediate effect of this opposition on our Lord's line of action is related at the time by St. Matthew, when he tells us how our Lord now retired from before His enemies. There is only one further similar step in the opposition to Him of which special mention is made, and it is that to which His enemies had recourse when they invented their blasphemous calumny about the league with Beelzebub, by virtue of which, as they said, He had the power of casting out devils. We shall see the importance of this in the Evangelical narrative, and the manner in which the miracles are introduced with reference to this calumny, and to our Lord's subsequent change of conduct in consequence, is one of the many arguments for the theory as to the miracles, of which we are now speaking.

After these miracles there is a kind of pause in the series of separate works of this kind—a pause probably occasioned by the fact, that our Lord was soon again occupied in one of His great missionary circuits. During this time, His miracles were immensely numerous, but they are related only in a general way by St. Mark and St. Luke. Then we have a few individual cases, each one of which has a character of its own, such as to make it a fitting subject for special relation. The first of these miracles is the healing of the Centurion's servant in Capharnaum,[21] a miracle which brought out our Lord's declaration that He had not found so great faith in Israel as in that Gentile officer. This miracle, again, is a kind of pendant or counterpart to that of the healing of the ruler's son the year before. The Centurion has learnt exactly the lesson which our Lord required of the ruler—the faith that His word only was enough for the healing of his servant. Again, the miracle is remarkable on other grounds, as showing that the mercies of the Incarnation were not to be confined to the Jewish nation only. Next to this in order is the raising to life of the widow's son at Naim, the first recorded instance of such a miracle on the part of our Lord. This also was an unsolicited miracle,—perhaps the faith of the crowd that was present did not rise so high as to expect the raising from the dead. It is not certain that our Lord was moved to this by no other impulse than that of His own ineffable mercy. He may perhaps have been looking on to the occasion of the next cluster of miracles which was to follow. This was to be wrought in consequence of the solemn embassy,[22] as it may be called, from St. John Baptist, then in prison, to our Lord, for the purpose, as we cannot doubt, of obtaining an opportunity, from the witness of his own disciples, of convincing them of the truth of the fulfilment in our Lord of the ancient prophecies. Thus St. John is said to have sent his disciples when he heard the 'works of the Christ,' that is, when he heard that our Lord was working those works which the Prophets had predicted as the works of the promised Messias. The answer which our Lord made was in keeping with this object of St. John; for the messengers were told to go and tell him what they had seen and heard—' the blind see, the lame walk, the lepers

---

[21] St. Matt. viii. 5—13; St. Luke vii. 1—10.
[22] St. Matt. xi. 2—6; St. Luke vii. 17—25.

are made clean, the deaf hear, the dead rise again, the poor have the Gospel preached to them.' These words of our Lord, which refer to a well-known passage in which the Prophet Isaias describes the wonders and blessings of the days of the Messias, are quite sufficient to explain the large number of miracles which He is said by the Evangelists in this place to have worked in the presence of the envoys of St. John. But it is also worthy of note, that, but for the miracle which immediately precedes these in the order of time —the raising of the widow's son—there would be no record up to this time, of the fulfilment of at least a part, and that the most striking part of the promise, namely, that the dead should rise. These two miracles, therefore, are in a certain sense necessary to the history, even if we set aside for the moment the reason for them which applies equally to all the other miracles, recorded or unrecorded. We cannot, indeed, be certain that no one had before this been raised from the dead by our Lord. His own words seem to imply that the resurrection of the widow's son was not a singular instance of the exercise of this great power. But they may be understood generally, as meaning that miracles of every class, this among others, had been wrought. The message of the Baptist, not long, as it seems, before his death, was an important point in the history. And, even if the instances of raising the dead had been more numerous than we find them in the Gospels, it may still have been well that St. Luke should give this particular instance in this place as a preface to his account of the question of the disciples of St. John.

The next in order among the miracles is one which gave occasion to a very diabolical outbreak of malice against Him on the part of the Scribes and Pharisees, who had now become His deadly enemies. They could not question the facts of His marvellous miracles, but, on the other hand, they were determined not to admit the natural and logical inference which was involved in those facts—that is, they would not admit Him to be the messenger of God, the truth of Whose words was ascertained by the witness of His miracles. Consequently, they were driven back on the only other alternative open to them, and were forced to assert that He worked His miracles, especially those which consisted in the dispossession of demoniacs, by means of a collusion with the prince of devils. This calumny, which amounted, as our Lord taught them, to the blasphemy against the Holy Ghost, is first heard of in connection with this next miracle, that on the blind and dumb demoniac.[23]

The taking up of this position of direct rebellion against God on the part of His enemies, was a turning-point in the conduct of our Lord towards them. He had retired before the persecution which had followed on His advancing His claims to be the Lord of the Sabbath, and to heal and do other good works on the Sabbath Day. Now He adopted a new method of teaching, that is, by parables, and we find Him henceforth preparing to quit altogether that part of the Holy Land in which He had spent so many blessed months. This is not the place to draw out all that might be said as to the change in our Lord's mode of teaching which begins from this moment, but what has been now said is sufficient for our purpose of explaining the importance of this miracle in the unfolding of the providential history of our Lord's ministry. We find no other miracle in the story until the close of His first systematic course of parables, if we may so speak, but on the evening of the day when He had concluded this teaching, we are told that He bade the disciples set sail for the opposite shore, and thus we begin that other short chain of beautiful miracles of which we have already spoken. As if our Lord wished to show that He was grieved with the hardness of heart with which He had been met at Capharnaum, and by the men whom He had so highly favoured, the next chain of miracles begins with the exertion of His miraculous power on the elements of nature and on

[23] St. Matt. xii. 22—31.

the world of evil spirits. The first of these miracles, as has been said, is the stilling of the tempest, and then follows the casting out of the legion of devils in the land of the Gerasenes. Our Lord is then compelled, by the inhospitable ingratitude with which the people meet Him, to return to the other side of the lake, where the crowd is waiting for Him, and where He first heals the woman with the issue of blood, then raises to life the daughter of Jairus, and finally heals the two blind men and the dumb demoniac, as has already been mentioned. These last miracles seem, as it were, to have been extorted from our Lord by the faith of those in favour of whom they were wrought, at a time when He had determined to have little more to do with Capharnaum. He was in fact driven away by the blasphemies of His enemies, with a second mention of which St. Matthew closes his account of these incidents. The blasphemies of His enemies, however, did not dry up the loving mercifulness of His Heart towards those to whom He was sent. After this series of miracles, we have again a sort of break in the continuity of the miracles, occasioned, as in the former case, by the fact that our Lord started again on one of His missionary circuits throughout the country. Before doing this, however, He went once more to His own city Nazareth. It would almost seem as if He courted the humiliation which was to meet Him there, as a fitting preparation for the labours of the missionary ministry which He was once more to begin. His servants have learnt from Him to practise humiliation and mortification before they undertake such labours, and it may be at least allowed us to see something of the kind in this visit, the last, as far as we know, that He ever paid, to His former fellow-townsmen. The Evangelists tell us that He could only work a few miracles there on account of their unbelief.[24] This visit was also the immediate prelude to another great onward step in the Gospel history; for it was just after this that the twelve

[24] St. Matt. xiii. 54—58; ix. 36; St. Mark vi. 1—6.

Apostles were sent out to preach in our Lord's Name. The miracles, therefore, of this immediately ensuing period were no doubt very multitudinous, but they were of that class which has escaped all particular mention in the Evangelical narrative, and they were also now worked by our Lord's Apostles as well as by Himself.

We have therefore to pass on for some short time before we come to any miracles of our Lord that are specially mentioned. But when the chain is once more resumed, the magnificence and grandeur of the miracles which now follow are quite sufficient to make up for the paucity of their number. For the next miracle of which we have a special record is the great wonder of the multiplication of the five loaves, which is immediately followed by our Lord's walking on the waters, and even bidding St. Peter come to Him on them. These are immediately followed by the miracle of the healing of the daughter of the Syrophœnician woman, and of the deaf and dumb man whom our Lord cured with the word 'Ephphetha,' and then we come to the second multiplication of the loaves for the feeding of the four thousand, and the miracle at Bethsaida on the blind man.[25] This brings us to the central point in the Gospel history, the confession of St. Peter, and the promise to him of the keys of the Kingdom of Heaven. Of this sequence of miracles, three are sacramental and prophetical, in the same way as the miracle at Cana and that of the first miraculous fishing. There can be no doubt as to the sacramental and doctrinal importance of the miracles of the multiplication of the loaves, nor is it difficult to see the prophetical meaning of the walking on the waters, especially when we consider the part of St. Peter in the miracle. The three other miracles have a beauty and a meaning of their own. The application of the cure performed, after so much apparent resistance on our Lord's part, in reward

[25] St. Matt. xiv. 14—20, 21—39; xvi. 13—29; St. Mark vi. 30—56; vii. 24—37; viii. 1—10, 23—30; St. Luke ix. 10—21; St. John vi. 1—24.

of the prayer of the Syrophœnician woman, to the doctrine of the extension of God's mercies beyond the strict limits of His covenants, is very obvious and very instructive. The other two miracles have a remarkable feature in common, which they share with one or two others of the recorded miracles of our Lord. For they seem to show a certain difficulty and weakness, as if some strange cause half paralyzed, for the moment, the lifegiving and healing virtues of the Sacred Humanity. In the case of the deaf and dumb, our Lord takes the poor sufferer apart from the crowd, puts His fingers into his ears, and spits and touches his tongue; He looks up to Heaven and sighs, before He says the word Ephphetha. In the case of the blind man at Bethsaida, He takes him by the hand and leads him out of the town—then He spits on his eyes and lays His hands on them, and asks the man whether he sees anything. The man replies that he sees men as trees walking. Then our Lord again lays His hands on his eyes and the man begins to see, and finally the cure is completed. It would be most unreasonable to suppose that all these particulars had not some special cause and meaning; but in any case, these miracles, if we may so speak, of difficulty, come in with a beautiful kind of contrast, in the midst of the splendid displays of power of which the narrative at this point is so full. They seem to hint at the operation of the causes which had been now for some time undermining the work of our Lord among the people, the lack of that ready and simple faith which had welcomed the first beginnings of the Gospel preaching, before the malice of the Pharisees had been roused to poison the hearts of His hearers against our Lord. Thus they lead up, as it may be said, to that striking contrast which has been made familiar to us in the great picture of the Transfiguration, the mystery which followed almost immediately on the confession of St. Peter and the preaching of the Cross, which then began.[26] We

[26] St. Matt. xvi. 1—22; St. Mark ix. 1—31; St. Luke ix. 28—45.

have our Lord in glory on the holy mountain, with His three chosen Apostles, and with Moses and Elias in ecstatic adoration of His Sacred Humanity. And below on the plain we have the poor lunatic boy writhing in torture, under the influence of the devil, from which the other Apostles were unable to free him, on account, in the main, as we gather from our Lord's words when He descends, of the faithlessness and perversity of the generation to which He had been preaching. Thus it is needless to point out that the miracle on this lunatic boy, as well as the Transfiguration itself, if it were to be counted among the miracles, has a character of its own, quite distinct from its evidential force.

The point at which we have now arrived, brings us almost within view of the last series of the miracles as they are recorded for us in the Gospels, and we shall take the opportunity of making here the break in this essay which the largeness of the subject requires. We have already had instances of all the various classes into which the miracles may be divided. Those of which we have last spoken, illustrate very well the difference between the solicited and the unsolicited miracles of our Lord. Those which are worked in answer to the faith of the petitioners, so to speak, are splendid, or not so splendid, in proportion to the strength of that faith. Our Lord's demeanour, and His words, in reference to what we may call the miracles of comparative difficulty, such as that on the lunatic boy, the blind man at Bethsaida, and the other just mentioned, seem to point to the weakness of the faith of the people as the reason for that difficulty. On the other hand, the unsolicited miracles are usually very splendid in their kind. Nor, as has been said, is it difficult to connect them with evident designs of our Lord as to the setting forth of Divine truths, either of doctrine, or in relation to the prerogatives of His new Kingdom. The only unsolicited miracle which seems at first sight to be one of simple mercy, is that of the raising of the widow's son, and we have seen good reason for thinking that in this case there may have been a purpose in our Lord's mind, independent of His ineffable mercy and compassion, the purpose of preparing the answer which He was to give to the envoys of St. John Baptist. And, further, we see the importance of the miracles on the execution of the Divine plan of His Life and Ministry, in another and a more lamentable way—that is, we see how certain of His miracles were to have the effect of driving His enemies to desperation, and of furnishing them with the pretext on which they based their inexorable hostility to Him. This effect on His enemies raises into a singular prominence the miracles which we have called 'Sabbatical,' all of which are unsolicited, and another class of cures which were connected with the deliverance, at the same time, of the sufferers who were cured, from the power of the devil. But, when we have given due consideration to the scandal taken so unjustly by the Pharisees at the cures wrought on the Sabbath, and to the reckless madness and blasphemous audacity of their charges about the supposed league with Beelzebub, we shall have gone far towards giving a full account of their opposition to our Lord. And, in the same way, when we have further taken sufficiently into account the effect which these measures on the part of His enemies had on our Lord, and on His manner of acting and teaching, we shall have enabled ourselves to enter, to no inconsiderable extent, into the plan of His Public Life—especially when we have added to this element the other, of His continual desire to prepare the ground for so many of the great doctrines and principles of His Kingdom. It remains to see, in another part of this essay, how the same considerations enable us to trace a Divine purpose in the sequence of His remaining miracles.

II.

THE confession of St. Peter, the beginning of the preaching of the Cross, and the great mystery of the Transfiguration which followed at a short interval, mark a great change in the manner of our Lord's acting, and also, as it seems, were followed, after no great lapse of time, by a change in the ordinary scene of His preaching. For it was soon after this that our Lord no longer preached in Galilee. He went up to Jerusalem for the feast of Tabernacles in the autumn of the year which immediately preceded His Passion, and during the months which followed the chief scene of His Ministry would appear to have been Judæa itself, with occasional visits to Jerusalem. He also spent a part of this time in Peræa, the country beyond the Jordan, and was at one time, at all events, on the confines of Galilee, though we have no certain intimation that He passed any time there. During this most important period we have comparatively but few miracles specially recorded, but these which are so recorded are remarkably interesting to us in our present inquiry. It has been already said, that a reason may be assigned for the absence of any mention of large numbers of miracles together. Our information as to this time comes almost exclusively from St. Luke and St. John, with the exception of the time spent in Peræa, which country was the place in which our Lord delivered some of His most important teaching, especially with relation to what we call the counsels of perfection and such matters as the law of marriage and divorce. This teaching is recorded by the two earlier Evangelists, as well as by St. Luke. But, as to the period before that teaching, the purpose of St. Luke, who is the historian of the Judæan preaching of our Lord, as distinguished from the Galilæan teaching, and of St. John, who has filled up the blank left by the former Evangelists as to the scenes in Jerusalem itself, is mainly didactic and doctrinal, and this fact supplies us with the reason for their comparative silence as to the miracles of our Lord in general, while it also gives the explanation of their mention of those miracles which they do insert. These, it will be seen, are mentioned by them precisely on account of their bearing on the course of the events of our Lord's life. This will be quite enough to enable us to see the importance of these miracles on the onward march of the Church history.

There are in all only five great miracles specially recorded by these two Evangelists before the point at which the three first Gospels again, so to say, meet, at the last journey of our Lord to Jerusalem before the last pasch, at which He was to suffer. Of these five miracles three are related by St. Luke and two by St. John. The two which St. John records are evidently most important in their bearing on the history. These two miracles are the healing of the man who had been blind from his birth, and the raising of Lazarus from the dead.[1] The first of these took place at Jerusalem itself, and the other at Bethany, close to Jerusalem. The first, the miracle on the man born blind, was wrought, like the miracle on the man at the pool, on the Sabbath Day. It led to a fresh outburst of the hatred which the Chief Priests had now conceived against our Lord, and also to the first instance of which we have any record of the passing of the sentence of excommunication on any one who professed his belief in Him. The fear of this sentence of excommunication is mentioned by St. John as the reason why some of the principal men among the rulers themselves did not avow themselves believers in our Lord.[2] And it appears from the history of the early Church that this was one of the great causes of the poverty of the Christian community at Jerusalem, who were excluded, by being treated as excommunicate from all share in the abundant alms which were sent from all parts of the world to the Holy City. That the sentence of excommunication from the Jewish Synagogue

[1] St. John ix. xi.   [2] St. John xii. 40.

was felt as a terrible disgrace, even by Christian Jews for many years after, seems to be implied by St. Paul's language to the Hebrews in a time of persecution, 'We have an altar,' he says, 'whereof they have no power to eat who serve the tabernacle. For the bodies of those beasts, whose blood is brought into the Holies by the High Priest for sin, are burned without the camp. Wherefore Jesus also, that He might sanctify the people by His own Blood, suffered without the gate. Let us go forth, therefore, to Him without the camp, bearing His reproach.'[3] This is enough to explain the importance of this miracle on the man blind from his birth, which is also one of the greatest of the miracles in itself, and which led to a very long discussion between our Lord and the Jewish rulers, for which alone it is very probable that St. John would have selected it for special mention. It is unnecessary to say anything about the great importance of the miracle of the raising of Lazarus. More than any other single action of our Lord, this miracle brought about the determination of the Jews to put Him to death, and it was immediately after this that Caiaphas gave his famous counsel that one man must die for the nation.[4] And it is also important on another account, because it is connected with the incident of the supper at Bethany, which determined the traitor Judas to take his step of treachery at once. And this miracle mainly produced the enthusiasm of the people who came out to meet our Lord on Palm Sunday, which, again, confirmed the resolution of Caiaphas and his compeers to bring about our Lord's death as soon as possible.[5] It is therefore clear, without further discussion, that the miracles which are chosen by St. John for insertion in his narrative at this point, have each of them a very marked importance in their bearing on the unfolding of the Divine plan by which His life was ordered.

If we turn now to the miracles which St. Luke records in

[3] Hebrews xiii. 10—13.
[4] St. John xi. 50.   [5] St. John xii. 17—19.

this period, between the Transfiguration and the ascent of our Lord for the last time to Jerusalem, we are struck with a fact which seems at first sight somewhat strange, and which must give some trouble to harmonists till they have mastered the right principle of understanding the purpose of the third Evangelist. For St. Luke, in his narrative of this time, relates exclusively miracles which are parallel to others which occur at an earlier period in the histories of St. Mark and St. Matthew. These miracles are four in number. Two of them are Sabbatical miracles, in the sense of the name already explained, that is, they were miracles wrought in public on the Sabbath Day, when our Lord was aware of the hostile criticism to which such acts as His would be exposed, and when—as it seems fair to conclude—He purposely braved that hostility, for the sake of asserting the principle of the right meaning of the law of the Sabbath and of His own authority as the Son of Man, Lord also of the Sabbath Day. These two miracles are those mentioned by St. Luke in the thirteenth chapter, the cure of the woman, whom our Lord spoke of as a daughter of Abraham, who had had a spirit of infirmity for eighteen years, and that on the dropsical man, mentioned in the fourteenth chapter. In both these cases, our Lord acted as He had done in the earlier part of His Ministry in Galilee, and healed these poor sufferers in spite of the opposition which would be aroused by the miracle. The other two miracles of St. Luke in this part are also repetitions of miracles which had been before worked. One of these is exactly parallel to the miracle already spoken of as having given occasion to the atrocious calumny of the Pharisees, who imputed the cure, which they could not question, to a league with Beelzebub. This is the miracle related by St. Luke in his eleventh chapter. It differs from the miracle in St. Matthew,[6] in that the demoniac out of whom the devil is cast, in the account of the earlier Evangelist is blind as well as dumb, and that

---

[6] St. Matt. xii. 22—24.

in St. Luke only dumb. The effect of the dispossession is the same in each case—that is, the sufferer regains the use of the sense or senses of which he had been deprived. And the effect on the enemies of our Lord is the same in each case—that is, the miracle is mentioned, as it would seem, for the purpose of informing us of the black calumny to which it gave occasion on the part of the Pharisees. Our Lord answers this calumny in much the same way in both passages. The other miracle of this time in St. Luke is the healing of the ten lepers, which is analogous to the first miracle of the same kind of which we have already spoken, as occurring quite at the beginning of a chain of works of wonder, which were designed to set forth the prerogatives of the Son of Man in His Kingdom.

Thus we have St. Luke, as it were, repeating the same notes as to the Ministry of our Lord in Judæa, which had already been struck with regard to the earlier Ministry in Galilee by the first two Evangelists. It has sometimes been a trouble to commentators, how to explain the apparent divergence between the narratives of miracles so much alike to one another as these in St. Luke on the one hand, and those in St. Matthew on the other, not to speak of the other difficulty as to the point of the history in which they are respectively placed. But the truth seems to be, that the miracles of this class were, in themselves and in their consequences, highly important in the effect which they produced on the rulers of the Jews. Before the incident of the raising of Lazarus, the chief occasions which had roused these rulers against Him had been just these—His healing on the Sabbath Day, and His casting out devils from persons who were not simply demoniacs, but also afflicted by the privation of the use of some of their natural organs of sense. The simplest account of the anger which these last miracles provoked in the Pharisees, seems to lie in the fact that exorcism were practised by themselves as a sort of ecclesiastical function, but that they could never attain to the cures which accompanied the deliverances worked by our Lord. This was something beyond the ordinary effect of exorcisms, as the Jews knew of them. The stages of the hostility to our Lord on the part of the Pharisees were marked in the first place, by the healing on the Sabbath, and in the second place by the instances of these dispossessions which were also cures. It may be thought also that the healing of the lepers had also some effect on their jealous and envious minds—inasmuch as the leprosy was a disease altogether different from others, humanly and ordinarily incurable, the recovery from which was reserved to the priests for examination and for certification.

It is well known to students of the Gospel Harmony, that there is very good reason for believing that the long series of incidents which are related by St. Luke, and, apparently, by him alone, and which fill up so large a portion of his whole Gospel—from the ninth to the eighteenth chapter—took place in Judæa, that is in the country round about Jerusalem, to the south-west of the Holy Land, and not in Galilee. This appears to be St. Luke's chief independent contribution to the history of our Lord, after his invaluable additions at the beginning of the whole. We shall assume this to be so, having elsewhere gone into the question at considerable length.[7] But if this is so, it is easy to understand why, if there were certain prominent historical features in the preaching of our Lord, especially as to the attitude of His enemies and the effect on His line of conduct which that attitude produced, and if these same features reappeared, as they were certain to reappear, in the course of His second period of popular preaching in the country parts of Judæa, as they had before appeared in his Galilæan preaching, the Evangelist to whom the narrative of that second period fell should have selected miracles which held the same prominence in their effects in this portion of the story as other miracles of the same sort held in the story of the Galilæan

[7] See *Life of our Life*, vol. i. Introduction p. iv.; vol. ii. ch. ii.

preaching. Thus, if it be true that the attitude of the Jewish rulers towards our Lord was determined in Galilee by His miracles on the leper, on the Sabbath Day, and on the possessed persons who were also blind or deaf or dumb as the consequence of their possession by Satan, or at least at the same time with that possession, it is shown by St. Luke to be equally true that the attitude of our Lord's enemies in Judæa was determined by incidents exactly similar to these. This is of itself a decided and most valuable addition to our knowledge of the history as a whole. It has already been said that St. Luke does not pause in this portion of his story to relate many miracles, but it is surely significant that he should have been guided in his selection of a few by the principle of which we speak.

After this cycle, so to call it, of miracles of the later period of our Lord's teaching, we have but few that remain of which we have any special account. These are, in the first place, the double miracle at Jericho on the blind men, then the few cures which are mentioned as having been wrought by our Lord on His entrance into the Temple on Palm Sunday, then the cursing of the barren fig-tree. These exhaust the list of miracles mentioned in the Gospels before the Passion. There remains the miracle on Malchus, wrought in the Garden of Olives at the very time of our Lord's capture by His enemies, and, after the Resurrection, we have one conspicuous miracle, the second miraculous fishing in the Lake of Galilee.[8] It is not difficult to justify, in regard to these miracles, the statement which has been already generally made, and on which the whole of this essay depends, that is, that the miracles which are specially mentioned by the Evangelists, are so specially mentioned for the sake of some particular relation which they bear to the development of the plan of our Lord's Public Life, except in a few cases when the Evangelists having from other reasons to relate the circumstances which led to them

[8] St. John xxi. 6.

The Sequence of the Miracles. 351

or with which they were historically connected, would naturally not omit them. We may assign this reason for the mention of the miracles at Jericho. That was a very memorable entrance and exit from Jericho, and it was natural that the miracles which then occurred should not be omitted, though indeed, it may very fairly be said that the two miracles taken together constitute a picture of our Lord's ineffable condescension and pity for suffering such as is hardly to be found elsewhere in the history. The same reason may be given for the mention of the healing of a few such persons in the Temple on Palm Sunday, while the miracle of the cursing of the fig-tree is a parable in action, and could not possibly have taken place at any other point of our Lord's history so well as at the particular moment at which it was wrought. It is also clear that the healing of Malchus is a work of a very different order from any ordinary miracle by which the same effect might have been produced, and that the miracle of the second miraculous fishing is also full of prophetical and even sacramental meaning, and is to be taken, as all the miracles mentioned by St. John are to be taken, in connection with the discourse which followed, in which, in this case, our Lord conferred on St. Peter the supreme pastorate in the Church.

Having thus run through, however rapidly, the whole series of these specially recorded miracles of our Lord, we are able to see their relation to at least two very important features in His history, on which it is clear that the whole course of that history mainly depended. One of these is the effect which His course of teaching and of miracles had on His enemies, and the other is the connection of certain miracles with some of the greatest doctrines and principles of His Church. It is clear enough that if our Lord had worked no miracles, the rulers at Jerusalem would probably have left Him alone. If His work had been confined to the promulgation of certain new truths and even to the assertion of certain new claims, Annas and Caiaphas might have afforded to let His movement work itself out, as they had passed, almost unnoticed, the movement of St. John Baptist. There were no doubt points in His teaching which they might have felt as attacks on themselves, or on the traditions which they were so careful to preserve. But that which gave His teaching force was that it was accompanied by displays of Divine power. It was this that gave Him His position in the minds of the people, and this position in the minds of the people forced the rulers of the people to deal with Him as they did. It made it necessary for them, either to acknowledge His claims, or to destroy Him in whatever way they could. For this reason a certain account of some of His miracles is essential in any true estimate of the history. It is mere childishness to suppose that the rulers would not have denied the miracles if they could. As it was they were driven by them to use two arguments against Him, one of which was captious and pharisaical, and the other diabolical. The first was that whatever might be the true explanation of His power, His miracles could not be the evidences of a truly Divine mission, because He wrought them on the Sabbath Day and thus violated the law. The other was, that the power which He showed over the devils was conceded to Him, not by God, but by virtue of a league with Satan himself, for the sake of imposing a false doctrine on the people. The first naturally preceded the other, the second grew out of the first. It has been already sufficiently pointed out how this accounts for the prominence given by the historical Evangelists to the 'Sabbatical' miracles, and to the instances in which the enemies of our Lord were forced to bring up the explanation founded on the supposed league with Satan, those instances, namely, in which, the devils having been cast out, the dumb spake or the blind saw.

These miracles, therefore, are in the strictest sense historical. They belong to the very foundations of the history of the three years of the Public Life. But there are also others which belong to that history in another way, namely, as having been connected with incidents and features which had a prominence of their own in the general history of our Lord. To this class we may assign the two instances of the cleansing of the Temple, considered as exertions of preternatural power. To the same class belong the clusters of miracles which occurred at the outset and at the close of our Lord's Ministry at Capharnaum. In the same list we may place the miracle on the lunatic boy which occurred when our Lord and His three disciples came down from the mountain on which the Transfiguration had taken place. The same may be said of the miracle on the blind men at Jericho, and of the few cures wrought by our Lord in the Temple on the evening, as it seems, of Palm Sunday. And lastly, the miracle of the healing of Malchus belongs naturally to any complete account of the Passion. It may be that none of these miracles had any special relation to the development of the Jewish opposition to our Lord, or on the onward flow of His Life as it had been ordained by the providence of the Father—that they asserted no new claim, and taught no new doctrine. But the outlines of the history being what they are, it would have been unnatural that such incidents as these, belonging to particular times and occasions, should have been omitted. We may say the same of the few miracles, mentioned because it might have been expected that they would have been far more numerous, which our Lord was able, as St. Mark puts it, to work at Nazareth on the occasion of His last visit to that place.

Besides these miracles, which may be called in various senses historical, it is clear that there are a certain number which are deeply significative, and even, in a certain sense, sacramental in their import. The great sacramental miracles are the miracle at Cana of the turning the water into wine, the miracle on the paralytic man, wrought in direct proof of our Lord's claim to have power on earth to forgive sins and the double miracle of the multiplication of the loaves, for the feeding of the five thousand and the four thousand. Nearly in the same class we may place the miracles which are doctrinal in the sense that they teach great principles of our Lord's Kingdom, such as those on the servant of the Gentile centurion, and on the daughter of the Syrophœnician woman. In the same way the miracles wrought on the Sabbath Day have a second kind of importance, inasmuch as they teach our Lord's doctrine as to the observance of the commandment which enjoined the keeping of the Sabbath. And we may place in the same class the two miracles of the healing of the lepers, which certainly have a significance in their relation to the Christian doctrine of the absolution of sin.

Another class of miracles contains those which may be considered as prophetical, or, at least, symbolical, of the powers or the fortunes of the Church. The miracles on the Lake of Galilee form a beautiful chain in this respect. They begin with the first miraculous fishing, a miracle altogether unsolicited, and, like the miracle at Cana, not strictly called for by the necessities of the moment, or, at least, going very far beyond them. Then comes the miracle of the stilling the tempest while our Lord was asleep in the boat. It is hardly possible for devout minds to contemplate this miracle, and not to see in it a promise and a prophecy of the fortunes of the Christian Church. Then follows the miracle of our Lord's walking on the waters, and calling St. Peter to Him to do the same, and the miracle of the didrachma, found in the mouth of the fish taken by St. Peter out of the lake, has the same sort of signification. Lastly, the whole series of miracles closes with the second unsolicited miraculous draught of fishes, in which again St. Peter plays a prominent part, and which introduces the great discourse in which the whole flock of Christ is committed to his charge. There is also another miracle, not on the lake, which may be classed among the prophetic miracles. This is that of the cursing of the barren fig-tree, which is clearly, as has been said, a parable in action, and which must be considered in connection with our Lord's saying about the fig-tree which had been found unfruitful for three years,[9] and was spared for one year more at the intercession of the gardener. We may also consider that the words about the blossoming of the fig-tree as a sign of the end of the world,[10] which are usually understood of the conversion of the Jews, may have reference to this figure also. That is, the fig-tree which is cursed, and which is sentenced to perpetual barrenness, is the synagogue, and thus our Lord's action in this miracle is equivalent to a solemn sentence of reprobation pronounced by Him on it, which sentence will be removed at the end of the world by the conversion of the Jews.

The importance of the miracles which we have classified as historical and doctrinal, or prophetical and symbolical, may be confirmed by the consideration how great a number of them were unsolicited by those for whose benefit they were wrought. We may suppose that on those occasions when our Lord is spoken of by the Evangelists as working a great multitude of miracles at once, as must have been the case in the ordinary course of His Ministry in Galilee and in Judæa, the miracles which were thus wrought were solicited by the people, who often, as we are told, brought their sick, even from a distance, to Him for the sake of the healing which they hoped to obtain from His mercifulness. In such cases the mere presentation to Him of a number of such sufferers was a plain and open appeal to His mercy, as well as a protestation of faith in His power. In a great many other instances, no doubt He was asked to do this or that miraculous cure. But in a great number out of the miracles of which we have a special account in the Gospels, our Lord Himself took the initiative. It is but reasonable to suppose that He had in such cases a design beyond and above the healing of the particular physical malady before

[9] St. Luke xiii. 6—9.
[10] St. Matthew xxiv. 32, 33 ; St. Mark xiii. 28, 29 ; St. Luke xxi. 29, 30.

His eyes. It is natural to look to such miracles for the development of the revelation concerning Himself which He had to make, or for the illustration of some doctrine or principle of His Church. Now, if we go through the list of the unsolicited miracles, we find that they include those of which we have been speaking in this connection. The miracle of Cana itself, the first of all, was not thought of by the bridegroom and bride for whose relief it was ostensibly worked. It was thought of and asked for by our Blessed Lady, but not by them, nor was it worked, as we may say, for them, but for the manifestation of the glory of the Incarnate Son of God to His few disciples. In the same way all the Sabbatical miracles—not all those that were worked on the Sabbath, but all those which were worked on the Sabbath with a special view to the doctrine connected therewith, and with the power of the Son of Man as Lord of the Sabbath—were unsolicited. But these are very considerable in number and in magnitude. They include the miracle at the Pool of Bethsaida, and that, at a later period, on the man who was blind from his birth. Both these were wrought in Jerusalem. The miracle on the man with the withered hand seems to have been wrought in Galilee, and there are, besides, two of these Sabbatical miracles mentioned by St. Luke, as has been seen, the case of a woman with a spirit of infirmity, and of the dropsical man. Both these seem to have occurred in the country parts of Judæa itself, and both were unsolicited.

The same is to be said of the miracles of the multiplication of the loaves—they were altogether unexpected by the Apostles, and unasked for by the multitude themselves, except in the way in which the simple sight of their need was enough to move the tender Heart of our Lord in their favour. The same, again, is to be said of the miracles on the lake, except the stilling of the storm, in which case the terror and danger of the disciples made them have recourse to our Lord, without, perhaps, any perfect anticipation of the manner in which He would extricate them from the difficulty. That is to say, both the miraculous fishings and the miracle of the walking on the waters were altogether due to our Lord's own choice and design. Again, as to the miracles of restoration of life, there is something of the same kind. The miracle of the widow's son was not thought of by the mourners or by the mother of the young man. Jairus, the father of the girl at Capharnaum, had set out from his house while she was yet alive, and was led on by our Lord's healing of the woman with an issue of blood to a higher faith than that with which he had begun, like the ruler, whose son was healed at a distance, and the sisters of Lazarus had to be carefully questioned, and by questioning instructed, by our Lord, before He wrought the last great miracle of this kind. If the cleansing of the Temple be numbered among the miracles, that also was unsolicited on both the occasions on which it took place; so was the healing of Malchus; so were the miracle of the didrachma, the miracle on the fig-tree, the casting out of the legion of devils, while the multitude of miracles that were wrought in the presence of the envoys of St. John Baptist, may well be considered as having been wrought for their benefit, as well as for that of the sufferers who were then delivered from various maladies, and even the miracle of the widow's son seems to have been worked, as has been already said, in order to prepare the answer which was to be made to the envoys of the Baptist on that occasion. Besides these miracles, which came forth spontaneously, as it were, from the Heart of our Lord, when He was not expected to work them, there are others in which His own Divine counsel influenced the manner in, or the conditions on, which they were vouchsafed, as in the case of the ruler's son, the paralytic who was let down in his bed before our Lord, and the woman with the issue of blood. In the deliverance of demoniacs, as that one who was dispossessed in the synagogue at Capharnaum, and that of the legion of devils, it seems to have been sometimes the case that the taunting and mocking or terrified cries of the devils, 'Art Thou come to torment us before the time?' and the like, furnished our Lord with the motive, we might almost say the provocation, on which He acted in working the miracle. He could not suffer such language from the enemies of God and man.

It is thus clear that the miracles which we have ventured to single out from among the rest, as having some special bearing on the unfolding of the counsels of God in the history of the Incarnation, may very likely have been selected by the Evangelists, under the guidance of the Holy Ghost, on account of that special bearing. It will be some confirmation of the general view thus taken of the miracles, if we find that it is borne out by the use made of them in the several Divine books of which we have been speaking. But it is remarkable that all three of the historical Evangelists agree in inserting some of the Sabbatical miracles, as well as in mentioning the miracles which occasioned the calumny about the league with Beelzebub. It is true that St. Luke seems to choose, as is always his method, different instances of miracles of these classes, as if to show us that the preaching of our Lord was exposed to the same phase of opposition in Judæa as in Galilee. It may be thought that in doing this, the third Evangelist to some extent impairs the exact order of time in the development of that opposition, because the occasions on which he mentions these Sabbatical miracles, and the calumny occasioned by the deliverance of the dumb demoniac, are to be placed, like all that occurs in that part of his narrative, at a later point in the general history than that at which the similar incidents in St. Matthew and St. Mark had occurred. It was, indeed, before our Lord transferred the scene of His general preaching from Galilee to Judæa, that the persecution on account of His miracles on the Sabbath Day had taken form, and that the calumny as to Beelzebub had been invented. But St. Luke is not writing a chronological history of the course taken by the adversaries of our Lord, and it is enough for him to show that their conduct towards our Lord was the same in Judæa that it had been in Galilee, or, rather, to give a general account of that conduct as prompted by the motives which actually did prompt it. Moreover, St. Luke fixes the outbreak of that persecution with great precision, mentioning the Sabbath in particular on which the remarks on the disciples eating in the cornfields were made by the Pharisees, and thus he has, in truth, done more than the others' towards making the point of time precise at which this line of opposition was taken up. In the same way, all the three Evangelists who are in the more strict sense historians, mention the healing of the leper and the miracle on the paralytic, as well as the great sacramental miracle of the multiplication of the loaves. Thus the reason why such miracles are selected by all the three earlier Evangelists may well be supposed to be their importance in the history itself.

If we turn to St. John, we must remember that he does not profess to do more towards the work of an independent historian than is implied in the supplementary character of his Gospel, considered as a narrative. And yet we find him bearing remarkable testimony to the importance of the points on which we have been insisting, as marking what may be called crises in the Public Life. His fifth chapter is invaluable in this respect. In that chapter he seems to explain silently, that is, without open allusion to it, the hostility of the Chief Priests to our Lord on the question of the Sabbath. He seems to tell us that it did not begin from the chance incident of the plucking of the ears of corn in the fields on the Sabbath Day, but that before that, and as it seems, only just before that, our Lord had worked the first of His Sabbatical miracles on the man at the Pool of Bethsaida, nor only this, but that He had held a long disputation on the subject with the authorities themselves, in which He had taken far higher ground than any which He took in the discussions with His critics on the same point in Galilee. That is, He had spoken of the unity of His work with the work of the Eternal Father, making Himself, as the scribes themselves perceived and said, 'equal with God.' This is St. John's contribution to this part of the Gospel history. He lays it down quite clearly, that it was on this account that our Lord's life was in danger in Judæa. Thus even the fourth Gospel is not without its witness—a point of detail more important than any which had been contributed before—to the truth as to this feature in the opposition to our Lord. But it may safely be said that this was the most important turning point in the whole history. The charge which was based on an imputation of a league with Satan, was far less probable than the charge about the Sabbath. And indeed, it seems to have sprung out of the other. We find no special mention of this in the Gospel of St. John, unless it be conveyed in the words of the Jews mentioned in the eighth chapter, 'Say we not well that Thou art a Samaritan and hast a devil?' On the other points which have been mentioned in reference to the prominent importance of certain miracles of our Lord, St. John is practically as plain as the other Evangelists. It is his peculiar work to draw out the policy pursued with regard to our Lord by the rulers at Jerusalem, and the latter half of that portion of his Gospel which precedes the account of the Last Supper and the Passion is infinitely valuable on this account. He alone mentions the strong hostility caused by the miracle on the man born blind, and he alone mentions the excommunication which was inflicted on the person cured by this miracle, a sentence the fear of which, as he tells us, kept back many of the principal men themselves from avowing their faith in our Lord. Lastly, St. John is the historian of the great crowning miracle of the raising of Lazarus, which, as has been said, had, more than any other miracle, to do with the final determination of Caiaphas and his colleagues to bring about the murder of our Lord.

In the same way it is clear, that all the Evangelists recognize the importance of the sacramental miracles. We may account for the silence of the first three as to the miracle of Cana, by remembering that they do not begin their history of our Lord's Ministry until the outset of His Galilæan preaching. The whole space of time covered by the first four chapters of St. John is outside the plan of their Gospels. But they mention with all due prominence the miracle on the paralytic, which has so close a connection with the doctrine of the Sacrament of Penance, and they also give great prominence to the miracle of the multiplication of the loaves, though the long discourse by which our Lord fixed for ever the sacramental meaning of that miracle is left to St. John.

It must be remembered that the scope of this essay is not to deny, or in any way to impair, the value and importance of the miracles of our Lord as evidences. When He enumerated, in His discourse reported in the fifth chapter of the Gospel of St. John, the various kinds of evidences by which His mission had been accredited by the providence of His Father, He placed the testimony of His works, that is, of His miracles, higher even than the witness borne to Him by St. John Baptist. It would be absurd to suppose that the Evangelists had not the evidential value of the miracles in view when they recorded them. But it is useful to remind ourselves that the miracles, and especially the recorded miracles, have a meaning and a bearing in relation to the Person and work of our Lord which are in many cases independent of their importance as simple evidences that God was with Him. St. Matthew has given us a beautiful instance of the manner in which they can be combined in a chain of such evidences, in the passage of his Gospel which follows immediately on the Sermon on the Mount. After that Sermon, of which he is the providential reporter for the Church of all ages, he proceeds to give us in succession, almost as if they had actually occurred one after the other, the miracles on the leper, on the centurion's servant, on the mother-in-law of St. Peter, and those that were wrought at Capharnaum on the evening of the same day, before our Lord left it to commence His first great missionary circuit. Then, after an interval of a few verses, he begins again with the miracle of the stilling the tempest, the deliverance of the man who was possessed by a legion of devils, the healing of the paralytic, which was the preface, as it were, to his own call to the Apostolate, the raising from the dead of the daughter of Jairus, the healing of the woman with an issue of blood, and the other miracles which took place at Capharnaum on the same occasion. It is clear that St. Matthew must have known, by personal knowledge, if any one in the world could know, that all these miracles did not take place at the same time, nor in the order in which he has placed them in his Gospel. But he uses them for a purpose in his own mind, in accordance with the main idea of that Gospel, and thus presents them to us, as it seems, in evidence of our Lord's exercise of Divine power in every conceivable manner, on the leprosy, on the disease of the servant who was cured at a distance in reward of the faith of his heathen master, then on all kinds of different diseases at once, then on the elements themselves and on the devils, and so on through the whole of this marvellous chain, including His power over death itself in the case of the daughter of Jairus. It would be absurd to deny this intention in St. Matthew, or the evident intention of St. Mark all through the second Gospel, to magnify our Lord by the chronicling of His works of power one after the other.

These facts are clear on a simple inspection of these two first Gospels. But it is also clear that both these Evangelists, and St. Luke also, had a very definite consciousness of the Divine purposes for which some of the miracles were wrought in respect of the course of the Life of our Lord, the doctrines He wished especially to enforce, and the laws of the Kingdom which He came to found on earth. One of the best evidences of the truth of this statement as to the Evangelists, would be found in the simple perusal of the Gospel of St. Mark, with this thought in the mind, of tracing therein the order of the miracles in their connection with the development of the external aspect of our Lord's Life, that is, of His relations with the authorities, the people, and His own disciples in particular, and again in their connection with the doctrines which it was important for Him to enforce, and the principle of His Kingdom which He wished to foreshadow. The Gospel of St. Mark is the simplest of the Gospels in construction. It may be considered as the most elementary expression of the idea of a Gospel as such. It does not follow that it was the earliest of the Gospels in actual existence, for it may well have been the case that the circumstances of the Church or Churches for which it was primarily written may have presented reasons why it is so elementary, though those Churches may only have required it at a time in the actual history of Christianity posterior in date to the full development of other Churches elsewhere, for which a more elaborate treatment of the subject-matter, such as we have in the Gospel of St. Matthew, may have been more opportune. This question need not be discussed at present. But if any one will take up the Gospel of St. Mark in the manner, and with the general view we have mentioned, he will find that the main outlines of the plan on which we have been supposing that the miracles which have been specially recorded by the Evangelists, were selected, will be easily traced in the book he holds in his hand. He will find the historical miracles, the miracles of doctrine, and the miracles which seem to indicate principles of the Gospel Kingdom, making up by far the greater part of the first ten chapters—that is, the whole of this Gospel until the beginning of the narrative of the events leading to the Passion—in what might seem at first sight almost an enumeration of one wonderful work after another, with but few interruptions for the sake of the insertion of some of the parables and other important heads of teaching. That is, St. Mark tells the story of the three years of our Lord's preaching very mainly by a series of miracles, and these miracles are, in the main, those which have the particular character of which we have been speaking. The same are found, in the main, in the Gospels of St. Matthew and St. Luke, though the latter makes it a rule to give fresh specimens of the same kind when he can, instead of the same specimens. The inference is not unnatural that the principles, so to speak, of the Gospel history, are to a great extent contained in these miracles, the purpose for which they were wrought, the doctrines with which they were connected, and the results which they produced.

APPENDIX II.

Harmony of the Gospels.

§ 37.—*The miraculous draught of fishes.*

Luke v. 1—11.

AND it came to pass that, when the multitudes pressed upon Him, to hear the Word of God, He stood by the lake of Genesareth. And He saw two ships standing by the lake, but the fishermen were gone out of them and were washing their nets. And going up into one of the ships that was Simon's, He desired him to thrust out a little from the land, and sitting down He taught the multitudes out of the ship.

Now when He had ceased to speak, He said to Simon, Launch out into the deep, and let down your nets for a draught.

And Simon answering, said to Him, Master we have laboured all the night, and have taken nothing, but at Thy word I will let down the net.

And when they had done this, they inclosed a very great multitude of fishes, and their net was breaking. And they beckoned to their partners that were in the other ship, that they should come and help them. And they came, and filled both the ships, so that they were almost sinking.

Which when Simon Peter saw, he fell down at Jesus' knees, saying, Depart from me, for I am a sinful man, O Lord. For he was wholly astonished, and all that were with him, at the draught of the fishes which they had taken; and so were also James and John, the sons of Zebedee, who were Simon's partners. And Jesus saith to Simon, Fear not, from henceforth thou shalt be taking men. And when they had brought their ships to land, leaving all things, they followed Him.

§ 38.—*The Healing of the Leper.*

Matt. viii. 2—4.	Mark i. 40—45.	Luke v. 12—16.
And behold a leper came and adored Him, saying, Lord, if Thou wilt, Thou canst make me clean.	And there came a leper to Him, beseeching Him, and kneeling down, said to Him, If Thou wilt, Thou canst make me clean.	And it came to pass, when He was in a certain city, behold, a man full of leprosy, who seeing Jesus, and falling on his face, besought Him, saying, Lord, if Thou wilt, Thou canst make me clean.
And Jesus stretching forth His hand, touched him, saying, I will, be thou made clean.	And Jesus having compassion on him, stretched forth His hand, and touching him, saith to him, I will, be thou made clean.	And stretching forth His hand, He touched him, saying, I will, be thou cleansed.
And forthwith his leprosy was cleansed.	And when He had spoken, immediately the leprosy departed from him, and he was made clean.	And immediately the leprosy departed from him.
And Jesus saith to him, See thou tell no man, but go, show thyself to the priest, and offer the gift which Moses commanded for a testimony unto them.	And He strictly charged him, and forthwith sent him away. And He saith to him, See thou tell no one, but go, show thyself to the high-priest, and offer for thy cleansing the things that Moses commanded for a testimony to them. But he being gone out, began to publish and to blaze abroad the word; so that He could not openly	And He charged him that he should tell no man, but Go, show thyself to the priest, and offer for thy cleansing according as Moses commanded for a testimony to them. But the fame of Him went abroad the more, and great multitudes came together to hear, and to be healed

Matt.	Mark i. 45.	Luke v. 15, 16.
	go into the city, but was without in desert places, and they flocked to Him from all sides.	by Him of their infirmities. And He retired into the desert, and prayed.

§ 39.—*The Healing of the Paralytic and the calling of St. Matthew.*

Matt. ix. 1—9.	Mark ii. 1—14.	Luke v. 17—28.
And He came unto His own city.	And again He entered into Capharnaum after some days. And it was heard that He was in the house, and many came together, so that there was no room, no, not even at the door, and He spoke to them the word.	And it came to pass on a certain day, as He sat teaching, that there were also Pharisees and doctors of the law sitting by, that were come out of every town of Galilee, and Judæa, and Jerusalem, and the power of the Lord was to heal them.
And behold they brought to Him one sick of the palsy, lying on a bed.	And they came to Him, bringing one sick of the palsy, who was carried by four. And when they could not offer him unto Him for the multitude, they uncovered the roof where He was, and opening it, they let down the bed wherein the man sick of the palsy lay.	And behold, men brought in bed a man who had the palsy, and they sought means to bring him in, and to lay him before Him. And when they could not find by what way they might bring him in, because of the multitude, they went up upon the roof, and let him down through the tiles, with his bed, into the midst before Jesus.
And Jesus, seeing their faith, said to the man	And when Jesus had seen their faith, He saith to the	Whose faith when He saw, He said, Man, thy

Matt. ix. 3—8.	Mark ii. 6—12.	Luke v. 21—26.
sick of the palsy, Be of good heart, son, thy sins are forgiven thee. And behold some of the scribes said within themselves, He blasphemeth.	sick of the palsy, Son, thy sins are forgiven thee. And there were some of the scribes sitting there, and thinking in their hearts, Why doth this Man speak thus? He blasphemeth. Who can forgive sins but God only?	sins are forgiven thee. And the scribes and Pharisees began to think, saying, Who is this who speaketh blasphemies? Who can forgive sins, but God alone?
And Jesus seeing their thoughts, said, Why do you think evil in your hearts?	Which Jesus presently knowing in His spirit, that they so thought within themselves, saith to them, Why think you these things in your hearts?	And when Jesus knew their thoughts, answering, He said to them, What is it you think in your hearts?
Whether is easier to say, Thy sins are forgiven thee, or to say, Arise and walk?	Which is easier, to say to the sick of the palsy, Thy sins are forgiven thee, or to say, Arise, take up thy bed, and walk?	Which is easier to say, Thy sins are forgiven thee, or to say, Arise and walk?
But that you may know that the Son of Man hath power on earth to forgive sins (then said He to the man sick of the palsy), Arise, take up thy bed, and go into thy house. And he arose, and went into his house. And the multitudes seeing it, feared, and glorified God that gave such power to men.	But that you may know that the Son of Man hath power on earth to forgive sins (He saith to the sick of the palsy), I say to thee, Arise, take up thy bed, and go into thy house. And immediately he arose, and taking up his bed, went his way in the sight of all, so that all wondered, and glorified God, saying, We never saw the like.	But that you may know that the Son of Man hath power on earth to forgive sins (He saith to the sick of the palsy), I say to thee, Arise, take up thy bed, and go into thy house. And immediately rising up before them, he took up the bed on which he lay, and he went away to his own house, glorifying God. And all were

Matt. ix. 9.	Mark ii. 13, 14.	Luke v. 27, 28.
		astonished, and they glorified God. And they were filled with fear, saying, We have seen wonderful things to-day.
	And He went forth again to the sea-side, and all the multitude came to Him, and He taught them.	
And when Jesus passed on from thence, He saw a man sitting in the custom-house, named Matthew, and He saith to him, Follow Me. And he arose up and followed Him.	And when He was passing by, He saw Levi the son of Alpheus sitting at the receipt of custom, and He saith to him, Follow Me. And rising up, he followed Him.	And after these things He went forth, and saw a publican named Levi sitting at the receipt of custom, and He said to him, Follow Me. And leaving all things, he rose up and followed Him.

§ 40.—*The Feast at St. Matthew's house.*

Matt. ix. 10—13.	Mark ii. 15—22.	Luke v. 29—39.
And it came to pass as He was sitting at meat in the house, behold many publicans and sinners came, and sat down with Jesus and His disciples.	And it came to pass, that as He sat at meat in his house, many publicans and sinners sat down together with Jesus and His disciples. For they were many, who also followed Him.	And Levi made Him a great feast in his own house, and there was a great company of publicans, and of others, that were at table with them.
And the Pharisees seeing it, said to His disciples, Why doth your Master eat with publicans and sinners?	And the scribes and the Pharisees seeing that He ate with publicans and sinners, said to His disciples, Why doth your Master eat and drink with	But the Pharisees and scribes murmured, saying to His disciples, Why do you eat and drink with publicans and sinners?

Matt. ix. 12, 13.	Mark ii. 17—21.	Luke v. 31—36.
	publicans and sinners?	
But Jesus hearing it, said, They that are in health need not a physician, but they that are ill. Go then and learn what this meaneth, 'I will have mercy and not sacrifice.'[1] For I am not come to call the just, but sinners.	Jesus hearing this, saith to them, they that are well have no need of a physician, but they that are sick. For I came not to call the just, but sinners.	And Jesus answering, said to them, They that are whole need not the physician, but they that are sick. I came not to call the just, but sinners, to penance.
	And the disciples of John and the Pharisees used to fast, and they come, and say to Him, Why do the disciples of John and of the Pharisees fast, but Thy disciples do not fast? And Jesus saith to them, Can the children of the marriage fast, as long as the bridegroom is with them? As long as they have the bridegroom with them, they cannot fast. But the days will come when the bridegroom shall be taken away from them, and then they shall fast in those days. No man seweth^c a piece of raw cloth	And they said to Him, Why do the disciples of John fast often, and make prayers, and the disciples of the Pharisees in like manner; but Thine eat and drink? To whom He said, Can you make the children of the bridegroom fast, whilst the bridegroom is with them? But the days will come when the bridegroom shall be taken away from them, then shall they fast in those days. And He spoke also a similitude

[1] Osee vi. 6.

Matt.	Mark ii. 22.	Luke v. 37—39.
	to an old garment, otherwise the new piecing taketh away from the old, and there is made a greater rent.	to them, That no man putteth a piece from a new garment upon an old garment, otherwise he both rendeth the new, and the piece taken from the new agreeth not with the old.
	And no man putteth new wine into old bottles, otherwise the wine will burst the bottles, and both the wine will be spilled and the bottles will be lost. But new wine must be put into new bottles.	And no man putteth new wine into old bottles, otherwise the new wine will break the bottles, and it will be spilled, and the bottles will be lost. But new wine must be put into new bottles, and both are preserved. And no man drinking old, hath presently a mind to new, for he saith, The old is better.

§ 41.—*The miracle at the Probatic Pool.*

John v. 1—15.

After these things was a festival day of the Jews, and Jesus went up to Jerusalem.

Now there is at Jerusalem a pond, called Probatica, which in Hebrew is named Bethsaida, having five porches. In these lay a great multitude of sick, of blind, of lame, of withered, waiting for the moving of the water. And an Angel of the Lord descended at certain times into the pond, and the water was moved. And he that went down first into the pond after the motion of the water, was made whole of whatsoever infirmity he lay under.

And there was a certain man there, that had been eight and thirty years under his infirmity. Him when Jesus had seen lying, and knew that he had been now a long time, He saith to him, Wilt thou be made whole?

John v. 7—15.

The infirm man answered Him, Sir, I have no man, when the water is troubled, to put me into the pond. For whilst I am coming, another goeth down before me.

Jesus saith to him, Arise, take up thy bed, and walk.

And immediately the man was made whole, and he took up his bed, and walked. And it was the sabbath that day. The Jews therefore said to him that was healed, It is the sabbath, it is not lawful for thee to take up thy bed. He answered them, He that made me whole. He said to me, Take up thy bed, and walk. They asked him therefore, Who is that Man Who said to thee, Take up thy bed, and walk? But he who was healed knew not Who it was, for Jesus went aside from the multitude standing in the place.

Afterwards, Jesus findeth him in the Temple, and saith to him, Behold thou art made whole, sin no more, lest some worse thing happen to thee. The man went his way, and told the Jews, that it was Jesus Who made him whole.

§ 42.—*Our Lord's dispute with the Jews.*

John v. 16—47.

Therefore did the Jews persecute Jesus, because He did these things on the sabbath.

But Jesus answered them, My Father worketh until now, and I work.

Hereupon therefore the Jews sought the more to kill Him, because He did not only break the sabbath, but also said that God was His Father, making Himself equal to God.

Then Jesus answered, and said to them, Amen, amen, I say unto you, the Son cannot do anything of Himself, but what He seeth the Father doing, for what things soever He doth, these the Son also doth in like manner. For the Father loveth the Son, and showeth Him all things which Himself doth, and greater works than these will He show Him, that you may wonder. For as the Father raiseth up the dead, and giveth life, so the Son also giveth life to whom He will. For neither doth the Father judge any man, but hath given all judgment to the Son, that all men may honour the Son as they honour the Father. He who honoureth not the Son, honoureth not the Father Who hath sent Him.

Amen, amen, I say unto you, that he who heareth My word, and believeth Him that sent Me, hath life everlasting, and cometh not into judgment, but is passed from

John v. 25—47.

death to life. Amen, amen, I say unto you, that the hour cometh, and now is, when the dead shall hear the voice of the Son of God, and they that hear shall live. For as the Father hath life in Himself, so He hath given to the Son also to have life in Himself, And He hath given Him power to do judgment, because He is the Son of Man. Wonder not at this, for the hour cometh, wherein all that are in the graves shall hear the voice of the Son of God. And they that have done good things, shall come forth unto the resurrection of life, but they that have done evil, unto the resurrection of judgment. I cannot of Myself do anything. As I hear, so I judge, and My judgment is just, because I seek not My own will, but the will of Him that sent Me.

If I bear witness of Myself, My witness is not true. There is another that beareth witness of Me, and I know that the witness which he witnesseth of Me is true. You sent to John, and he gave testimony to the truth. But I receive not testimony from man, but I say these things, that you may be saved. He was a burning and a shining light, and you were willing for a time to rejoice in his light.

But I have a greater testimony than that of John, for the works which the Father hath given Me to perfect, the works themselves, which I do, give testimony of Me, that the Father hath sent Me. And the Father Himself Who hath sent me, hath given testimony of Me. Neither have you heard His voice at any time, nor seen His shape. And you have not His Word abiding in you, for Whom He hath sent, Him you believe not.

Search the Scriptures, for you think in them to have life everlasting, and the same are they that give testimony of Me. And you will not come to Me that you may have life. I receive not glory from men. But I know you, that you have not the love of God in you. I am come in the name of My Father, and you receive Me not, if another shall come in his own name, him you will receive. How can you believe, who receive glory one from another, and the glory which is from God alone, you do not seek? Think not that I will accuse you to the Father. There is one that accuseth you, Moses, in whom you trust. For if you did believe Moses, you would perhaps believe Me also, for he wrote of Me. But if you do not believe his writings, how will you believe My words?

§ 43.—*The disciples plucking corn on the Sabbath.*

Matt. xii. 1—8.	Mark ii. 23—28.	Luke vi, 1—5.
At that time Jesus went through the corn on the sabbath, and His disciples being hungry, began to pluck the ears, and to eat.	And it came to pass, again, as the Lord walked through the cornfields on the sabbath, that His disciples began to go forward, and to pluck the ears of corn.	And it came to pass, on the second first sabbath, that as He went through the cornfields, His disciples plucked the ears, and did eat, rubbing them in their hands.
And the Pharisees seeing them, said to Him, Behold, Thy disciples do that which is not lawful to do on the sabbath-days.	And the Pharisees said to Him, Behold, why do they on the sabbath-day that which is not lawful?	And some of the Pharisees said to them, Why do you that which is not lawful on the sabbath-days?
But He said to them, Have you not read what David did when he was hungry, and they that were with him? How he entered into the house of God, and did eat the loaves of proposition, which it was not lawful for him to eat, nor for them that were with him, but for the priests only? Or have ye not read in the law, that on the sabbath-days the priests in the Temple break the sabbath, and are without blame? But I tell you, that there is here a greater than the Temple.	And He said to them, Have you never read what David did when he had need, and was hungry himself, and they that were with him? How he went into the house of God, under Abiathar the high-priest, and did eat the loaves of proposition, which was not lawful to eat, but for the priests, and gave to them who were with him?	And Jesus answering them, said, Have you not read so much as this, what David did, when himself was hungry, and they that were with him? How he went into the house of God, and took and ate the bread of proposition, and gave to them that were with him, which is not lawful to eat but only for the priests?

Matt. xii. 7, 8.	Mark ii. 27, 28.	Luke vi. 5.
And if you knew what this meaneth, I will have mercy, and not sacrifice, you would never have condemned the innocent.	And He said to them, The sabbath was made for man, and not man for the sabbath.	
For the Son of Man is Lord even of the sabbath.	Therefore the Son of Man is Lord of the sabbath also.	And He said to them, The Son of Man is Lord also of the sabbath.

§ 44.—*Another miracle on the Sabbath.*

Matt. xii. 9—14.	Mark iii. 1—6.	Luke vi. 6—11.
And when He had passed from thence, He came into their synagogue. And behold there was a man who had a withered hand, and they asked Him, saying, Is it lawful to heal on the sabbath days? that they might accuse Him.	And He entered again into the synagogue, and there was a man there who had a withered hand. And they watched Him whether He would heal on the sabbath-days, that they might accuse Him.	And it came to pass also on another sabbath, that He entered into the synagogue, and taught. And there was a man, whose right hand' was withered. And the scribes and Pharisees watched if He would heal on the sabbath, that they might find an accusation against Him.
But He said to them, What man shall there be among you, that hath one sheep, and if the same fall into a pit on the sabbath-day, will he not take hold on it and lift it up? How much better is a man than a sheep? Therefore it is lawful to	And He said to the man who had the withered hand, Stand up in the midst. And He saith to them, Is it lawful to do good on the sabbath-days, or to do evil? to save life or to destroy? But they held their peace. And looking round about on	But He knew their thoughts, and said to the man who had the withered hand, Arise, and stand forth in the midst. And rising he stood forth. Then Jesus said to them, I ask you, if it be lawful on the sabbath-days to do good, or to do evil, to save

Matt. xii. 13, 14.	Mark iii. 6.	Luke vi. 10, 11.
do a good deed on the sabbath-days. Then He saith to the man, Stretch forth thy hand. And he stretched it forth, and it was restored to health even as the other. And the Pharisees going out made a consultation against Him, how they might destroy Him.	them with anger, being grieved for the blindness of their hearts, He saith to the man, Stretch forth thy hand. And he stretched it forth, and his hand was restored unto him. And the Pharisees going out immediately, made a consultation with the Herodians against Him, how they might destroy Him.	life, or to destroy? And looking round about on them all, He said to the man, Stretch forth thy hand. And he stretched it forth, and his hand was restored. And they were filled with madness, and they talked one with another, what they might do to Jesus.

§ 45.—*Our Lord retiring before His enemies.*

Matt. xii. 15—21.	Mark iii. 7—12.
But Jesus knowing it, retired from thence, and many followed Him, and He healed them all. He charged them that they should not make Him known.	But Jesus retired with His disciples to the sea, and a great multitude followed Him from Galilee and Judæa, and from Jerusalem, and from Idumæa, and from beyond the Jordan. And they about Tyre and Sidon, a great multitude, hearing the things which He did, came to Him. And He spoke to His disciples that a small ship should wait on Him because of the multitude, least they should throng Him. For He healed many, so that they pressed upon Him for to touch Him, as many as had evils. And the unclean spirits, when they saw Him, fell down before Him, and they cried, saying, Thou art the Son of God. And He strictly

Matt. xii. 17, 21.	Mark iii. 12.
	charged them that they should not make Him known.
That it might be fulfilled which was spoken by Isaias the prophet, saying, 'Behold My servant Whom I have chosen, My beloved in Whom My soul hath been well pleased. I will put My Spirit upon Him, and He shall show judgment to the Gentiles. He shall not contend, nor cry out, neither shall any man hear His voice in the streets. The bruised reed He shall not break, and smoking flax He shall not extinguish, till He send forth judgment unto victory. And in His name the Gentiles shall hope.'[2]	

[2] Isaias xlii. 1.

A LIST OF BOOKS

WRITTEN OR EDITED

BY

Fathers of the Society of Jesus.

LONDON: BURNS AND OATES,
PORTMAN STREET AND PATERNOSTER ROW.

TO BE HAD ALSO AT
St. Joseph's Library, 48, South Street, Grosvenor Square, W.

Works by the Rev. H. J. Coleridge.

Vita Vitæ Nostræ meditantibus proposita.
Cloth 7s. 6d.; calf 10s. 6d.

[This volume is a Latin Harmony of the Gospels, arranged in parts and sections according to the chronological order of our Lord's life.]

The Life of our Life. Two vols. 15s.

[This volume is an English version of the above, with two introductory chapters to each Part of the Life, explaining first the general history, and secondly the part taken by each Evangelist in recording it. Notes illustrating the Harmonistic difficulties in each Part of the Life are also subjoined.]

CONTENTS.
VOL. I.

Preface.—On the Harmony of the Gospels.
Chapter I.—The Life of our Blessed Lord as independent of its records.
Chapter II.—Divisions of the Life of our Lord in the Gospels.
Chapter III.—Earlier Mysteries of our Lord's Life.
Chapter IV.—The Infancy and Hidden Life as related in the Gospels.
Chapter V.—Harmony of the Gospels as to the first part of the Life of our Lord Jesus Christ.
Chapter VI.—First period of our Lord's Public Life.
Chapter VII.—The first stage of our Lord's Ministry in the four Gospels.
Chapter VIII.—Harmony of the Gospels as to the first period of our Lord's Public Life.
Note I.—Harmonistic Questions as to the first period of our Lord's Public Life.
Chapter IX.—Second period of our Lord's Public Life.
Chapter X.—The second stage of the Public Life in the four Gospels.
Chapter XI.—Harmony of the Gospels as to the second period of the Public Life.
Note II.—Harmonistic Questions as to the second period of our Lord's Public Life.
Appendix.—On the Theology of the Parables.

VOL. II.

Chapter I.—Third period of our Lord's Public Life.
Chapter II.—The third stage of the Public Life in the four Gospels.
Chapter III.—Harmony of the Gospels as to the third period of the Public Life.
Note I.—Harmonistic Questions as to the third period of our Lord's Public Life.
Chapter IV.—First days of Holy Week.
Chapter V.—The first days of Holy Week in the four Gospels.
Chapter VI.—Harmony of the Gospels as to the first days of Holy Week.
Note II.—Harmonistic Questions as to Holy Week.
Chapter VII.—The Passion of our Lord.
Chapter VIII.—The Passion in the four Gospels.
Chapter IX.—Harmony of the Gospels as to the Passion of our Lord Jesus Christ.
Note III.—Harmonistic questions as to the Passion.
Chapter X.—Resurrection and Ascension of our Lord.
Chapter XI.—Resurrection and Ascension in the four Gospels.
Chapter XII.—Harmony of the Gospels as to the Resurrection and Ascension.
Note IV.—Harmonistic questions as to the Resurrection and Ascension.

The Public Life of our Lord. Part I.
    Vol. 1. THE MINISTRY OF ST. JOHN BAPTIST.
    Vol. 2. THE PREACHING OF THE BEATITUDES.
    Vol. 3. THE SERMON ON THE MOUNT (*to the end of the Lord's Prayer*).
    Vol. 4. THE SERMON ON THE MOUNT (*concluded*).
    Vol. 5. THE TRAINING OF THE APOSTLES (Part I.).
    Price 6s. 6d. each.

[These five volumes contain a full commentary on the Second Part of the *Life of our Life*, that is, on the first Part of the *Public Life of our Lord*. The volumes on the Second Part of the *Public Life* will, it is hoped, be published in the course of the present year.]

The Sermon on the Mount. Three vols.
(the second, third, and fourth vols. of the above bound up separately).

The History of the Sacred Passion. By Father Luis de la Palma, of the Society of Jesus. Translated from the Spanish. With Preface by the Rev. H. J. Coleridge, S.J. Fourth Edition. Price 7s. 6d.

The Dialogues of St. Gregory the Great. An Old English Version. Edited by the Rev. H. J. Coleridge, S.J. Price 6s.

Biographies.

The Life and Letters of St. Francis Xavier. By the Rev. H. J. Coleridge, S.J. Two vols. Third Edition. Price 18s.

The Story of St. Stanislaus Kostka. Edited by the Rev. H. J. Coleridge, S.J. 3s. 6d.

The Chronicle of St. Anthony of Padua, 'The Eldest Son of St. Francis.' Edited by the Rev. H. J. Coleridge, S.J. In Four Books. Price 5s. 6d.

The Life of St. Jane Frances Fremyot de Chantal. By Emily Bowles. With Preface by the Rev. H. J. Coleridge, S.J. Second Edition. Price 5s. 6d.

The Life of St. Thomas of Hereford. By R. Strange, S.J. Price 6s. 6d.

The Life of the Blessed Peter Favre, First Companion of St. Ignatius Loyola. From the Italian of Father Boero. With Preface by the Rev. H. J. Coleridge, S.J. Price 6s. 6d.

The Life of the Blessed John Berchmans. By the Rev. F. Goldie, S.J. Second Edition. Price 6s.

A Gracious Life, being the Life of Barbara Acarie (Blessed Mary of the Incarnation), of the Reformed Order of our Blessed Lady of Mount Carmel. By Emily Bowles. Price 6s.

An English Carmelite. The Life of Catharine Burton, Mother Mary Xaveria of the Angels, of the English Teresian Convent at Antwerp. Collected from her own writings and other sources by Father Thomas Hunter, S.J. Price 6s.

The Life of Mother Margaret Mostyn, Prioress of the Discalced Carmelites of Lierre, Flanders. Edited from the Manuscripts preserved at Darlington, by the Rev. H. J. Coleridge, S.J. Price 6s.

(N.B. *The Life and Letters of St. Teresa,* by the Rev. H. J. Coleridge, is in preparation.)

The Life of Anne Catharine Emmerich. By Helen Ram. With Preface by the Rev. H. J. Coleridge, S.J. Price 5s.

The Life of Doña Luisa de Carvajal. By Lady Georgiana Fullerton. Price 6s.

The Life of Pope Pius the Seventh. By M. Allies. Price 6s. 6d.

The Life of Christopher Columbus. By Rev. A. G. Knight, S.J. Price 6s.

The Life of Henriette d'Osseville (in Religion, Mother Ste. Marie), Foundress of the Institute of the Faithful Virgin. Edited by J. G. MacLeod, S.J. Price 5s. 6d.

Three Catholic Reformers of the Fifteenth Century. I. St. Vincent Ferrer. II. St. Bernardine of Siena. III. St. John Capistran. By Mary H. Allies. Price 5s.

The Suppression of the Society of Jesus in the Portuguese Dominions. From documents hitherto unpublished. By the Rev. Alfred Weld, S.J. Price 7s. 6d.

The Sufferings of the Church in Brittany during the Great Revolution. By Edward Healy Thompson. Price 6s. 6d.

The Prisoners of the Temple; or, Discrowned and Crowned. By M. O'C. Morris. With Preface by the Rev. H. J. Coleridge, S.J. Price 4s. 6d.

The Christian Reformed in Mind and Manners. By Benedict Rogacci, S.J. The Translation Edited by the Rev. H. J. Coleridge, S.J. Price 7s. 6d.

The Manna of the Soul. Meditations for Every Day in the Year. By Father Segneri, S.J. Four vols. Price 29s.
    Vol. 1. January—March. Price 6s. 6d.
    Vol. 2. April—June. Price 7s. 6d.
    Vol. 3. July—September. Price 7s. 6d.
    Vol. 4. October—December. Price 7s. 6d.

Preces Xaverianæ. Price 1s. 6d.
1. Devotions for the Ten Fridays in honour of St. Francis Xavier.
2. Daily Exercise of a Christian, by St. Francis Xavier.
3. The Novena in honour of St. Francis Xavier.
4. Other Meditations for the Ten Fridays.

Sermons by Fathers of the Society of Jesus.

Vol. 1. Sermons by the Rev. FF. Coleridge, Hathaway, Gallwey, Parkinson, and Harper. Price 6s. 6d.

Vol. 2. Sermons by Rev. Fr. Harper. Price 6s. 6d.

*Vol. 3. Sermons by Rev. FF. Kingdon, Pur-*brick, Coleridge, Weld, and Anderdon. Price 6s. 6d.

Pietas Mariana Britannica. A history of English Devotion to the Most Blessed Virgin Marye, Mother of God, with a Catalogue of Shrines, Sanctuaries, Offerings, Bequests, and other Memorials of the Piety of our Forefathers, by Edmund Waterton, F.S.A., Knight of the Order of Christ, of Rome.

Price One Guinea.

The Virtues of Our Lord Jesus Christ. By Father Francis Arias, S.J.

1. The Virtue of Charity. Price 3s.

[This is a part of the famous work so much recommended by St. Francis de Sales. The chapters on the *Virtue of Charity* will be reprinted from the *Messenger of the Sacred Heart*, and appear in a separate volume at the beginning of Lent, 1880. It is hoped that other portions of the same great work may speedily follow.]

The Prisoners of the King. Thoughts on the Catholic Doctrine of Purgatory. By the Rev. H. J. Coleridge. Price 6s. 6d.